ECONOMIC RESEARCH CENTRE

REPORT OF THE
HUNDRED AND FIFTH ROUND TABLE
ON TRANSPORT ECONOMICS

held in Paris on 7th-8th November 1996
on the following topic:

INFRASTRUCTURE-INDUCED MOBILITY

EUROPEAN CONFERENCE OF MINISTERS OF TRANSPORT

EUROPEAN CONFERENCE OF MINISTERS OF TRANSPORT (ECMT)

The European Conference of Ministers of Transport (ECMT) is an inter-governmental organisation established by a Protocol signed in Brussels on 17 October 1953. It is a forum in which Ministers responsible for transport, and more specifically the inland transport sector, can co-operate on policy. Within this forum, Ministers can openly discuss current problems and agree upon joint approaches aimed at improving the utilisation and at ensuring the rational development of European transport systems of international importance.

At present, the ECMT's role primarily consists of:

- helping to create an integrated transport system throughout the enlarged Europe that is economically and technically efficient, meets the highest possible safety and environmental standards and takes full account of the social dimension;
- helping also to build a bridge between the European Union and the rest of the continent at a political level.

The Council of the Conference comprises the Ministers of Transport of 39 full Member countries: Albania, Austria, Azerbaijan, Belarus, Belgium, Bosnia-Herzegovina, Bulgaria, Croatia, the Czech Republic, Denmark, Estonia, Finland, France, the Former Yugoslav Republic of Macedonia (F.Y.R.O.M.), Georgia, Germany, Greece, Hungary, Iceland, Ireland, Italy, Latvia, Lithuania, Luxembourg, Moldova, Netherlands, Norway, Poland, Portugal, Romania, the Russian Federation, the Slovak Republic, Slovenia, Spain, Sweden, Switzerland, Turkey, Ukraine and the United Kingdom. There are five Associate member countries (Australia, Canada, Japan, New Zealand and the United States) and three Observer countries (Armenia, Liechtenstein and Morocco).

A Committee of Deputies, composed of senior civil servants representing Ministers, prepares proposals for consideration by the Council of Ministers. The Committee is assisted by working groups, each of which has a specific mandate.

The issues currently being studied – on which policy decisions by Ministers will be required – include the development and implementation of a pan-European transport policy; the integration of Central and Eastern European Countries into the European transport market; specific issues relating to transport by rail, road and waterway; combined transport; transport and the environment; the social costs of transport; trends in international transport and infrastructure needs; transport for people with mobility handicaps; road safety; traffic management, road traffic information and new communications technologies.

Statistical analyses of trends in traffic and investment are published yearly by the ECMT and provide a clear indication of the situation in the transport sector in different European countries.

As part of its research activities, the ECMT holds regular Symposia, Seminars and Round Tables on transport economics issues. Their conclusions are considered by the competent organs of the Conference under the authority of the Committee of Deputies and serve as a basis for formulating proposals for policy decisions to be submitted to Ministers.

The ECMT's Documentation Service is one of the world's leading centres for transport sector data collection. It maintains the TRANSDOC database, which is available on CD-ROM and accessible via the telecommunications network.

For administrative purposes the ECMT's Secretariat is attached to the Organisation for Economic Co-operation and Development (OECD).

Publié en français sous le titre :
LA MOBILITÉ INDUITE PAR LES INFRASTRUCTURES

Further information about the ECMT is available on Internet at the following address:
http://www.oecd.org/cem/

TABLE OF CONTENTS

AUSTRIA

Peter CERWENKA and G. HAUGER
Institute for Transportation Systems Planning
University of Technology
Vienna
Austria

5

SUMMARY

Vienna, March 1996

INTRODUCTION

"He who sows roads, shall reap traffic" has been the cry throughout the land for some years now. Somewhat less poetic and more sober, the maxim in certain traffic planning circles has been: *"New roads create new traffic"*. This "created" traffic is known as "new traffic", "induced traffic" or "generated traffic". Characteristic of the perception and discussion of this concept of new traffic is the extraordinarily strong polarisation of the positions adopted by the different ideological camps: while the "green" lobby tries to prevent any further infrastructure construction with the argument that it will only "create" more traffic, the opposing lobby argues that new transport infrastructures do not create new transport demand, but simply make it possible to satisfy existing demand "more efficiently" (i.e. faster and cheaper). Intermediaries between these two irreconcilable positions often resort to the "percentage trick", i.e. they give percentages for new traffic in concrete cases, without the 100 per cent being unambiguously defined. *"Where there is shouting, there is no real knowledge"*, as Leonardo da Vinci said nearly half a millennium ago[1]. The aim of this contribution is to improve knowledge a little, to the detriment of shouting, which means above all:

- -- Introducing crystal-clear, precise terms and using them consistently throughout;
- -- Building a clear, theoretical concept on the basis of these terms, which can interpret both the traffic engineering standpoint (e.g. constant traffic interconnection matrix or constant mobility time budget) and economic approaches (e.g. elasticities);
- -- Using an unambiguous case study to demonstrate the limits to the empirical verification of new traffic, the necessary assumptions and hence the limited meaningfulness of theoretical concepts and the starting points which lead to the improper use for ideological purposes.

In addition, a distinction should be made between the **volume** of new traffic and its **perception**. The latter lies outside the scope of this contribution.

2. CLARIFICATION OF CONCEPTS

The popular definition of infrastructure-induced new traffic (i.e. "that traffic which is created by new transport infrastructures") creates a misleading impression, assigning a causality to an anonymous thing, namely "transport infrastructure" (or its constructor), so that it is forgotten that traffic is always and without exception caused by transport-demanding people. We therefore wish to define infrastructure-induced new traffic as follows, admittedly somewhat more long-windedly but less misleadingly, whereby, first, the attribute "infrastructure-induced" is dropped for the purposes of generalisation and replaced by the attribute "supply-enhancing":

Definition: New traffic is that traffic which:

a) is made **additionally possible** through enhanced transport supply (in the case of transport infrastructure: extended or upgraded); **and**
b) as a result is **caused by transport participants** who partly or fully realise this potential.

Or identically, but complementarily defined: New traffic is that traffic which would not arise without the enhancement of the transport supply.

Basically, it is immaterial whether the enhanced infrastructure concerned is a road, rail or some other infrastructure, even though in the literature attention is focused on roads. Generally, the enhancement is understood as the extension of a transport network, whether it be through adding a new link to an existing network or through increasing the capacity of an existing link through adding further lanes or tracks, etc. In the very broadest sense, however, it may be a matter of other than technical measures (above all economic) with which the attractiveness of the transport supply is altered. If the attractiveness of a transport infrastructure is reduced, for example, by restrictive or economic measures, then according to the definition there must be new traffic with a negative sign or a reduction in traffic as compared with the baseline situation before the attractiveness-reducing measures.

The use of the term "traffic" is not conducive to clear analysis, however, because it is too vague. In order to clarify the phenomenon of new traffic, it is absolutely necessary to distinguish between the two quite different dimensions:

-- traffic volume; and
-- traffic performance (transport output).

Here we agree to limit ourselves to passenger transport. The unit for traffic volume is therefore **Passenger trips/unit of time (PW/t).** Transport performance is the product of the number of journeys (traffic volume) by the average journey length and will therefore take the form of passenger-kilometres per unit of time. (It should be said in passing that, when considering new goods traffic, there are certainly some differences to be seen but, on the whole, there are strong similarities with the new passenger traffic we are dealing with here.) The "passenger trip" is defined as a person's change of location, regardless of the transport mode used and regardless of the length of the trip. "Passenger trip" is a term which covers both walking and using a vehicle.

With this so far agreed glossary of terms, we can introduce an initial analysis of transport volume growth. To this end, we first take up three different positions adopted with regard to new traffic:

a) Improvements in the road network result in **no additional traffic;**
b) Improvements in the road network enhance the attractiveness of road transport. The main beneficiaries are private car transport and road haulage. On the whole this leads to the **substitution** of public transport trips, walking and cycling;
c) Improvements in the road network lead not only to the effects described in b), but also to **new trips** and **longer trip lengths** by private motorised transport[2].

If we are inclined to accept view c) and if we also postulate a "general" growth in traffic (not brought about by any infrastructural change), then an increase in traffic can be interpreted over a precisely defined cross-section q of a precisely delimited "corridor" between a point in time t_0 and a point in time t_1 as the sum of:

-- general traffic growth;
-- (spatially and/or modally) switched traffic;
-- new traffic (as defined here);

where, at a point in time t_A (where $t_0 < t_A < t_1$), a supply attractiveness enhancement is introduced. However, the term "corridor" generally used in the literature is imprecise and often -- though unknowingly -- rather arbitrarily delimited. This is made clear by Figures 1, 2 and 3 below.

Figure 1 shows an existing road network S (full lines), an existing railway line (dashed line) B and nodal points i, j, k, l, m, n, o, which to simplify are also singular creators of traffic (sources and destinations). At time t_A a new road N (double line) is opened to enhance the attractiveness of the infrastructure. Figure 2 shows in graph form the changes in passenger traffic volume P [passenger trips/unit of time (PW/t)] for differently delimited corridor cross-sections (A) to (E) to illustrate the stages of interpretation following on from one another. Figure 3 shows in graph form a possible final situation after accumulated changes.

Figure 1. **Schematic diagram showing the difficulties involved in defining the term "corridor"**

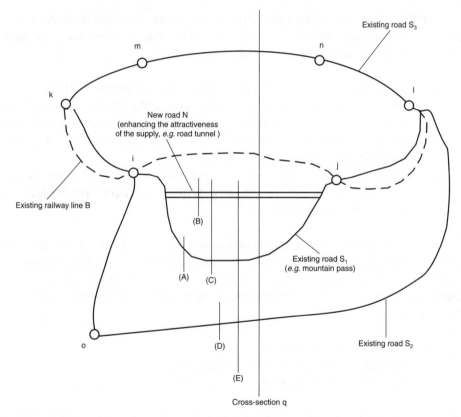

i, j, k, l, m, n, o: Nodal points or singular causes of traffic

12

Figure 2. **Graphical representation of trend in passenger traffic volume P passenger trips/unit of time (PW/t) for differently delimited corridor crossings (A) to (E) of cross-section q of Figure 1**

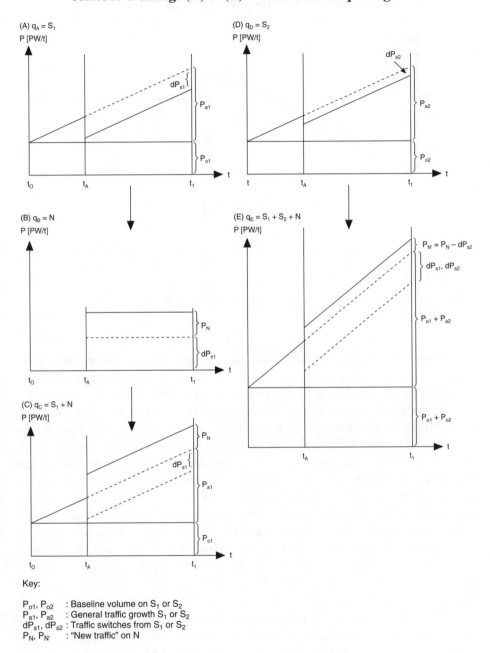

Key:

P_{o1}, P_{o2} : Baseline volume on S_1 or S_2
P_{a1}, P_{a2} : General traffic growth S_1 or S_2
dP_{s1}, dP_{s2} : Traffic switches from S_1 or S_2
P_N, $P_{N'}$: "New traffic" on N

13

Figure 3. Graphical representation of trends in passenger traffic volume P (PW/t) for an extended "corridor cross section" q = S₁+S₂+S₃+…+B+N of Figure 1

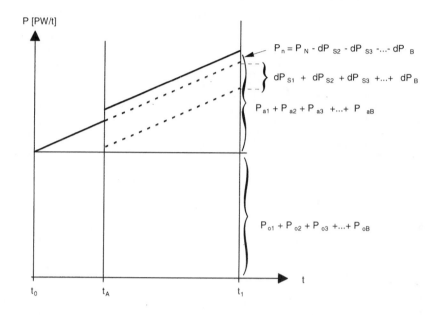

We first limit our considerations to a corridor (A) that consists only of the existing road S_1. After the new relief road N comes into operation, the trend in passenger traffic volume on S_1 can be registered as (A). Similarly, the trend in passenger traffic volume on N itself can be registered as (B), which, for the sake of simplicity, is assumed to be constant over time. Virtually all the studies we know of focus and base their statements on version (C), i.e. there are only switches from (A) and (B) to (C), in which **one** existing road S_1 and its new relief road N are combined into a "corridor cross-section". As a rule, P_N is then designated "new traffic volume" or even more simply "new traffic" and the quotient $p_N = P_N : (P_{o1}+P_{a1})$ is the "new traffic share". "Percentages of new traffic" calculated in this way are found all over the place. However, we want to go a step further in our interpretation phase and turn our attention to section (D) of Figure 2. This shows the possible trend in passenger traffic volume in corridor S_2 before and after the opening of N. (E) now shows the switches from (C) and (D) or from (A), (B) and (D). This reveals that what was originally interpreted as new traffic volume P_N was falsely labelled new traffic and should in fact be reduced by traffic volume diverted from S_2, dP_{S2}. At the same time, the base (what was in the denominator of our fraction) of $P_{o1}+P_{a1}$ has increased to $P_{o1}+ P_{o2}+P_{a1}+ P_{a2}$, so that including the correction for S_2 the new

14

traffic share $p_{N'}$ is reduced from $p_N = P_N : (P_{o1}+P_{a1})$ to $p_{N'} = (P_N - dP_{S2}) : (P_{o1}+P_{o2}+P_{a1}+P_{a2})$. With the inclusion of S_2 it is, furthermore, already questionable whether we can still speak of a "corridor". This would be completely meaningless if we now went a step further and included all the possible road links, S_3, S_4... and the railway line B as competing links, from which the introduction of N attracts switches to N. This final situation is shown in Figure 3 and we see that the originally suspected new traffic volume P_N fuses into $P_n = P_N - dP_{S2} - dP_{S3} - ... - dP_B$ and the final "new traffic share" becomes:

$$p_n = (P_N - dP_{S2} - dP_{S3} - ... - dP_B) : (P_{o1} + P_{o2} + P_{o3} + ... + P_{oB} + P_{a1} + P_{a2} + P_{a3} + ... P_{aB})$$

which tends asymptotically towards zero, because with each new "corridor" extension the numerator becomes smaller and the denominator larger. Obviously, this "corridor" concept is most unsatisfactory from the theoretical standpoint, especially when it is restricted to (C). This concept becomes particularly dubious when it is used to try to determine the additional environmental pollution caused by new traffic. But precisely such an aim is very helpful if we want to improve the concept. A first important step towards this is to **drop traffic volume on a corridor cross-section** and **take up traffic performance in a network**.

To embark upon this, we first use Figure 1 to list all possible behavioural reactions of a traffic participant to the introduction of attractiveness enhancement N (as an example, let us take N here to be a new motorway):

Effect 1: Instead of staying at home go for a drive on N (new traffic **volume**)

Before N opens: Stay at home (in i);
After N opens: Drive on N by car from i to j.

Effect 2: Slight change of route using the same mode

Before N opens: Drive by car from i to j on S_1 ;

After N opens: Drive on N by car from i to j [under the conditions shown in Figure 1 this would mean a negative new traffic **performance** because the drive is shorter on N than on S_1. As regards traffic volume, this drive is new traffic neutral on cross-section (C)].

Effect 3: Longer trip (new traffic **performance**, usually combined with effect 2)

Before N opens: Drive by car from i to j on S_1 ;

After N opens: Drive by car from i to l, using N [this trip does not appear as new traffic in corridor (C), but does on the stretch j-l].

Effect 4: Big change of route using the same mode. (This effect differs from Effect 2 only in scale, not in principle. It is listed separately here, however, because as a rule Effect 2 is taken into account in concrete cases, whereas Effect 4 is virtually without exception ignored and therefore necessarily interpreted as new traffic.)

Before N opens: Drive by car from k to l via m and n on S_3 ;

After N opens: Drive on N by car from k to l via i and j, using N.

Effect 5: Modal switch

Before N opens: Travel by train from i to j;

After N opens: Drive on N by car from i to j.

Effect 6: Change of destination and direction using the same mode

Before N opens: Drive by car from i to k on S_1 ;

After N opens: Drive on N by car from i to j.   [This trip appears in corridor (C) as new traffic performance and over stretch i-k as negative new traffic performance. If stretches i-k and i-j over N are of the same length, this reaction is new traffic neutral as regards performance.]

These effects can overlap to some extent. Only Effects 1 and 3 are to be regarded as true new traffic effects. Furthermore, they must be balanced against Effect 2 and, where appropriate, 4.   According to the usual assumptions concerning the fairly constant number of trips per person per day (mobility rate), Effect 1 should be negligible or scarcely demonstrable. Effects 3 and 6 are similar to one another: in both cases there is a change of destination. They differ not in principle but in scale: in the case of Effect 3 a known route to the original destination is extended to a more distant destination, while in the case of Effect 6 a known route is abandoned altogether and another chosen (which may in fact be shorter than the original one).

Having described the possible reactions of individual traffic participants to an enhanced supply, the verbal definition of new traffic (from now on regarded exclusively in terms of new traffic **performance**) given at the beginning of this chapter can be expressed mathematically: if in a spatially delimited area we designate as V_A the traffic performance of all trips f (leading from source i to destinations j) of respective length L, which **after** the completion of a supply enhancement use this attractiveness enhancement somewhere (n_A = number of such trips) and V_0 the traffic performance of all the trips made **before** the enhancement (possibly partly from difference sources and possibly partly to different destinations; n_0 = number of such trips), then the new traffic performance V_n is defined by:

$$V_n = V_A - V_0$$

and the new traffic share v_n as a percentage is defined by:

$$v_n = 100 \cdot \frac{V_A - V_0}{V_0} [\%] \quad (1),$$

where:

$$V_A = \sum_{k_A=1}^{n_A} f_{k_A} \cdot L_{k_A} \ (\text{pkm/t}),$$

$$V_0 = \sum_{k_0=1}^{n_0} f_{k_0} \cdot L_{k_0} \ (\text{pkm/t}).$$

If we are interested in the absolute quantity of new traffic (V_n) rather than the percentage v_n, then it is empirically much easier to add to both V_A and V_0 a constant (but generally unknown) value V_C, such that $V_A + V_C$ represents the **total** ascertainable traffic performance in a transport system **after** the attractiveness has been enhanced (i.e. not only the trips which use N) and similarly $V_0 + V_C$ the **total** traffic performance in the same system **before** the attractiveness has been enhanced. In the case of percentage data (v_n) this is misleading, however (in the same way as the consideration of corridors), because then, as the system is extended (represented by V_C), this share tends asymptotically towards zero. (Beware of the percentage trick: through extending the system any desired small percentage can be produced, whereas through contracting the system the percentage can be inflated.)

Because of the impact estimates (energy consumption, travel times, emission quantities, etc.) usually associated with the determination of new traffic, it is advisable to break traffic down by mode from the outset: while V_A by definition can only include the mode in which the supply enhancement is made; V_0 can (as a rule will) also include other modes.

It is obvious that such a definition of new traffic performance is very much more difficult to apply in a concrete empirical case than a simple corridor-specific definition of new traffic volume. However, it appears indispensable to construct a theoretically correct, consistent and plausible definition, even if it cannot be fully applied empirically, so that the gaps in an empirical study can be filled by **meaningful** assumptions consistent with this concept.

The definition is based on the following (fictional) experimental approach: after the introduction of a supply enhancement, during a specific period, each traffic participant on the enhanced stretch is asked about the source and destination of the trip. This makes it possible to establish the "traffic spider" and also average trip lengths and hence V_A. (It follows from this that, strictly speaking, a spatial delimitation appropriate to the problem can be made only

after the survey has established the spider.)   Subsequently, the supply enhancing measure is reversed and another survey is made, to determine the trip pattern that the traffic participants who used the enhanced stretch now use after the disappearance of the enhancement, where (broken down by mode, m = number of modes):

$$V_0 = \sum_{e=1}^{m} V_{0,e}$$

and hence also $V_n = V_A - V_0$ can be calculated.

3. THE TWO "CULTURES" OF THE TOPIC AND THEIR ORIGINS

Right at the beginning of the introduction (Chapter 1) it was established that the topic of new traffic threatened to split those interested in the transport system into two irreconcilable camps. This division is connected with the very different interests of the two camps and is thus easy to understand.   It is doubtless much less well known and understood, however, that the two interest groups derive the "scientific" justification for their respective positions from different scientific disciplines, both of which are of the greatest importance for the transport system, but represent different "cultures" or views of the world. Furthermore, they unfortunately do not hold clarifying exchanges of ideas and are generally based in different universities.   On the one side is traffic engineering and, on the other, transport economics. (Not infrequently, the latter claims the all-embracing title of "transport science" exclusively for itself.)

The **traffic engineer's view** regarding new traffic can probably be summed up as follows:

--   As infrastructure designers, traffic engineers always think in terms of concrete transport networks and spatial connections;
--   (Real) transport engineers always work from the outset with precisely defined and specified dimensional data (e.g. passenger-kilometres per unit of time in a defined area);

-- Transport engineers (in the classic tradition) take survey data for source-destination trips to be objective, fixed data which change only with changes in the type and intensity of land use. Any change beyond this is seen as not empirically sound and therefore as more or less arbitrary manipulation or speculation;

-- A mobility pattern established by surveys, questionnaires or traffic counts (i.e. the attribution of sources and destinations or the trip interconnection matrix) is therefore varied only in connection with changes in land use and **not in connection with changes in transport infrastructure** (though the modal choice between the same source and destination may be switched with a change of infrastructure).

With this view, only Effects 2, 4 and possibly 5 of the traffic participant's possible reactions to a change in the attractiveness of the transport supply, as listed in Chapter 2, can be taken into account. Effects 1, 3 and 6 are totally ignored.

The **transport economist's view,** on the other hand, can be summed up as follows:

-- In general, there is no direct reference to a concrete transport network or to detailed land use of the specific area. Symbolic corridors are constructed as simplified aggregations of transport networks;

-- In general, there is a lack of concrete dimensional data. The talk is mainly of "transport demand" and "generalised costs";

-- For transport economists, "transport" is a consumer good like any other, the demand for which can basically be controlled through a "demand function" (i.e. through a dependency on costs or prices). This demand function is, however, to be understood more as an abstract working hypothesis than as a tool which can be used for concrete action;

-- A mobility pattern established by surveys, questionnaires or traffic counts is therefore seen as certainly useful and necessary baseline information, but not as fixed; **on the contrary, it reacts elastically to variations in supply which alter its attractiveness**, including infrastructural changes. The spatial disposition of these modifications is not, as a general rule, part of the transport economists' discussions.

With this view, it is certainly possible in theory to explain all the possible reactions of transport participants relevant to new traffic, as listed in Chapter 2, but any attempt at concrete empirical confirmation of the abstract demand function model and the corresponding practical translation into altered traffic burdens over individual sections of a given transport network comes up against enormous difficulties.

It is the task of transport science to combine these two views in the future in such a way that the positive aspects of the models interact synergistically while the negative aspects are attenuated or even eliminated. This discussion is intended to contribute one small stone to this edifice.

Simplifying somewhat, this means that, on the one side, the rigidity of the source-destination interconnection matrix of the transport engineer's view must be abandoned so that the attribution of sources to destinations can react **elastically** to changes in the attractiveness of the transport infrastructure and, on the other side, the transport economist's usual restriction to abstract demand functions must be abandoned and demand elasticities must be considered in relation to concrete changes in the traffic burden over specific stretches of actual transport networks.

4. THE CONCEPT OF ELASTICITIES

For this we need, first of all, to examine very closely the economic concept of elasticities, so often used and abused in connection with the transport system.

4.1. The transport demand function

The basic concept is the already-mentioned transport demand function, i.e. the dependence of volume of demand N on the attractiveness of the transport supply or -- expressed in different terms -- on the (generalised) cost K of mobility (transport economists' terminology) or resistances (transport engineer's terminology) to mobility. In line with the argumentation of Chapter 2, the volume of transport demand is always expressed in "passenger-kilometres per unit of time" (pkm/t), while costs are in "currency units per passenger-kilometre" (WE/pkm) or physical consumption of resources per passenger-kilometre [e.g. time in hours required per passenger-kilometre (h/pkm)] or again in price-weighted linear combinations of resource consumption ("generalised costs") per passenger-kilometre. As regards **infrastructure-induced** new traffic, it can be stated right away that, from the standpoint of the traffic participant, the resource time is as a rule the most important decision variable. The demand function is shown graphically in Figure 4. This graph corresponds to the representation used by economists, who (for unknown reasons) always have the dependent variable N as the abscissa and the independent variable K as the ordinate. (No natural scientist or engineer would dream of doing this but, in the case of economists, this representation is so ingrained that we have to go along with it if we wish to avoid confusion.)

Figure 4. **Basic principle of the transport demand function**

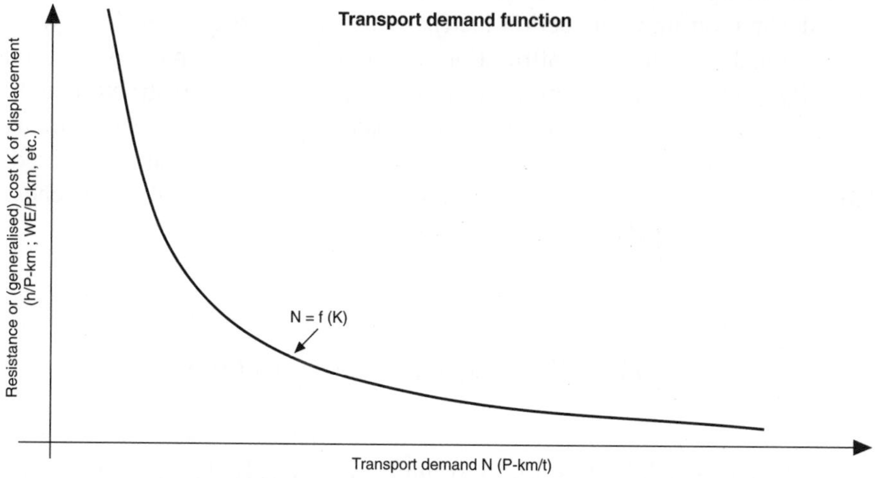

This graph shows the way of thinking of the economist, for whom it is true of any consumer good that: the more the consumer good costs the consumer (**other things being equal!**) per unit quantity, i.e. the higher the price of the consumer good, the less will be the demand for this consumer good within one and the same unit of time. In mathematical terms, this means that the transport demand function is a **monotonic falling function**. This, however, already fully describes just about the only agreed characteristic of the transport demand function because a more complete and empirically-tested specification of the concrete form of this function has virtually never been documented for the field of transport demand. The precise form of this function therefore, as a rule, remains in the dark. For didactic reasons and for considerations of practicability, two possible special cases are worth mentioning, namely:

-- the linear formulation

$$N = a + b \cdot K \qquad (2)$$

-- and the power formulation

$$N = c \cdot K^{\varepsilon} \qquad (3),$$

where, because of the required property of monotonic falling, b or ε must be negative (a, b, c and ε are parameters to be determined empirically).

4.2. The economic concept of elasticity

We now need to bring in the economic concept of **elasticity**. It is generally defined as the quotient of the **relative** change in an effect parameter and the **relative** change in a suspected or actual causal parameter. Thus, for example, for infrastructure-induced new traffic the relevant time elasticity ε_T of transport demand (in pkm) is the percentage by which traffic performance N changes when transport time T changes by 1 per cent. In mathematical terms, this means:

$$\varepsilon_T = \frac{\dfrac{N_1 - N_0}{N_0}}{\dfrac{T_1 - T_0}{T_0}} \qquad (4),$$

where the index 0 indicates a baseline situation and the index 1 a changed situation (time saving) due to an infrastructural enhancement.

If we go from considering final differences to considering infinitesimal differentials, then Equation (4) takes the form:

$$\varepsilon_T = \frac{dN}{dT} \cdot \frac{T}{N} \qquad (5).$$

4.3. Advantages and dangers of using elasticities

The economic concept of elasticity has two seductive advantages which have made it enormously popular:

-- Since elasticities are ratios of **relative** changes in two variables and hence have no dimension, it is easy to bring in concrete dimensional data and use the "percentage trick", i.e. work with the ratios of percentage changes without always having to know and be aware of precisely how the 100 per cent of the numerator and denominator are defined;

-- Elasticity is a very clear and neat but, at the same time, somewhat **abstract** working hypothesis, which is difficult to verify empirically and therefore in concrete applications leaves nice grey areas where discretionary powers can be used to suit any ideological need.

These convenient advantages of elasticity hide serious drawbacks connected with their use, however. With regard to infrastructure-induced new traffic and its extremely sensitive position in the clash of interests, these drawbacks must not be swept under the carpet, especially when, for example, the time elasticity ε_T is given a concrete value (e.g. $\varepsilon_T = -0.3$).

First, the biggest drawback: from Equation (5) it can be directly derived by transformation and subsequent integration **that ε, according to Equation (3), represents such an elasticity and the demand function of the power formulation according to (3) is the only mathematical form, for ε to be constant over the whole of the transport demand function curve.** But this means that **for any other function curve, the elasticity then depends on the area of the independent variables considered.** However, this also means that setting a fixed value (e.g. $\varepsilon_T = -0.3$) and just going ahead and making the calculations always assumes this particular type of curve. Also, even if a range is given (such as $\varepsilon_T = -0.2$ to -0.5), then this statement only uses something which indicates for which area the determinant T is valid for the lower and which for the upper limit. Even for the mathematically simplest form, i.e. the linear form according to Equation (2), ε is already dependent on T (or K), as can easily be shown:

$$\varepsilon_T = \frac{dN}{dT} \cdot \frac{T}{N} = \frac{b \cdot T}{a + b \cdot T}$$

It should also be noted how the concept is used with empirical data in the first place. In the most favourable case, two points can be found on the transport demand function through approximation to the "other things being equal" condition. To integrate these two points into an elasticity without

24

knowing the true curve of the function and then to use this elasticity, further extrapolating, to estimate the effects of measures can lead to totally false conclusions. This is shown in Figure 5, where, generalising, instead of transport time T the consumer cost K is the independent variable.

For didactic and computing reasons and because of the general lack of any more detailed specification of elasticity data in the literature, further discussion and example calculations (see Chapter 5) will be limited exclusively to the power formulation according to Equation (3).

Figure 5. **Extrapolation of transport demand using elasticity data (K_0, N_0; K_1, N_1 ... "measured" values; K_{neu} ... cost to the user of an envisaged measure, N_{neu} ... estimated transport demand effect of K_{neu})**

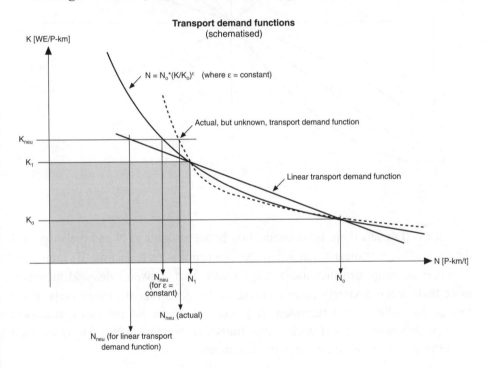

4.4. Relationships between traffic demand functions and elasticities

First, we need to say a little about the relationship between transport demand functions and the range of values for elasticities ε, as shown in Figure 6.

Figure 6. **Transport demand function curves of the form**
$$N = c \cdot K^\varepsilon \text{ or } N = c \cdot E^\varepsilon, \text{ depending on the value of } \varepsilon$$
(K ... e.g. cost, E ... e.g. income)

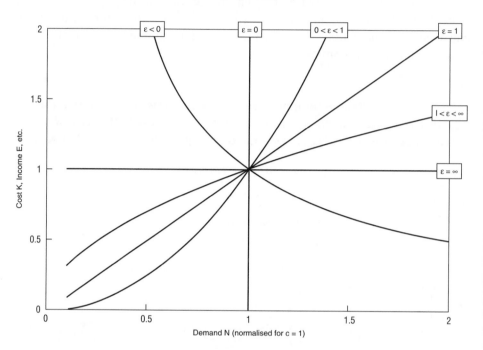

Transport demand functions
(schematised)

If $\varepsilon = 0$ means there is no connection between demand N and the suspected determinant, $\varepsilon > 0$ means that when the determinant (e.g. income E) increases, transport demand also increases; $\varepsilon > 1$ means that transport demand increases more than proportionately to an increase in the determinant. Conversely, $\varepsilon < 0$ means that when the determinant (e.g. cost of travel K) increases, transport demand decreases; $\varepsilon < -1$ means that transport demand decreases "more than proportionately" to an increase in the determinant.

4.5. Combined effect of several determinants

Up to now, we have considered only a single determinant in each case. The extraordinary difficulty in empirical application, however, lies precisely in the fact that there are always several determinants affecting transport demand at the same time. In mathematical terms, using the basic formulation (3) with constant elasticities, this can be expressed as follows, for example:

$$N = N_0 \cdot \left(\frac{E}{E_0}\right)^{\varepsilon_E} \cdot \left(\frac{K}{K_0}\right)^{\varepsilon_K} \cdot \left(\frac{T}{T_0}\right)^{\varepsilon_T} \qquad (6),$$

where:

E_0:   Incomes (of private households, for example) in the baseline situation;

K_0:   Perceived out-of-pocket costs in the baseline situation;

T_0:   Travel time in the baseline situation;

N_0:   Transport demand in the baseline situation;

E,K,T,N: Corresponding parameters in the changed situation;

ε_E: Income elasticity of transport demand;

ε_K: Out-of-pocket cost elasticity of transport demand;

ε_T: Time elasticity of transport demand.

If we adopt the concept of "generalised costs", then Equation (6) has to be written:

$$N = N_0 \cdot \left(\frac{E}{E_0}\right)^{\varepsilon_E} \cdot \left(\frac{K + p_T \cdot T}{K_0 + p_T \cdot T_0}\right)^{\varepsilon_{Kg}} \qquad (7),$$

where:

p_T: monetary value of the unit of time (WE/h);

ε_{Kg}:   generalised cost elasticity of transport demand.

4.6. Considering competition by using "cross elasticities"

So far, we have assumed that there is only one "transport" consumer good. But in the field of transport we very often have competing transport supplies, as, for example, in long-distance passenger transport where, in addition to a "private car transport" consumer good, we also have a "rail transport" consumer good. There then arises the question of how a change in a determinant in one consumer field changes demand in another. It is well known that an estimate of this type can be made using "cross elasticities" (e). They logically have the opposite sign to the corresponding "direct" elasticities (ε).

If we take two competing systems [for example, private car (index P) and rail (index B)], then Equation (6) is extended as follows:

$$N_P = N_{P,0} \cdot \left(\frac{E}{E_0} \right)^{\varepsilon_E} \cdot \left(\frac{K_P}{K_{P,0}} \right)^{\varepsilon_{K,P}} \cdot \left(\frac{T_P}{T_{P,0}} \right)^{\varepsilon_{T,P}} \cdot \left(\frac{K_B}{K_{B,0}} \right)^{e_{K,P}} \cdot \left(\frac{T_B}{T_{B,0}} \right)^{e_{T,B}} \tag{8}$$

The cross elasticities are indicated by the letter "e". The cross elasticity $e_{K,B}$ would thus be the percentage change in private car transport demand resulting from a relative change of 1 per cent in the out-of-pocket cost of rail transport and, similarly, $e_{T,B}$ the percentage change in private car transport demand resulting from a relative change of 1 per cent in the travel time of rail transport.

4.7. Law of the constant travel time budget

Together with the concept of elasticity, it is essential at this point to discuss the suspected **"Law of the constant travel time budget"** which is enjoying increasing popularity. Briefly summarising, it says: time savings made possible by an enhanced transport system (and this includes, for example, an improved infrastructure), in that the time taken to travel from a fixed source to a fixed destination is shortened, will be fully reinvested (through new or longer trips) in the enhanced transport system; there is therefore no real saving of travel time. (How this phenomenon -- if it exists -- is to be **evaluated** is not discussed here.)

We can now show, by means of Equation (8), what this law would mean in economic terms:

--   All the elasticities and cross elasticities of Equation (8) except for the direct and cross time elasticities would have to be exactly zero. The total transport demand would depend exclusively on travel times;

--   The transport demand function would have to take the form of a power function according to Equation (3). Even a formulation for generalised costs according to Equation (7) would be excluded;

-- In the case of restricting to simply one transport system (i.e. no cross time elasticities exist), the time elasticity of transport demand ε_T would have to take precisely the value -1, because then and only then is the total travel time in the system constant, $N_0 \cdot T_0 = N_1 \cdot T_1 = N \cdot T = const$ (shaded area in Figure 5, there with K instead of T).

It is fairly reasonable to suppose that it is most improbable that these three conditions are fulfilled in reality. Instead it might be possible to use this "law" simply as a working hypothesis if it is desired that "**other things being equal" conditions apply for all other determinants** (other than travel time) and if the changes in travel times remain within modest limits.

4.8. Time phases of elasticities relevant to traffic demand

Lastly in this chapter on elasticities, there is one more aspect to consider, namely the **changes over time** of these elasticities. When infrastructure-related time and cost elasticities are being considered, it is usual to distinguish between three phases:

-- Short-term phase: this is the phase in which "attraction traffic[3]" appears, i.e. transport demand which arises immediately after a new transport infrastructure is opened, arousing the curiosity of transport participants, who want to visit and admire the new stretch. This short-term phase is not the subject of this paper;
-- Stable phase: this is the new equilibrium reached after the short-term phase and is the main subject of this paper;
-- Long-term phase: gradual shift in the equilibrium through changes in land use (in the vicinity of the new infrastructure) made possible by this more attractive transport supply. This phase is taken into account indirectly in the case study (Chapter 5) insofar as in a longitudinal study these changes in land-use structures result in increasing real household incomes, which are empirically included.

4.9. Survey of empirical problems

When using the concept of elasticities in concrete cases to estimate infrastructure-induced new traffic, three fundamental problem areas are encountered:

--   The problem of delimiting an area which is, on the one hand, manageable and, on the other, representative of the actual conditions (discussed in Chapter 2);

--   The problem of the never completely realisable "other things being equal" condition in the "with" case and the "without" case. Above all, in a longitudinal analysis, as time goes on there is a transition from a singular increase in the attractiveness of the transport infrastructure to a complex with many reasons for "new traffic";

--   The problem of demonstrating causality (of enhanced attractiveness of supply, for example), even where the "other things being equal" condition more or less applies, because of the fundamental impossibility of replicating a real "experiment" on a 1:1 scale in the socioeconomic field in a real geographical area.

There are thus, basically, three fundamental problem areas as they appear in classical physics: space, time and causality.

5. CASE STUDY

In what follows, as announced in the introduction, we present and discuss a case study. The aim here is not to provide a generally applicable calculation algorithm for determining traffic -- there is probably no such thing -- but rather to empirically work out the elasticity concepts discussed in Chapter 4 [on the basis of Equation (8)], strictly applying the terms agreed in Chapter 2.

This work proceeds in the following stages:

--   Description of the situation (Section 5.1.);
--   Documentation of the data used (Section 5.2.);
--   Longitudinal analysis to estimate income elasticities and out-of-pocket cost elasticities (Section 5.3.);
--   Estimation of performance of infrastructure-induced mobility and examination of the "law of the constant travel time budget" (Section 5.4.);
--   Discussion, interpretation and relativisation of results (Section 5.5.).

5.1. Description of the situation

The main criteria for the choice of a suitable example are: the best possible data, possibility of good spatial delimitation and the most decisive, significant and radical enhancement of the attractiveness of supply introduced at a single point in time. As the few examples in the literature show, it is scarcely possible to get anything like satisfactory fulfilment of the first condition. This is also true of the case study chosen, the Arlberg Road Tunnel. Here we consider **private car traffic only**.

The Arlberg Road Tunnel was opened on 1 December 1978, establishing a sure road link in winter between the two Austrian *Länder* of Tirol and Vorarlberg. It was planned to be a toll road with a maximum speed of 80 kph. Before, there had only been a steep, winding mountain pass road which was not always negotiable in winter. This road still remained after the opening of the tunnel. Between the fork in Tirol (near St. Anton am Arlberg) and that in Vorarlberg (near Langen) the mountain road is about 20 km long and the tunnel road about 16 km. Parallel to the road tunnel there is a railway, also with a long tunnel (see Figure 7). The advantage of this example lies in the fact that **in the immediate vicinity** there is no practical alternative other than the mountain pass, the tunnel or the railway.

Figure 7. **Sketch map of the selected example**

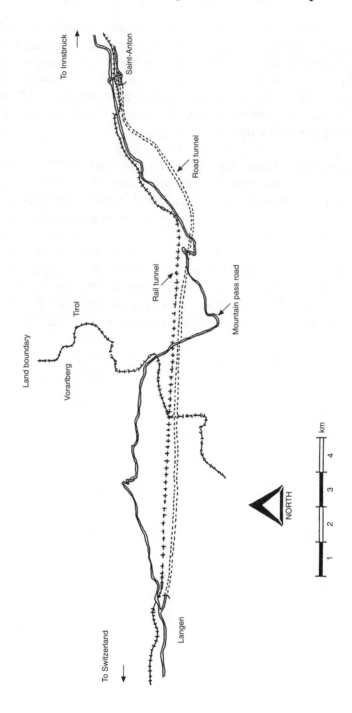

5.2. Documentation of the data used

To carry out the longitudinal analysis to estimate elasticities (see Section 5.3.), it is necessary to have or to construct the longest possible time series (before and after the opening of the tunnel), both for the parameter to be explained (here, traffic performance in pkm) at least for the road tunnel and the mountain road and for the determinants. Here, already, certain serious limitations must be noted.

-- Because of the limited availability of data, only the period 1970 to 1994 can be considered. (Automatic road traffic counts were introduced for the first time in Austria in 1970; 1994 was the last relevant year available when this paper was completed.) Data is available for whole years only. Data were collected and published for the year the road tunnel was opened (1979) and the two following years (1979 and 1980), but were not included in the calculations in order to eliminate the effect of the short-term "attraction traffic" (see Section 4.8.).

-- The trend in rail passenger transport demand, which is not very certain due to the size of the sample and the type of survey, shows no identifiable connection with the opening of the road tunnel and is therefore not taken into account in what follows.

5.2.1 *Private car passenger transport demand for the mountain pass road and the road tunnel*

Here, it is first necessary to state the unit used for the parameter "passenger transport demand". In accordance with the exposition in Chapter 2, this is passenger-kilometres per day (pkm/d), since, in our opinion, only this is suitable for evaluating new (passenger) traffic. This means, however, that the usual unit of vehicles per day (veh/d) has to be abandoned, which leads to considerable additional work in an empirical study. Starting with the usual "average daily traffic volume" used in road traffic counts, with the unit (veh/d), the following additional steps are required:

a) Determination of the average vehicle volume on the mountain road and the road tunnel;
b) Determination of the private car share of all vehicles;
c) Attribution of an average transport distance to convert the volume of cars into traffic performance (car-kilometres);
d) Conversion of the daily car-kilometres (ckm/d) into daily passenger traffic performance (pkm/d), using car occupation rates.

Regarding (a): The vehicle traffic volume (veh/d) at the permanent traffic monitoring stations relevant for the mountain pass (99) and the road tunnel (81) were taken from the annual reports[4] on the automatic road traffic counts. However, monitoring station 99, relevant for the mountain road, did not come into operation until 1977. The years 1970 to 1976 were estimated backwards from 1977 using the growth rates of monitoring station 36 on a similar corridor not far away. A similar reconstruction also had to be made for the year 1989, however, for which there are no figures, no doubt due to a fault in the recorder.

Regarding (b): The private car share of the total traffic was determined using the five-yearly Europe-wide standardized manual road traffic counts, which distinguish between types of vehicle. The counts usable were those for 1970, 1975, 1980, 1985 and 1990[5]. For the years between the manual survey years, the car share was interpolated linearly. The results are presented in column (1) of Table 2.

Regarding (c): The inclusion of an attributable trip distance represents, in our opinion, an important extension of the usual way of considering the problem. It is also, however, an indispensable part of the elasticity concept used here. This was possible with empirical support solely due to the fact that, for the case examined here, what are known as "traffic spiders" were produced both for the road tunnel and for the mountain pass road. These spiders are graphic representations of the intensity of source-destination routes for all vehicles passing over a specific stretch during a specific period of time. This made it possible to calculate average trip distances for all vehicles passing over the designated stretch. Since the data for the spiders can be obtained only by stopping vehicles, they involve a great deal of work, are extraordinarily costly and they also disturb the traffic flow during the survey itself. They can therefore be produced only rarely and only on a sample of traffic on individual days. For our example, we have data from two survey cycles (1979-80[6] and 1990-91[7]), for which the data from the single-day surveys[8] are presented in Table 1.

Table 1. **Data from the traffic spider surveys in Arlberg**

Survey date	Traffic volume: number of passenger vehicles(*)	Average trip distance (km)
Mountain road		
31.7.79 (Tuesday)	3 999	399
21.7.90 (Saturday)	9 625	420
3.10.91 (Thursday)	2 844	317
Tunnel road		
31.7.79 (Tuesday)	4 880	474
24.4.80 (Thursday)	2 422	339
21.7.90 (Saturday)	7 943	606
3.10.91 (Thursday)	3 165	428

(*)   Cars, motorcycles and coaches (no further breakdown possible).

Figure 8 shows the example of the traffic spider from the survey day Saturday, 21 July 1990 for the Arlberg Road Tunnel.   Now, three or four individual survey days undeniably constitute an extremely small empirical basis for a period of 25 years, but it is nevertheless better than nothing and we must now try, by applying theory, to exploit this small database as efficiently as possible, while remaining conscious of the limited nature of the empirical basis. In short, after much trial and error, comparing the individual traffic spiders made it seem plausible to formulate a positively correlated relationship between daily traffic volume TV and the corresponding average trip distance W, of the following form:

$$W = W_0 \cdot \left(\frac{TV}{TV_0}\right)^{\alpha}$$

Figure 8. Traffic spider for counting station 45, Arlberg Tunnel, on Saturday, 21 July 1990

Source: Bundesministerium für wirtschaftliche Angelegenheiten: *Straßenverkehrserhebung Verkehrsspinnen*, Vol. 2, Paper 1/3, Vienna.

The index "0" refers to a defined baseline situation, while α can be understood as the trip distance elasticity of the daily traffic volume. It falls in the period after the opening of the road tunnel for the mountain road with $\alpha = 0.1$, much smaller than for the road tunnel with $\alpha = 0.5$. If we take the values of survey year 1979 [column (2) of Table 2] as the base, then we have the following equations for the years $j = 1979 \ldots 1994$ after the opening of the tunnel (survey figures are available only for these years):

$$\text{Mountain road (j = 1979 ... 1994)}: W_j = 375 \cdot \left(\frac{DTV_j}{DTV_{1979}} \right)^{0.1} \qquad \text{(km)}$$

$$\text{Road tunnel (j = 1979 ... 1994)}: W_j = 350 \cdot \left(\frac{DTV_j}{DTV_{1979}} \right)^{0.5} \qquad \text{(km)}$$

If we adhere consistently to this principle, then for the mountain road for the years $j = 1970 \ldots 1978$ before the opening of the tunnel, again taking 1978 as the base, then, working from the 1979 traffic spiders for the mountain road and the road tunnel, we can use a mixed formulation of the following form:

$$\text{Mountain road (j = 1970 ... 1978)}: W_j = 338 \cdot \left(\frac{DTV_j}{DTV_{1978}} \right)^{0,3} \qquad \text{(km)}.$$

The trip distances W_j thus determined appear in the time series in column (2) of Table 2.

Regarding (d): Neither direct, example-relevant nor overall territorial time series of car occupancy rates are available for Austria. We, therefore, assuming similar occupancy rates, used the appropriate German time series instead, as they appear annually as the quotient of the passenger traffic performance of motorised private vehicles including taxis (deducting two-wheelers) and the associated car traffic performance[9]. The occupancy rates appear in column (3) of Table 2.

After carrying out these individual steps in the analysis, it is now possible to calculate the relevant daily passenger traffic performance in car traffic as the product of the daily car volume over the stretch, the average trip distance and the car occupancy rate. This appears in column (4) of Table 2. In addition, the trend over time of these important parameters is shown graphically in Figure 9.

Table 2. Trends in private car passenger traffic demand on the Arlberg mountain road and Road Tunnel 1970-94

	Year	Car traffic volume (Cars/d) (1)	Average trip distance (km) (2)	Occupancy rate (P/car) (3)	Traffic performance (pkm/d) (4) = (1)(2)(3)
Mountain road	1970	2771	307	1.747	1485097
	1971	3222	321	1.740	1799365
	1972	3623	332	1.708	2057794
	1973	3664	334	1.698	2075249
	1974	3439	327	1.681	1891707
	1975	3598	332	1.650	1969850
	1976	3750	336	1.631	2054796
	1977	3886	340	1.621	2138162
	1978	3827	338	1.600	2070427
	1979	2174	**375**	1.591	1296406
	1980	2182	375	1.569	1284699
	1981	2259	376	1.563	1329002
	1982	2658	383	1.547	1573416
	1983	2682	383	1.537	1578574
	1984	2813	385	1.523	1649099
	1985	2731	384	1.518	1589895
	1986	2982	387	1.501	1731718
	1987	3130	389	1.473	1793384
	1988	3176	389	1.462	1808316
	1989	3502	393	1.448	1994280
	1990	3591	**394**	1.464	2073263
	1991	3751	396	1.460	2168573
	1992	3428	392	1.459	1963576
	1993	3612	395	1.459	2079511
	1994	3633	395	1.459	2092592
Road tunnel	1979	2597	**350**	1.591	1445450
	1980	2444	340	1.569	1302321
	1981	2322	331	1.563	1201197
	1982	2377	335	1.547	1231124
	1983	2443	339	1.537	1274677
	1984	2601	350	1.523	1387543
	1985	2561	348	1.518	1351133
	1986	2811	364	1.501	1536462
	1987	3105	383	1.473	1750824
	1988	3499	406	1.462	2078521
	1989	3730	419	1.448	2264846
	1990	3885	**428**	1.464	2435563
	1991	4059	438	1.460	2592339
	1992	4258	448	1.459	2785242
	1993	4229	447	1.459	2756093
	1994	4366	454	1.459	2891015

Figure 9. **Trend in daily car passenger traffic performance over the Arlberg Pass and through the Road Tunnel, 1970-94**

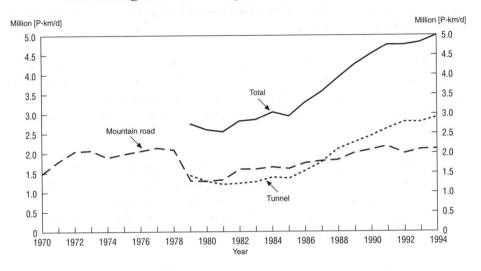

5.2.2   *Data for the independent variables*

As input parameters for the longitudinal elasticities model, according to Equation (8), the following determinants are necessary:

a) Private household incomes;
b) Transport costs perceived by the car driver (car transport costs);
c) Rail transport costs.

In addition, it would be necessary to have travel time data for the average trip distance over the pass and through the tunnel as well as for rail travel in order to be able to calculate the model fully. There are no data available for this, however. We therefore work on the following basis: for the time period before the opening of the tunnel, on the one hand and after the opening of the tunnel, on the other, it is assumed that the values of the stretch-specific time required (= the reciprocal values of the speeds) remain virtually unchanged and that any reduction in travel time is due exclusively to the singular process of opening the road tunnel. In the period considered (1970-94) rail travel time did not change over relevant distances either. Under this assumption, discussed more fully in Section 5.3., the above-mentioned input data suffice.

39

Regarding (a): The data on household incomes (for 1970-94) are from the Austrian Central Statistical Office. The raw data are at current prices, which are then converted to 1994 prices using the consumer price index. These values are shown in column (1) of Table 5.

Regarding (b): As costs perceived by the car driver and hence affecting his choices, fuel costs are generally used. In the case of a road-use charge over specific stretches (toll for using the road tunnel), this is also to be taken into account. In order to arrive at the dimension required here (ASch/pkm), a number of steps are necessary:

-- First, a gasoline price[10] series is to be determined. Data on this (average annual sales prices of different types of fuel) at current prices were kindly made available by the ÖMV Aktiengesellschaft[11]. These were again converted to 1994 prices. The values are shown in column (1) of Table 3.

Table 3. Perceived car transport costs over the Arlberg Pass, 1970-94
(all cost data adjusted to 1994 prices)

Year	Gasoline price (ASch/l)	Specific gasoline consumption (l/100 car-km)	Occupancy rate (P/car)	Perceived car transport cost (ASch/P-km)
	(1)	(2)	(3)	(4)=(1).(2)/[100.(3)]
1970	11.03	9.63	1.747	0.61
1971	10.59	10.00	1.740	0.61
1972	10.53	10.28	1.708	0.63
1973	10.70	10.00	1.698	0.63
1974	13.92	9.91	1.681	0.82
1975	13.14	10.00	1.650	0.80
1976	13.49	10.10	1.631	0.84
1977	12.76	10.20	1.621	0.80
1978	12.65	10.30	1.600	0.81
1979	12.53	10.10	1.591	0.80
1980	12.09	10.20	1.569	0.79
1981	11.61	10.20	1.563	0.76
1982	11.28	10.20	1.547	0.74
1983	11.19	10.20	1.537	0.74
1984	10.83	10.20	1.523	0.73
1985	10.74	10.20	1.518	0.72
1986	10.80	10.20	1.501	0.73
1987	10.88	10.10	1.473	0.75
1988	10.91	10.00	1.462	0.75
1989	10.85	9.80	1.448	0.73
1990	10.72	9.70	1.464	0.71
1991	10.59	9.50	1.460	0.69
1992	10.39	9.40	1.459	0.67
1993	10.22	9.40	1.459	0.66
1994	10.12	9.30	1.459	0.64

-- Also to be taken into account is the specific fuel consumption of the car, which changes over time. As in the case of the car occupancy rate, because of the lack of traffic performance weighted time series in Austria, the German values for internal combustion engines were used[12]. The values are shown in column (2) of Table 3.

-- Lastly, the product of the gasoline price and the specific fuel consumption is divided by the occupancy rate, the determination of which has already been discussed and which is again shown in column (3) of Table 3. The results are shown in column (4) of Table 3.

-- As already mentioned, in the case of the road tunnel there are additional toll charges: regardless of the occupancy rate, each car has to pay a toll when using the road tunnel. Rather as in the case of commuter travel, there are concession rates or quantity discounts for "frequent users". It was possible to obtain an average cost per car on the basis of survey data communicated by the Alpen Straßen Aktiengesellschaft [13] and the toll charges contained in this company's annual reports as time series at current prices. Again, these data were converted to the standard 1994 price using the consumer price index [column (1) of Table 4]. In order to obtain the dimension required here (ASch/pkm), these values had to be divided by the already-determined occupancy rate [shown again in column (2) of Table 4] and the also previously determined average trip distance [shown again in column (3) of Table 4]. The result is presented in column (4) of Table 4. (It is worth noting that, in terms of cost per passenger-km, the **real** cost had fallen by one-third in 15 years.)

Table 4: **Additional perceived car transport costs (toll) for using
the Arlberg Road Tunnel 1979-94**
(all cost data adjusted to 1994 prices)

Year	Average toll per car trip (ASch/car trip) (1)	Occupancy rate (P/car) (2)	Average trip distance (km) (3)	Toll cost (ASch/pkm) (4) = (1)/[(2).(3)]
1979	162.36	1.591	350	0.29
1980	159.25	1.569	340	0.30
1981	173.03	1.563	331	0.33
1982	158.83	1.547	335	0.31
1983	151.82	1.537	339	0.29
1984	144.69	1.523	350	0.27
1985	138.25	1.518	348	0.26
1986	135.56	1.501	364	0.25
1987	131.84	1.473	383	0.23
1988	129.03	1.462	406	0.22
1989	131.33	1.448	419	0.22
1990	133.62	1.464	428	0.21
1991	133.00	1.460	438	0.21
1992	130.35	1.459	448	0.20
1993	127.26	1.459	447	0.20
1994	123.68	1.459	454	0.19

Regarding (c): To determine rail fares per pkm, because of the digressive tariffs it would be necessary to know the average trip distance in the case of rail passengers on the Arlberg line, too but, despite considerable efforts, no information could be obtained on this. We therefore took one average distance of 150 km and another of 300 km. The tariffs were taken from the official timetables of the ÖBB (Austrian Federal Railways), using the standard case of a full-fare second class express train ticket. In the case of tariff changes in the course of a calendar year, the tariffs before and after the change were weighted by the respective number of days of the year. The rail transport costs thus obtained were in current prices and again had to be converted to 1994 prices using the consumer price index. The results appear in columns (2) (for 150 km) and (3) (for 300 km) of Table 5.

43

Table 5. **Additional determinants of passenger traffic demand 1970-94**
(all cost data adjusted to 1994 prices)

Year	Income of private households in Austria (billion ASch/yr) (1)	Second class express train fare for 150 km (ASch/pkm) (2)	Second class express train fare for 300 km (ASch/pkm) (3)
1970	693.16	1.59	1.41
1971	740.87	1.52	1.34
1972	763.86	1.80	1.57
1973	787.91	1.74	1.51
1974	816.23	1.59	1.38
1975	855.05	1.46	1.28
1976	911.95	1.36	1.19
1977	917.27	1.37	1.21
1978	942.66	1.49	1.33
1979	991.18	1.54	1.39
1980	998.08	1.45	1.31
1981	983.26	1.52	1.42
1982	1025.29	1.52	1.36
1983	1054.66	1.50	1.32
1984	1051.88	1.53	1.34
1985	1078.24	1.51	1.33
1986	1131.91	1.49	1.30
1987	1182.89	1.47	1.29
1988	1210.45	1.41	1.32
1989	1266.09	1.37	1.29
1990	1324.53	1.33	1.24
1991	1370.86	1.32	1.23
1992	1382.73	1.31	1.21
1993	1384.50	1.33	1.23
1994	1443.32	1.44	1.25

5.3. Longitudinal analysis to estimate income elasticities and out-of-pocket cost elasticities

As already indicated in Section 5.2.2, the aim of the longitudinal analysis is to separate the income and transport cost trend effects from the suspected new traffic effect caused by the increased speed, it being assumed that, with the exception of the opening of the road tunnel itself, there were no significant speed-increasing measures during the observation period. From the computational standpoint, this means that in Equation (8) the factors can be set with the time elasticity equal to 1, insofar as in the comparison of two successive situations (years) the "big leap" of the opening of the tunnel is excluded. Applied to the present problem, Equation (8) with N_P as the relevant passenger traffic performance in car traffic takes the following form:

$$N_{P,j+1} = N_{P,j} \cdot \left(\frac{E_{j+1}}{E_j} \right)^{\varepsilon_E} \cdot \left(\frac{K_{P,j+1}}{K_{P,j}} \right)^{\varepsilon_{K,P}} \cdot \left(\frac{K_{B,j+1}}{K_{B,j}} \right)^{e_{K,B}} \qquad (9).$$

Here, the index j can cover three situations, with n each time representing available equations:

a) Mountain pass values $j = 1970$ to $j = 1976$ $(n = 7)$
b) Mountain pass values $j = 1981$ to $j = 1993$ $(n = 13)$
c) Road tunnel values $j = 1981$ to $j = 1993$ $(n = 13)$

For each of these sets and for the union of all three sets it is possible, after finding the logarithm of Equation (9), to estimate the unknown elasticities ε_E, $\varepsilon_{K,P}$ and $e_{K,B}$ by linear regression. This was done. The only elasticities with the correct sign and at least a 90 per cent significance level were those shown in the constellation of Table 6, with two alternative rail transport costs being calculated for two alternative trip distances (W = 150 km and W = 300 km), as explained in Section 5.2.2.

Table 6. **Constellation of significant elasticities**
(R^2 = degree of certainty)

No.	Situation	Direct elasticities ε		Cross elasticities e		R^2
		Income	Car transport costs	Rail transport costs (W = 150 km)	Rail transport costs (W = 300 km)	
1	(a)	1.810	-0.542	-	-	0.649
2	(b)	2.185	-0.459	0.592	-	0.862
3	(c)	2.214	-0.445	-	0.629	0.867
4		1.531	-0.468	-	-	0.522
5		1.865	-0.366	-	0.616	0.599

5.4. Estimation of performance of infrastructure-induced mobility and examination of the "law of the constant travel time budget"

Using the elasticities calculated in Section 5.3, it is now possible, on the basis of the transport demand on the mountain pass road in 1977 ($N_{pass,1977}$), to calculate a fictitious transport demand for this road in 1981 ($N_{pass,1981,fict}$) (i.e. the year after the suspected decline of the "attraction traffic", as it probably would have been had the road tunnel **not** been opened). But now we have the problem of deciding which of the constellations in Table 6 should be selected. We first exclude constellations 2, 3 and 5, because in these the cross elasticities of the rail transport costs are higher than the direct elasticities of the car transport costs, which does not seem very plausible. Of the remaining constellations, we select No. 1, because this has a higher degree of certainty than No. 4 and in addition is extrapolated from situation (a) (i.e. from 1977). This choice gives:

$$N_{pass,1981,fict} = N_{pass,1977} \cdot \left(\frac{E_{1981}}{E_{1977}} \right)^{1.810} \cdot \left(\frac{K_{P,1981}}{K_{P,1977}} \right)^{-0.542} = 2.493 \text{ million pkm/d}$$

This figure can now be compared with the two actual transport demand figures for the mountain pass and the road tunnel in 1981. This is shown graphically in Figure 10. If we now assume that there was **no switch** from other roads (other than the pass) or from other modes, then under these assumptions the difference of 1.301-1.164 = 0.037 million pkm, shown in Figure 10, can be regarded as the new car traffic performance. The new traffic share as defined in Equation (1) thus amounts to:

$$V_n = 100 \cdot \frac{1.201 - 1.164}{1.164} = 3.18\%$$

Figure 10. Estimate of the "new traffic" generated by the opening of the Arlberg Tunnel for the first year after the probable disappearance of attraction traffic (1981)

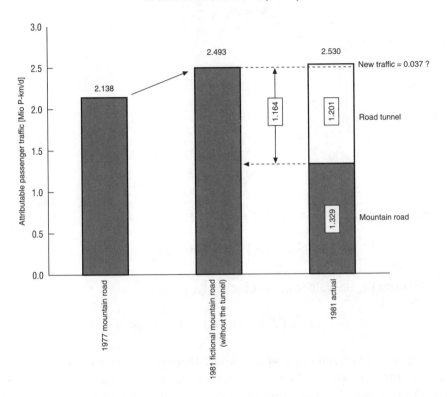

Lastly, with this result we can reconstruct a time elasticity from the transition from the system **without** the road tunnel to the system **with** the tunnel for 1981 and hence test the "law of the constant travel time budget".

The methodology is as follows: in 1981, the average trip distance for a car using the tunnel was estimated at 331 km (see Table 2). If we assume that the average speed of a car over the 16 km tunnel stretch is 80 kph, over the relatively steep and non-motorway-standard approach and existing roads, totalling some 80 km, about 70 kph, and over the flat and largely motorway standard remaining distance (331 - 16 - 80 = 235 km) 90 kph, then the average speed over the whole trip V = 83.7 kph. The comparable situation for an identical source-destination trip over the mountain pass (20 km of mountain road at 50 kph instead of 16 km of tunnel at 80 kph, otherwise identical conditions) gives an average speed of V_0 = 80.6 kph.

Using the basic formula derived from Equation (5):

$$N = N_0 \cdot \left(\frac{T}{T_0} \right)^{\varepsilon_T}$$

then with the identity:

$$T{:}T_0 = V_0{:}V$$

and the formulation:

$$\frac{N}{N_0} = 1 + v_n$$

the time elasticity can be calculated as follows:

$$\varepsilon_T = -\ln(1 + v_n) / \ln(V / V_0) \ .$$

Substituting the values in our case study, we get:

$$\varepsilon_T = -\ln(1 + 0.0318) / \ln(83.7 / 80.6) = -0.829 \ .$$

This value is greater than -1 and would therefore not satisfy the "law of the constant time budget", which -- as demonstrated in Section 4.7. -- requires exactly the value -1. The value of $\varepsilon_T = -0.829$ indicates that only part of the travel time saved by using the tunnel is reinvested in traffic performance, not the whole of it.

5.5. Discussion, interpretation and relativisation of results

The results of Section 5.4. are misleading because, although they fit well into the philosophy of modern, economically-oriented transport science, our delight in their plausibility threatens to make us forget the many assumptions, the many gaps in the data filled by analogous experience, the many simplifications and the altogether shaky empirical base. In what follows -- as is appropriate in serious scientific endeavour -- we adopt the role of our own devil's advocate and, through documenting our own misgivings and objections, we call our own results into question. This is also intended to prophylactically prevent those lobbyists who find our results particularly appealing from using them to justify their political action and also to take the wind out of the sails of the arguments of those counter-lobbyists whom our results do not suit, by ourselves drawing attention to:

-- The representation of decision behaviour for modelling purposes as, for example, in the choice of transport route or mode, should be oriented towards individual characteristics (such as the incomes of individual households whose members undertake a trip) and not macroscopically surveyed aggregate data (such as the incomes of all Austrian private households). We are constantly with this dilemma of having to use only macroscopic aggregate or average values rather than the decision-relevant microscopic data. (This applies also, for example, to car occupancy rates and specific fuel consumption where, to make matters worse, comparable foreign data had to be used.)

-- The empirical basis for the average trip distance leaves much to be desired.

-- As shown in Chapter 4, the elasticity concept as formulated in Equation (8) represents one calculable special case among an infinite number of other possible models. We know virtually nothing about the concrete shape of demand functions and, above all, about their transferability.

-- The regression estimates for the different elasticities, as shown in Table 6 for different equation constellations, need to be interpreted with corresponding caution. If, instead of constellation No. 1 (selected for good reasons) we had taken No. 4, for example, then, otherwise making the same assumptions, there would have been a new traffic share of 8.49 per cent (as against 3.18 per cent); if we had taken No. 2, 3 or 5 (i.e. a constellation including the cross elasticity of the rail transport cost), then there would have been a considerable **negative** new traffic share (from -13 per cent to almost -20 per cent).

-- The new traffic share, as calculated in Section 5.4., is distorted by the fact that there is a toll charge for using the tunnel and not for using the pass. This means that it can be assumed that without the toll there would be considerably more traffic through the tunnel and really this higher value should be considered in calculating new traffic. This value could also be used to calculate the changed car transport costs and the corresponding elasticities. However, the result would be completely misleading for an interpretation of new traffic: since, with the exception of source and destination traffic from and to the pass and with the exception of excursionists who want to enjoy the beautiful view from the pass in good weather, if the toll were removed there would be no logical reason **not** to use the tunnel, so that it would essentially be a case of traffic switched from the pass, which cannot be recognised as such by the elasticity model. One possible development of the model might be to make the calculations separately for the mountain pass road (as a "competing consumer good" vis-à-vis the road tunnel) with it becoming a factor with an (unknown) cross elasticity to the road tunnel cost. Only the remaining difference between the two model calculations could then be interpreted as new traffic.

-- Besides the (local area) alternative route over the Arlberg Pass, which is relatively simple to take into account, it was not possible to consider any (broad area) alternative road routes. The estimates are therefore limited exclusively to Case (C) of Figure 2.

-- Over the average trip length of 300 to 400 km for traffic using the tunnel, there were, over the period considered, a number of larger and smaller infrastructural improvements, but it is not possible to determine their impacts on travel times. (Small proportions of time elasticities are probably hidden in the car transport cost elasticities estimated by regression.)

-- As shown by the estimates in Section 5.4., there are sensitive small differences in the computed values. The computation must always be as precise as possible. (The most precise calculation can never compensate for the imprecisions in the data, of course, but simply prevents further imprecision in the results.)

6. CONCLUSIONS

The following conclusions can be drawn from the theoretical discussion and the effort to establish an empirical basis for the problem area of "infrastructure-induced new traffic":

-- On fundamental economic grounds, it makes sense to postulate infrastructure-induced new traffic. This can be seen very easily from the fact that without infrastructure there would be no traffic.

-- However, saying that "new roads **create** new traffic" leads to a completely erroneous view and the "anonymisation" or wrong imputation of blame. The fact is that "new roads **permit** new traffic", which is "created", as it always has been, by ourselves.

-- The "law of the constant travel time budget" implies a very particular case of the transport demand function, in which all the possible determinants other than travel time must also be held constant. The concept of "generalised costs" (out-of-pocket costs + time costs) is fundamentally incompatible with the "law of the constant travel time budget".

-- The empirical estimates made here do not permit any clear statement about the value of the time elasticity of transport demand. For our example we calculated a time elasticity of about -0.8 but, as pointed out in Section 5.5., this value is subject to many uncertainties.

-- An important question -- bordering on the philosophical -- in the economic discussion of new traffic can be illustrated by an analogy: if the price for the consumer good "apple" falls, then according to economic theory -- other things being equal -- more apples will be consumed. And what else happens? Will less pears and/or less plums be consumed? Perhaps in total exactly as much fruit (= apples + pears + plums) will be consumed and the increase in apple consumption will be compensated by a fall in pear and plum consumption. Is the analogy road tunnel = apple, mountain pass = pear, railway = plum now valid? Or should it be road tunnel = apple, mountain pass = different variety of apple, all other (unknown) alternative routes = other varieties of apple? Does new traffic correspond to more apples of a specific variety or simply more apples or more fruit? Or perhaps even less fruit?

These conclusions are intended to be an essential component of our contribution, so that the results will not be misused for ideological purposes.

7. SUMMARY

Infrastructure-induced new traffic has, for some years, been the subject of very controversial discussion and evaluation in transport policy circles, but there are very few studies on the topic which deserve the appellation "scientific". It is therefore a very good thing that the ECMT has taken up this topic and devoted a Round Table (No. 105) to it.

It is not the intention of this paper to present a model for calculating new traffic which will be generally applicable (this would probably be just as impossible as squaring the circle), but rather:

-- to introduce clear, precise terms;
-- to build a clear theoretical concept on the basis of these terms, capable of taking into account and interpreting both transport engineering and economic concepts;
-- to carry out an empirical case study.

The theoretical concept is based on the income, cost and time elasticities of transport demand and shows the relationships between demand functions, elasticities and cross elasticities. The "law of the constant time budget" is found to be a (somewhat improbable) special case among an infinite number of conceivable demand functions, in which **only** travel time appears as an independent variable.

In the selected case study, the income and transport cost influences are first filtered out by longitudinal analysis, in order to then be able to designate the remaining excess transport demand resulting from a singular, major transport supply enhancement (the opening of the Arlberg Road Tunnel in Austria on 1 December 1978) as infrastructure-induced new traffic. We then try to construct a time elasticity in order to be able to interpret infrastructure-induced new traffic in economic terms, using time elasticities.

An absolutely essential part of this contribution, to which the authors attach great importance, is the concluding discussion with its self-critical relativisation of the meaningfulness of the findings and the resulting set of conclusions, which should be taken to heart in future work on this topic.

NOTES

1. Leonardo Da Vinci: *Traktat von der Malerei,* Teil 1, Faszikel 1, No. 6 (deutsche Ausgabe: Jena, 1909, 5.5).

2. Arnold, T. *et al.: Umweltwirkungen von Verkehrsbehinderungen und verkehrsflußfördernden Maßnahmen im Straßenverkehr. Studie des Instituts für Verkehrsplanung und Straßenverkehr der Technischen Universität Dresden im Auftrag des Amtes für Umweltschutz der Stadt Dresden,* Dresden, 1995, p. 30. The report is concerned only with measures which alter attractiveness in the road mode, but the ideas can be generalised to some extent.

3. Würdemann, G.: Neuverkehr -- die unbekannte Größe; in: *Internationales Verkehrswesen,* 35(1983), No. 6, pp. 403-408.

4. Bundesministerium für Bauten und Technik BZW (Ab 1986) Bundesministerium für Wirtschaftliche Angelegenheiten (Eds.): *Auswertung und Darstellung der Ergebnisse der automatischen Straßenverkehrszählung, Jahrgänge* 1970 ff. Vienna, 1971 ff.

5. Österreichisches Statistisches Zentralamt (Ed.): *Straßenverkehrszählung* 1970, 1975, 1980, 1985. *Beiträge zur österreichischen Statistik,* Heft 281 (Vienna, 1972) inklusive Heft 339 (Vienna, 1973), Heft 543 (Vienna, 1979), Heft 750 (Vienna, 1985), Heft 865 (Vienna, 1987). The figures for 1990 were no longer published, but were made available in list form by the Österreichischen Statistischen Zentralamt.

6. Bundesministerium für Bauten und Technik (Ed.): *Straßenverkehrserhebung Verkehrsspinnen,* Vienna.

7. Bundesministerium für Wirtschaftliche Angelegenheiten (Ed.): *Straßenverkehrserhebung Verkehrsspinnen,* Vienna.

8. In these two surveys, the relevant traffic count stretches are Numbers 45 (road tunnel) and 46 (mountain pass).

9. For 1975 to 1994 (from 1991 the old *Bundesländer* only): Bundesverkehrsministerium (Ed.): *Verkehr in Zahlen 1995*, pp. 158-159 and pp. 214-215; Bonn, 1995. For 1970 to 1974 the corresponding tables from *Verkehr in Zahlen 1991* were used, taking into account the subsequent revision of the corresponding time series.

10. For the sake of simplicity, it is assumed that all cars use carburetted fuel.

11. ÖMV Aktiengesellschaft: *Jahresdurchschnittspreise für Treibstoffe*. Vienna, communication of 11.1.1996.

12. For 1975 to 1994, Bundesverkehrsministerium (Ed.): *Verkehr in Zahlen 1995*, pp. 286-286, Bonn, 1995. For 1970 to 1974, the corresponding tables from *Verkehr in Zahlen 1991* were used, taking into account the subsequent revision of the corresponding time series.

13. Alpen Strassen Aktiengesellschaft: Communication of 7.2.1996, Innsbruck.

SPAIN

José Maria MENÉNDEZ
Universidad Politecnica de Madrid
Madrid
Spain

NEW TRANSPORT INFRASTRUCTURES IN MADRID-SEVILLE CORRIDOR. ANALYSIS OF SOME EFFECTS REGARDING INDUCED TRAFFIC

SUMMARY

Madrid, March 1996

1. INTRODUCTION

The aim of this paper is to analyse certain aspects of traffic generation in two newly completed infrastructures: the Andalucía Expressway *(Autovía)* and the high-speed train linking Madrid and Seville. The objective is not to define a model that allows a forecast of future traffic as a function of certain parameters believed to be significant, but rather to analyse the process emerging from the transformation of the Madrid-Seville corridor, dating from 1992, on the basis of available information concerning the various coexisting means of transport.

To this end, our intention has been to gather as much information as possible regarding this period which, as may be imagined, has occasionally been very difficult due to the fact that certain data, given the current process of market liberalisation, have a direct bearing on the marketing strategies of operating companies. On the other hand, data concerning private transport are indirect, since the Spanish Administration does not carry out systematic origin-destination surveys for road passenger transport.

This paper has mainly been based on the following information:

- Number of passengers on each of the public transport modes (railroad, aeroplane, bus) for the more important connections in the area under study, 1992-1995;
- Evolution of tariffs and availability for the same connections and period;
- Evolution of traffic intensity in key points within the road network linked to the corridor;
- Significant results related to traffic induction deduced from periodic RENFE surveys of AVE (high-speed) passengers.

2. THE CONCEPT OF GENERATED TRAFFIC

The concepts "substitution effect" and "generated effect" are apparently clearly differentiated but, expressed in numerical values, always seem *hidden* within the results indicating total demand met by the various operating companies in any given service.

Traditionally, the various modalities were imbued with a certain nature of complementarity in such a way that, according to parameters such as income, reason for travelling or distance travelled, each passenger decided to use a single means of transport. It seems evident that over the last few years this doctrine has become obsolete, especially in Europe and particularly due to the presence of high-speed railroads and a drastic reduction in air tariffs, as a result of the liberalisation of price structures proposed by Brussels.

Highways, high-speed railroads and air transport currently compete within wide margins yet to be clarified but, at the same time, include most of the traffic connections included in the present analysis.

Concerning generated demand and for the purposes of our analysis, we define the term as an increase in traffic within a certain relation resulting from the appearance of certain new elements in the infrastructure or in the services provided within it, as long as this increase is not due to travellers who simply change modality or as a result of a subjective reason hindering the use of alternative means.

A global analysis shows clearly that this concept includes two distinct considerations: on the one hand, what is simply an increase in number of passengers, that is, people who under different circumstances would not travel (although they could do so) and now, under the new circumstances, do travel. Secondly, there is an increase in mobility, that is, in the number of passengers who make more than the usual number of trips given the new circumstances.

From the point of view of a time-series study, these definitions could be completed by establishing a distinction between short- and mid-term generation, on the one hand and long-term generation on the other. The first would relate strictly to the new characteristics of supply and would tend to disappear after a period yet to be determined but probably under six years.

The latter type, however, could evolve over a very long term and would be linked to considerations such as indirect job creation, development of new enterprises or redistribution of inhabited areas.

It appears obvious that the nuances we have tried to establish so far are especially difficult to analyse, particularly if we attempt to apply them to an infrastructure and services featuring entirely new components, as is the case with the high-speed Madrid-Seville railroad; more so if, as will be shown further, a new infrastructure (the Expressway, or *Autovía*) is put into operation almost in parallel to the existing one. This circumstance will make it more difficult, if not impossible, to establish a distinction between what is "generated" or "induced" and what is "transferred" in the types of traffic subject to analysis. We will at least try to define the new elements in the increased demand versus the "natural evolution" of the various types of traffic.

3. A RETROSPECTIVE ANALYSIS: THE MADRID-SEVILLE-CADIZ ROUTE AT THE EMERGENCE OF THE RAILROADS

We hope the reader is not surprised if we begin our analysis by going back 150 years, but the number of analogies to be considered is large enough and each of them is of sufficient interest to justify our plunge into the past.

The Madrid-Seville-Cadiz line was started around 1850 with the support of foreign capital, French to a large extent. The first section, sharing the Valencia route, was completed by 1855, at which time work was started on the opposite end, with completion of the Cadiz-Cordoba section by the end of 1860. The complete line, 730 km long, (572 km Madrid-Seville and 158 km Seville-Cadiz) was finished around 1865. Construction therefore lasted some fifteen years, although partial sections, both in the north and south ends, were under operation by various companies as and when the corresponding works projects were completed.

The introduction of the railroad meant a qualitative jump in reference to the transport services provided up to that time (stagecoaches), whose importance can be assessed by comparing specific operating data (tariffs, number of passengers, duration of trip) for each of the two modes.

The Madrid-Seville-Cadiz stagecoach worked regularly as of 1822, although long before then an attempt had been made to establish this service, in 1771. This initial project failed, among other reasons, because the deficiencies in the infrastructure made it impossible, at the time, to guarantee the regularity of a passenger service operating on wheeled vehicles. The main obstacle, as continues to be the case today, was the Sierra Morena Pass which was not to be overcome, with a modern road, until 1783.

The reason for waiting four additional decades for the availability of a regular passenger transport service between the capital of Spain and the main city in Andalucia is obviously closely related to the contents of this Round Table and is perfectly expressed in the introductory chapter of *Stagecoaches. Handbook of Activities for the Year 1830*, from which we have drawn some of the data here incorporated: *"Due to the lack of passengers, there was no means of travel and due to the means of travel, there were no passengers."*

3.1. Duration of trips

The service, providing mail stagecoaches covering the Madrid-Cadiz line, left the capital, around 1830, on Mondays, Thursdays and Sundays (at midday in winter and at 3 p.m. in the summer) and reached destination in four and a half days. The Madrid-Seville stagecoach, taking three and a half days for the trip, left Madrid on Wednesdays and Saturdays. This service became daily during the following decade.

It should be noted that the duration of these trips was a major breakthrough in the days when the road through the Despeñaperros Range was not yet modernised. These trips took some ten days, around 1775, for the Madrid-Seville route and thirteen days for Madrid-Cadiz.

3.2. Available seats

The average stagecoach, during the first part of the 19th century, had four types of ticket: Berlin, Interior, Cabriolet and Rotunda, derived from analogous French terminology. Vehicle features were as shown in Figure 1 and carrying capacity (far superior to that in coaches of the previous century) hovered between 16 and 20 passengers. This meant the annual availability of regular seats, for the period previous to the introduction of the railroad, of some 3 000 passengers each way for the Madrid-Seville-Cadiz route, besides some 2 000 more on the Madrid-Seville route.

Figure 1

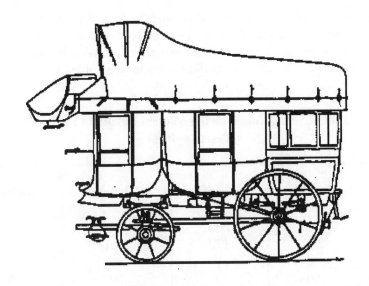

The modest size of these indicators is evidenced by the number of inhabitants in the largest cities in the corridor around 1850, besides which we have listed data from 1995 as a benchmark for the remainder of the study (Table 1).

Table 1. **Population**

	1850	**1995**
MADRID	281 000	3 041 000
SEVILLE	112 000	714 000
CORDOBA	42 000	315 000
MALAGA	94 000	531 000
GRANADA	68 000	271 000
CADIZ	70 000	155 000

Towards the middle of the century, but prior to the appearance of the railroad, the type of vehicle had evolved on some of the routes (particularly the one described) to become an omnibus (*gondola* was the expression used at the time) with capacity for some 45 places, which represented slightly over 16 000 places per year on the Madrid-Seville route alone.

3.3. Tariffs

Given the lack of specific data concerning the evolution of demand covered in the period prior to the introduction of the railroad in this corridor, tariffs are probably, along with data concerning the provision we have just mentioned, the more precise indicators concerning traffic evolution (see Table 2).

Table 2. **Stagecoach tariffs Madrid-Seville 1822-1854**
(Peseta values)

	Berlin	Interior	Cabriolet	Rotunda
1822		200	165	
1832	200	170	140	120
1846	130	110	80	
1854	90	80	70	70

It should be noted that the data provided concerns monetary units in current value for each year and, if a deflator were applied, even approximate, the resulting differences would be spectacular.

Although the data may be incomplete, both the evolutions of services offered and of tariffs seem to indicate that satisfied demand must have evolved, through the period considered, continuously and in a lively fashion.

What are the implications of the introduction of the train (new infrastructure and newly available services) in relation to the period prior to its appearance? We will attempt to describe these by comparing a number of relevant data.

Concerning the duration of trips, commercial speeds reached on Spain's initial railroad network ranged between 30 and 40 km per hour and, although on the Madrid-Seville route these speeds were mainly in the bottom end of the range (31.5 km/h), this implies that the travel time on the Madrid-Seville route was 18 hours and 23 hours on the Madrid-Cadiz route. The frequency of service was one trip daily in each direction from the beginning of operations.

The normal configuration for trains on this route was ten cars, whose characteristics are shown in Figure 2. This meant slightly more than 200 seats per day and direction, four times more than the previous phase for the stagecoach service.

Figure 2

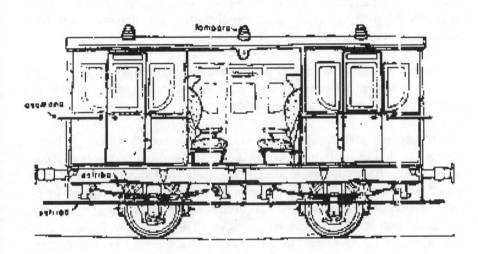

Tariffs remained fairly stable over the early years of operation. We have data provided by the two main operating companies of the time, Compañía del Norte and MZA. The practically total concordance of data (Table 3) allows us to affirm that their application to the Madrid-Seville-Cadiz route provides trustworthy results.

Table 3. **Railroad company tariffs/km (1864) (Pesetas)**

Passengers	COMPANY NORTE	MZA COMPANY
1st class	0.10	0.10
2nd class	0.075	0.075
3rd class	0.0475	0.0475

If we apply these tariffs to the Madrid-Seville route, the result is a price per ticket totalling 57 pesetas in first class, 43 ptas. in second class, and 27 ptas. in third class, i.e. between one-half and one-third of the stagecoach tariffs.

Taking all of the above into consideration, it is no wonder that the stagecoach service disappeared immediately following the inauguration of the railroad, after that time providing only complementary functions to the railroad. It is also not abnormal that the sharp decrease in generalised costs (both in tariffs and in travel times) resulted in an important generation of traffic. It is important, however, to note two interesting aspects.

The first is that the level of this generation of traffic was not proportional to the new provision of services; in fact, operating companies were forced to lower supply since sales did not match forecast values.

The second is that, for some years, Spanish society (users, technicians, politicians) allowed itself to be deluded by the "mirage" of the new mode of transport and believed that the road was to be abandoned as a means of connecting the territory and to play no more than a secondary role as a support for local traffic. This historical mistake led to decisions which, in hindsight, might appear to be absurd but, at the time, seemed almost inevitable. Specifically, around 1870, the Ministry of Development, then responsible for the road system, decided to abandon a total of 2 600 km of roads (of which 1 800 were first class) in the belief that they were a useless duplication of the communications network. It is unnecessary to remark on the economic costs to the State which would result from this measure in the long term.

4. TERRITORIAL CONSIDERATIONS.
SUPPLY OF INFRASTRUCTURE AND SERVICES

4.1. High-speed railroad

Around 1980, the rail network linking Madrid and Seville through the Despeñaperros Range, the only rail access to the Guadalquivir River Valley, was fully congested. This circumstance, together with the sinuous design of the line for over 570 km (straight distance barely over 380 km), led the experts to generate the "New Railroad Access to Andalucia" (NAFA) project, announced by the Government in October 1986.

This project, which did away with 100 km, was to be included in the Railroad Transport Plan, approved in April 1987. Work started on the Brazatortas-Cordoba section in October of that year and, slightly over a year later, in December 1988, the Government made the decision to build the new high-speed lines on the international gauge.

Work was completed during 1989-1991, and the first running trials took place in December of that year. Commercial operations began concurrently with the inauguration of the Seville Universal Expo, on 21 April 1992 (Figure 3).

Figure 3

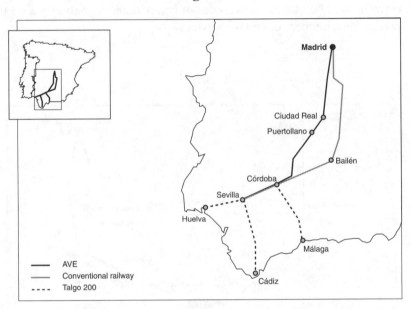

A number of advances have taken place since that date in relation to service operations. Specifically, since October 1992, a number of "shuttles" (no intermediate stops) link Madrid with Puertollano and Ciudad Real, cities which before the AVE (high-speed train) ran were outside the Andalucian railroad network.

On the other hand, the first Talgo 200 services were launched in January 1993, linking Madrid to Malaga. This line employs Talgo units running on the AVE track and continuing on the conventional network, which requires a change of gauge. The second service of this type, Madrid-Huelva-Cadiz, began operating in June of that year.

For this reason, we believe it convenient, in the analysis of mobility generated by the new infrastructure of the Madrid-Seville corridor, to take into consideration not just these two cities and some other intermediate stops, but also the system resulting from the cities of Malaga, Cadiz and Huelva, as shown in Figure 4, since, for analytical purposes, they constitute a deeply interconnected system. We will also include the city of Granada which, although not part of the AVE network, will be of use for purposes of comparison in analysing road traffic flows and the development of certain services.

Figure 4

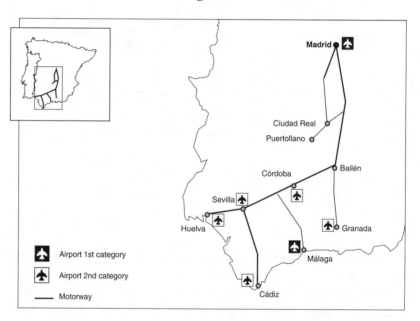

Concerning the volume of supply on the market provided by AVE services, Table 4 shows in some detail the evolution in the number of weekly trains for the period 1992-1995 and for the main connections in the corridor.

Table 4. **Number of weekly trains**

	MADRID-SEVILLA	MADRID-MÁLAGA	LANZADERAS	MADRID-CADIZ	MADRID-HUELVA
18.10.92	56+56		35+35		
31.01.93	59+59	14+14	43+37		
23.5.93	72+72	15+15	48+42		
26.7.93				7+7	7+7
26.9.93	70+70	14+15	48+42	7+7	7+7
18.3.94	70+70	14+15	48+42	7+7	7+7
18.4.94		15+22			
29.5.94	70+70	25+25	48+42	7+7	7+7
11.9.94	76+71		48+42		
16.11.94				7+7	7+7
2.1.95	76+71	25+25	48+47	7+7	7+7
12.3.95	76+71	25+25			
28.5.95		26+25		7+7	7+7
10.9.95	86+86				
16.10.95		26+26		7+7	7+7

4.2. The Madrid-Seville-Huelva and Seville-Cadiz Expressway

The changeover to expressway of the Madrid-Seville-Cadiz route was already part of the ambitious Programme of the Spanish National Highways (PANE), drafted in 1964, and practically cancelled before initiation. At the end of the '60s, this route benefited from the REDIA programme (Network of Asphalt Routes) which substantially improved quality for some 5 000 km of the Spanish road network, upgrading them to European standard (two 3.5 m lanes and lateral shoulders of 2.5 m). At this time, the Andalucia road underwent its first significant transformation since it was first laid in 1783.

One of the few sections of highway (in this case, a toll highway) completed as part of the PANE was finished in 1972, linking Seville and Cadiz. However, the remaining sections (Madrid-Seville and Seville-Huelva) had to wait for the approval and initiation of the National Road Plan, 1984-1991. Table 5 shows the construction stages for each route for the period 1987-1992.

Table 5. Madrid-Seville-Huelva Expressway. Construction process
(in kms)

	1987		1988		1989		1990		1991		1992	
	In oper	Under constr	In oper	Under constr	In oper.	Under constr	In oper	Under constr	In oper.	Under constr.	In oper.	Under constr
Madrid-Seville	30.5	484.1	136.0	379.4	208.0	311.6	408.2	116.6	450.2	66.4	519.8	
Seville-Huelva	9.0	55.0	9.0	55.0	23.8	40.2	64.0		64.0		64.0	

It should therefore be noted that two infrastructures as important as the high-speed train (481 km) and the expressway (520 km) were begun and completed almost simultaneously and aimed at providing service for the same traffic link.   This makes the analysis of the resulting mobility especially interesting, both in its configuration and particularly concerning induced effects but, at the same time, makes it extremely difficult to establish any reflection or attempt to draw definitive conclusions to extrapolate on any comparable future set of circumstances.

4.3. Public road transport services

Before approval of the Enabling Act for Land Transport (July 1987), existing legislation dated from 1947 and 1949, and emphasized rail transport over road transport, which gave RENFE the right of prevention, or "bumping" right concerning possible future regular passenger lines to be put into operation.

To give an idea of the scenario prior to 1987, it should be enough to note that a Madrid-Cadiz bus trip required two transfers (Bailén and Seville) and the purchase of tickets from three different operating companies.

The new law abolished preferential treatment and gave equal status to both means of transport. However, a number of years went by before the new services could be put into operation, after solving a number of remaining administrative procedures.   Specifically, the Madrid-Seville-Huelva line was inaugurated in February, 1992 and shortly after -- in May of that year -- the Madrid-Cadiz line also started operating, both lines managed by the same company. As may be observed, 1992 was a milestone year and, as such, is the basis for the present analysis.

The Madrid-Malaga and Madrid-Granada lines began running in the summer of 1995 and therefore there are as yet no significant operating data. The Madrid-Ciudad Real line, however, is one of the few that underwent no change in the period under analysis, since it began operating before 1987. The number of seats provided by the operating companies in this corridor (1995 data) is shown in Table 6.

Table 6. **Buses (1995). Number of seats**

	PER WEEK (SUMMER)	PER WEEK (WINTER)	PER YEAR
MADRID-SEVILLE	3 240	3 060	164 520
MADRID-CADIZ	1 512	900	62 712
MADRID-CORDOBA	1 548	1 044	62 346
MADRID-C. REAL	1 650	1 650	85 800
MADRID-MALAGA	2 546	2 014	114 304
MADRID-GRANADA	3 952	2 698	157 852

4.4. Airport infrastructure and services

Figure 4 shows the breakdown of the territory under analysis into six operating airports, two of them first category (Madrid and Malaga) and the remaining four regional (Seville, Jerez, Granada and Cordoba). The Jerez airport may be considered, for practical purposes, as serving Cadiz, since the distance between the two cities is barely 30 km of highway. The Cordoba airport is not as active in commercial traffic compared with the others.

Global activity for the set of airports (national and international traffic) is shown in Table 7.

71

Table 7. **Airports. Global activity. 10^3 passengers**

	1987		1988		1989		1990		1991		1992	
	In oper	Under constr	In oper	Under constr	In oper.	Under constr	In oper	Under constr	In oper.	Under constr.	In oper.	Under constr
Madrid-Seville	30.5	484.1	136.0	379.4	208.0	311.6	408.2	116.6	450.2	66.4	519.8	
Seville-Huelva	9.0	55.0	9.0	55.0	23.8	40.2	64.0		64.0		64.0	

If we specifically centre our attention on the services under study, Table 8 shows data on weekly flights for the four routes linking Madrid with airports in Andalucia.

Table 8. **Weekly flights**

	1992		1993		1994		1995	
	MAX.	MIN.	MAX.	MIN.	MAX.	MIN.	MAX.	MIN.
Madrid-Sevilla	125	53	57	45	42	15	31	31
Madrid-Málaga	64	58	64	47	56	55	48	48
Madrid-Cádiz	25	24	24	19	24	24	19	19
Madrid-Granada	13	13	13	13	13	13	16	16

5. ANALYSIS OF TRAFFIC EVOLUTION

Generally, it may be said that the period 1992-95 -- the first four years of operation for the new infrastructure -- was a time of clear growth for the corridor, in both public and private transport.

The former is evident for the Madrid-Seville route in Diagram 1 and will be shown in successive diagrams and tables for the remaining sections of the corridor.

Diagram 1. **Public transport. Madrid-Seville. Passengers transported**

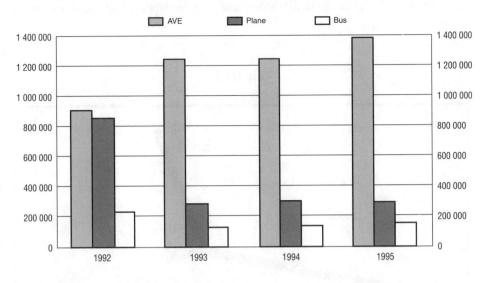

5.1. Private traffic

As mentioned above, the Spanish Administration unfortunately does not carry out systematic mobility surveys concerning private transport to provide precise information on the flows and origin-destination of this type of trip. However, the evolution of average annual daily traffic (AADT) in specific key points of the network may not be of use in quantifying real traffic volumes, but at least it will allow an estimate of evolution through the period. Here, Diagram 2 is quite significant. It shows the evolution of light vehicle traffic in the period 1987-1995 at the two more significant census stations for long-distance travel analysis, both on the Madrid-Cordoba (Station E-195) and Cordoba-Seville (Station E-200) routes. Locations are shown in Figure 5. For purposes of comparison, we also include data generated in Station E-196, located between Bailén and Granada, a section which underwent no substantial transformations in infrastructure during the period of analysis. The diagram shows three quite distinct sections. The first (1987-90) features very similar percentile growth in the three stations with annual variations of little significance, and could be defined by natural evolution compatible with general growth in car ownership and mobility at a time of sustained economic growth. The second period (1990-1992) corresponds to a time of stagnation, resulting from the deepening of the economic crisis and traffic recession. However, as may be noted, the stagnation continues at Station E-196, but disappears radically at the two other stations and enters a phase of traffic growth, featured by a much more pronounced slope than the one showing global traffic growth throughout the network or general economic growth.

Figure 5

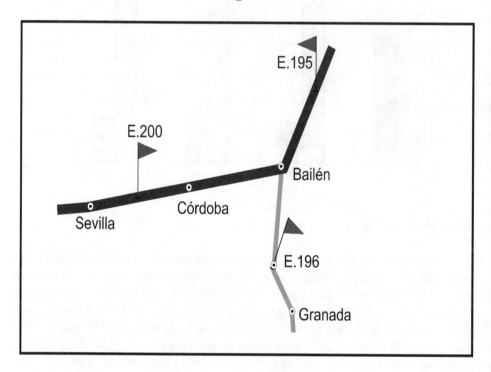

Diagram 2. **Evolution of AADT**

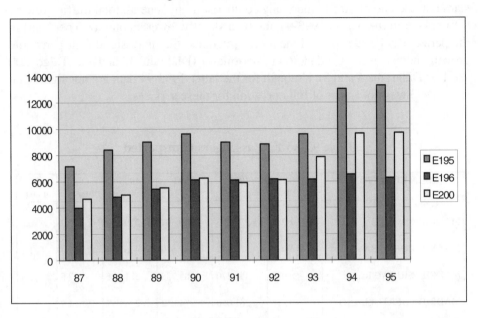

Specifically, data from Station E-195 show a growth from 8 835 vehicles/day in 1992, the year when the expressway was opened, to 13 041 vehicles/day in 1994 (+ 47.6 per cent). Station E-200 showed a growth of 57.4 per cent over the same period. We emphasize the fact that these data are in no way an attempt to show the increase in number of trips between Madrid and Seville, since it is impossible to eliminate the fraction that corresponds to an increase in local or intraregional mobility, but are in any case undeniable proof of the induction effect resulting from the new infrastructure.

As a general indicator, and taking into account that the latest trustworthy data on private vehicle passenger flows between Madrid and Seville, dating from 1989, reached some 590 000, a fairly conservative estimate could lead us to a figure of around 880 000 passengers/year in 1995.

5.2. Rail transport

The case of AVE is, in general, remarkable and includes a number of noteworthy considerations. Table 9 shows data regarding passengers transported in some of the more important relations covered by the new high-speed train as well as total number of passengers. It appears obvious that 1992 data are not relevant for analytical purposes; the Universal Expo and the fact that operations started at the end of April hinder any comparison. In general, total traffic grew by 9.1 per cent in the period 1993-94 and by a slightly lower amount (8.6 per cent) in the period 1994-1995. As a function of relations, the more significant percentile growth indices were Ciudad Real-Puertollano (Diagram 3) and the Talgo 200 service (Diagrams 4 and 5), although for the latter 1993-94 data are not significant since 1993 was not a year of full operation for these services.

Table 9. **AVE. Passengers transported**

MAIN RELATIONS	1992	1993	1994	1995	% 94/93	% 95/94
MADRID-SEVILLE	902 282	1 237 897	1 240 507	1 379 400	0.2	10.8
MADRID-CORDOBA	115 039	371 172	421 570	426 264	13.4	1.1
MADRID-CIUDAD REAL	60 077	451 270	485 733	521 086	7.5	7.4
MADRID-PUERTOLLANO	40 518	261 050	274 012	294 057	4.9	10.9
CIUDAD REAL- PUERTOLLANO	26 000	206 048	231 978	283 249	12.6	21.9
MADRID-MALAGA		351 740	434 833	476 201	23.6	9.6
CADIZ-HUELVA		100 379	184 6112	188 463	84.0	2.0
TOTAL JOURNEYS	1 314 035	3 256 098	3 553 653	3 861 571	9.1	8.6

Diagram 3. **Shuttle (Lanzaderas) Ciudad Real-Puertollano Passengers transported**

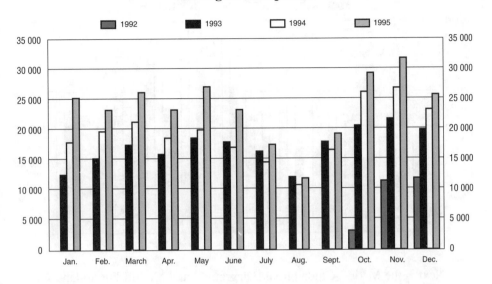

Diagram 4. **Talgo 200. Madrid-Cádiz-Huelva. Passengers transported**

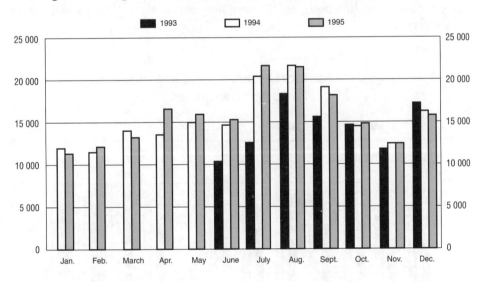

Diagram 5. **Talgo 200. Madrid-Málaga. Passengers transported**

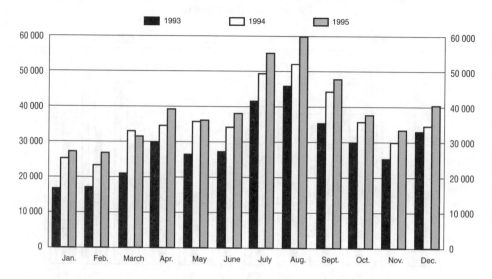

Next is the Madrid-Ciudad Real (Diagram 6) and Madrid-Puertollano service (Diagram 7). It continues to appear surprising that the "Shuttle" services, whose operation was decided as a complementary commercial strategy, inaugurated quite some time after the line itself, are the ones that register the highest growth indices for the period.

Diagram 6. **Shuttle (Lanzaderas) Madrid-Ciudad Real Passengers transported**

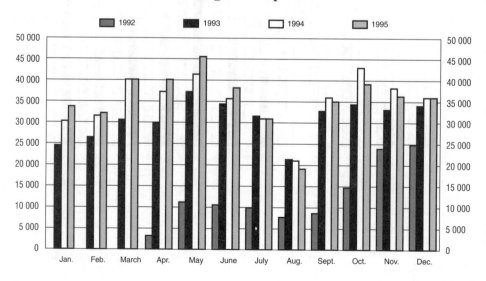

Diagram 7. **Shuttle (Lanzaderas) Madrid Puertollano**
Passengers transported

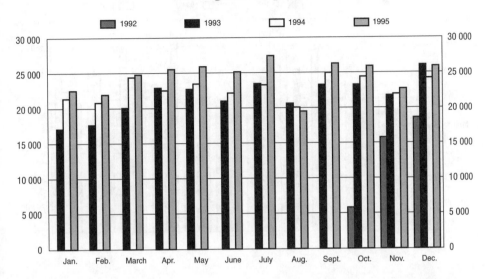

The remaining links [Madrid-Seville (Diagram 8) and Madrid-Cordoba (Diagram 9) are the most outstanding] feature increases of varying importance but that respond to very similar patterns, both concerning seasonal variations and the months where interannual increase is more marked, with the exception in both cases of the Madrid-Malaga route which, for obvious reasons (its nature as a summer resort) shows trends that in some ways are inverse to the other connections.

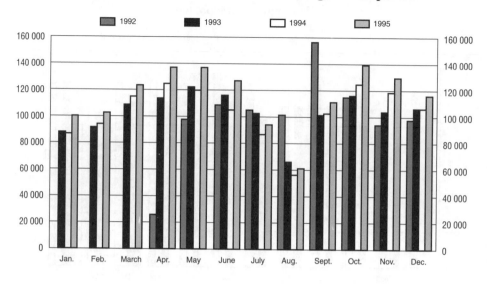

Diagram 8. **AVE Madrid-Seville. Passengers transported**

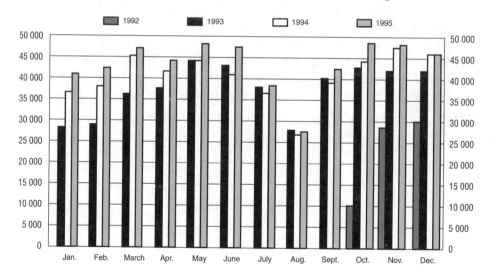

Diagram 9. **AVE Madrid-Cordoba. Passengers transported**

5.3. Buses

As mentioned in point 4.3. above, 1992 was the year when the Madrid to Seville, Cadiz and Huelva services were inaugurated. Data reflecting the number of passengers on these three lines are shown in Tables 10 (a, b, c). Total indicators (it must be remembered that the service structure is a single unit) show that growth rates in the period under analysis were very similar to those of the AVE (8.7 per cent in 1993-1994 and 8.9 per cent in 1994-1995).

It should be noted that there is no seasonal factor on the Madrid-Seville line, where the only peak observed takes place in April, as opposed to that seen for the AVE in the other two cases.

Taking into consideration the data available for that period, it appears evident that, concerning bus transport and the AVE routes covering Madrid-Seville-Cadiz, the determining aspect is the complementary nature of the modalities and therefore the marked increase of demand satisfied will be the result, for bus transport, of an inductive effect due to the new expressway while, in the case of the AVE, we must take into account data on air transport, which will be analysed below.

Table 10 a. **Buses Madrid-Seville. Passengers transported**

	1992	1993	1994	1995
January		8 084	8 399	10 008
February	1 381	7 669	8 278	9 723
March	10 507	9 019	11 612	10 666
April	21 264	14 171	16 150	18 784
May	24 550	10 643	10 041	12 138
June	22 203	8 721	9 783	10 941
July	27 917	11 834	13 055	13 403
August	26 445	10 234	11 425	11 331
September	46 509	11 715	13 539	13 563
October	29 986	11 261	12 260	13 690
November	8 718	9 598	10 082	11 303
December	11 564	11 958	13 900	15 705
TOTAL	231 044	124 907	138 524	151 255

Table 10 b. **Buses Madrid-Cadiz. Passengers transported**

	1992	1993	1994	1995
January		2 405	2 304	2 989
February		3 476	3 679	3 914
March		2 863	3 255	2 860
April		3 912	3 350	4 426
May		2 755	2 802	2 816
June		3 032	2 831	3 242
July	226	4 960	4 837	4 985
August	1 929	4 491	4 833	4 829
September	2 101	4 175	4 491	4 477
October	1 939	3 380	3 439	4 019
November	1 215	2 500	2 654	2 972
December	1 705	3 662	3 932	4 073
TOTAL	9 115	41 611	42 407	45 602

Table 10 c. **Buses Madrid-Huelva. Passengers transported**

	1992	1993	1994	1995
January		1 663	1 735	2 011
February	158	1 379	1 484	1 702
March	1 409	1 594	2 293	1 903
April	2 624	2 811	2 396	3 533
May	2 195	1 954	2 268	2 321
June	2 440	2 042	1 987	2 358
July	3 374	3 360	3 558	3 491
August	3 718	3 261	3 843	3 895
September	3 205	2 687	3 084	3 301
October	2 279	2 047	2 238	2 654
November	1 581	1 579	1 684	1 940
December	2 094	2 293	2 538	2 752
TOTAL	25 077	26 670	29 108	31 861

The fact that bus and the AVE complement one another is not, however, a constant for the corridor, as can be deduced if we analyse Table 11. As may be observed, the Madrid-Ciudad Real-Puertollano bus connection undergoes a strong decrease in traffic after 1992, whose interpretation is especially simple if we study AVE operating data. Indeed, the shuttle (direct Madrid to Ciudad Real and Puertollano service) was not yet in operation in 1992, but a large number of the new trains stopped in either one of these two stations. This fact breaks, although not too spectacularly, with what until 1991 had been a growth line in the type of service under consideration. After 1993, once the shuttles are operative the process as a whole becomes more acute, which is not the case, however, for the Madrid-Ciudad Real route where the cause must be located in the other infrastructure under analysis, the Madrid-Seville expressway. Indeed, as we shall note when commenting on running time, the considerable reduction in journey time resulting from the expressway must have been the cause of the recovery this service experienced after 1993, although never attaining pre-1992 levels.

Table 11. **Buses Madrid-Ciudad Real-Puertollano. Passengers transported**

	1990	1991	1992	1993	1994	1995
Madrid-Ciudad Real	18 495	19 783	16 552	11 169	14 011	14 417
Madrid-Puertollano	26 781	32 424	28 281	27 237	26 078	
C. Real-Puertollano	53 516	57 087	56 005	41 514	42 141	

Figure 6

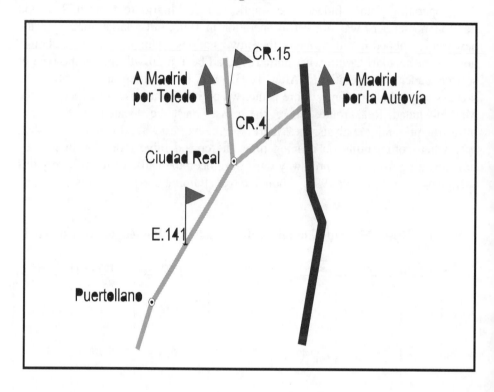

Analysis of road traffic in the vicinity of Ciudad Real and Puertollano will complement this series of reflections. In this case we have defined as reference points Stations E-141, CR15 and CR4 (Fig. 6) which, due to their location, are the ones best indicated for interpretation of long-distance traffic. As may be observed (Diagram 10) the period 1988-91 shows moderate but constant growth for traffic in all three stations. In fact, this growth is even stronger at CR4, since in 1991 the section of expressway connecting with Madrid was already in operation.

Diagram 10. **Evolution of AADT**

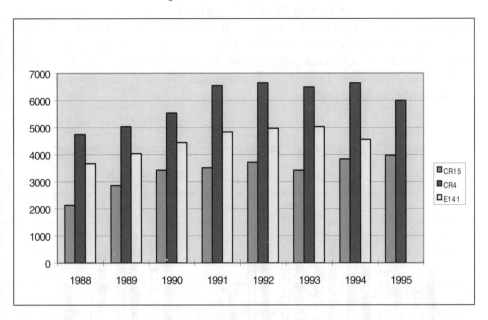

After this period, the trend is towards a decrease in Stations CR4 and E-141, while CR15, covering the connection with Toledo -- which is neither on the AVE line nor on the Andalucia expressway -- shows a slight recovery.

5.4. Aeroplane

We have mentioned several times the fact that 1992 was an extraordinary year concerning traffic in the corridors under study and thus its use as a reference point for analysis of the evolution of demand might be misleading. In reference to air transport, and particularly the Madrid-Seville route, it must be said that 1990 and 1991 were also not fully typical insofar as they saw an unusual flow of passengers directly related with preparations for the 1992 Expo. It is clear that demand growth rates for air transport in those years could not have been maintained after 1992, even if the high-speed trains had not been operative.

In any case, total air passengers between Madrid and Seville fell from 846 437 in 1992 to 283 429 in 1993, by almost exactly two-thirds. At the time, it was thought that the process had only just begun and, considering the results generated on the Paris-Lyons route over the first four years of operation, it was believed that passenger transfer would continue with a certain intensity. The fact is that, as Diagram 11 shows, the period 1993-1995 has been, at the least, acceptable for air service, with 299 000 passengers in 1994, that is 5.6 per cent more than in 1993, and 288 000 in 1995 (3.6 per cent less than in 1994). Analysis of the diagram shows an interesting seasonal evolution with an upward trend throughout the period, in June, July, August, September and October. The trend is reversed in November, December, January and February, and becomes more diffuse in March, April and May.

Diagram 11. **Aeroplane Madrid-Seville. Passengers transported**

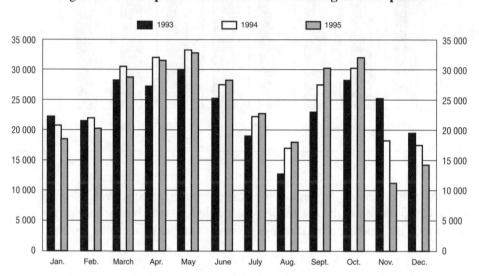

The routes covering Madrid to Malaga and Cadiz, of which only the latter, as a result of its proximity to Seville, enjoyed the 1992 "boom" with a certain intensity, have grown in number of passengers as appears in Diagrams 12 and 13. As a whole, air traffic between Madrid and Malaga, which dropped four percentage points in the period 1992-1993, has remained almost stable over the last three years (576 000 passengers in 1993, 573 000 in 1994 and 574 000 in 1995). Unfortunately, at the time of completing this report, data concerning passengers on the Madrid-Malaga connection carried by a new private operator, AIR-EUROPA, which provides service since early 1995, are not available. These data will have a certain effect on total traffic distribution.

Diagram 12. **Aeroplane Madrid-Malaga. Passengers transported**

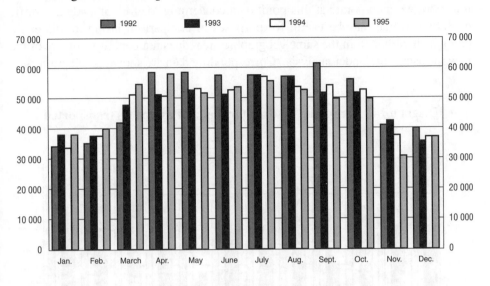

Diagram 13. **Aeroplane Madrid-Cadiz. Passengers transported**

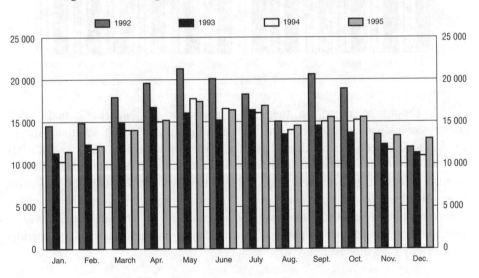

An identical model applies for the Madrid-Cadiz route, where passenger traffic reached 168 000 in 1993, 168 500 in 1994 and 175 000 in 1995, although in this case the decrease between 1992 and 1993 was even more intense, some 22 per cent.

In completing this section, and as was done above when analysing private transport, we incorporate at this point data concerning Madrid-Granada air traffic evolution, which may be useful for purposes of comparison, using to this end a city which, although in the same geographic area, does not benefit from any of the new infrastructure under analysis. Corresponding data are shown in Diagram 14.

Diagram 14. **Aeroplane Madrid-Granada. Passengers transported**

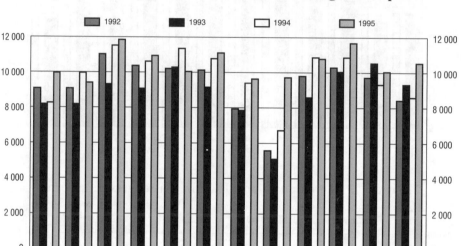

It should be noted, in the first place, that the Madrid-Granada route underwent a significant decrease in 1993, although in this case it was more similar to the Malaga connection than that of Cadiz. Specifically, traffic went from 111 500 in 1992 to 105 000 in 1993 (-5.7 per cent). 1994 and 1995 showed intense percentile growth, reaching 118 000 in 1994 and 125 000 the following year, increases of 12.3 per cent and 5.9 per cent, respectively. These values, obviously not to be used other than for purposes of orientation, may provide a indication of the number of passengers truly lost to the aeroplane in the corridor under study over the last few years.

6. EVOLUTION OF PUBLIC TRANSPORT TARIFFS

It seems evident that an analysis of the tariff framework is, in principle, an important element when interpreting traffic evolution. In our case, this is especially relevant for the AVE but is harder to interpret for the expressway, since the single factor for analysis is the bus tariff structure: inasmuch as it is free of charge, there is no financial expenditure to consider.

In any case, it should be noted that, of the tariffs subject to analysis, those corresponding to bus services are under the control of the Administration as a result of the clause included in the licence contracts, according to which operating companies are under monopoly status on each line. This means that tariff increases in this sector are nothing but a reflection of the corresponding increases in each year's index of general prices (CPI). On the other hand, although the air transport sector and the railroads can currently set their tariffs with no restriction, the fact that this is a practically new situation and that, with very few exceptions (the Madrid-Malaga line), companies operate under a single-operator system, means that the tariff increase policy is quite similar to the bus model. In any case, it will be interesting to learn of the evolution of tariff levels throughout the period under study so as to verify the greater or lesser impact on traffic generation.

6.1. Rail transport

The most significant feature in defining the AVE's tariff system is diversity. Following the French model, the operating company decided to establish three tariff levels: "Valley", "Plain" and "Peak", according to the time of day of the trip. There are also three levels of service quality: "Tourist", "Preferential" and "Club" which, in principle, generate nine different tariffs for each relation. The trend in the period has been to introduce one or, at the most, two tariff changes per year. Data concerning the Madrid-Seville relation, the most important in the service, are shown in Table 12.

Table 12. AVE Madrid-Seville. Tariffs in pesetas

| | Tourist | | | Preferential | | | Club | | |
	Valley	Plain	Peak	Valley	Plain	Peak	Valley	Plain	Peak
21.04.92	6 000	7 200	8 400	8 400	10 100	11 800	11 800	14 100	16 500
26.09.93	6 600	7 900	8 900	9 100	10 800	12 500	12 100	14 300	16 500
18.03.94	6 800	8 400	9 100	9 400	11 500	12 800	12 500	14 400	16 500
02.01.95	6 900	8 500	9 100	10 400	11 700	12 800	12 500	14 500	16 500
10.09.95	7 600	8 900	9 200	11 400	12 700	13 200	13 700	15 600	16 500
% 92-95	26	23.6	14	35	25.7	11.8	16.10	10.6	0

The company's commercial policy has been to increase the tariffs of the lower service levels and retain unchanged the higher ones. As a result, the "valley" modality in the "tourist" and "preferential" classes has grown through the period by 26 per cent and 35 per cent respectively. At the opposite end, the "peak" tariff in "club" class remains constant at 16 500 ptas. since the inauguration of the line.

The shuttles, for which Table 13 shows information covering the Madrid-Ciudad Real route, were subject to different treatment. These services did not require a breakdown into valley, plain and peak and thus, from the start of operations, only two types of seating were provided. The novelty in this case is the availability of monthly tickets (by name reservation or bearer) and, as of end-1994, to weekday vouchers. These tariff structures show most clearly the effects of traffic induction (in terms of increase in the number of trips, or the generation of new users) resulting from the introduction of the high-speed train.

Table 13. Shuttle Madrid-Ciudad Real. Tariffs in pesetas

	Single ticket		Monthly ticket				Monthly ticket (Monday to Friday)			
			Nominative		To bearer		Nominative		To bearer	
	Tourist	Club	Tourist	Club	Tourist	Club	Tourist	Club	Tourist	Club
18.10.92	1 800	2 400	50 000	65 000	60 000	80 000				
29.09.93	2 000	2 500	50 000	65 000	60 000	80 000				
18.03.94	2 200	2 600	55 000	65 000	66 000	80 000				
11.09.94	2 200	2 600	55 000	65 000	66 000	80 000	45 000	53 000	55 000	65 000
10.09.95	2 300	2 700	57 000	68 300	69 300	84 000	47 500	55 900	58 000	68 600
% 92-95	27	12	14	5	15.8	5	5.5	5.4	5.4	5.5

If measured in percentage terms, the general trend has resembled, in the case of the single ticket, that already described for "long distance" (Madrid-Seville). However, for monthly vouchers, the effect has been much more subdued and, in fact, tariff increases in that period, between 14 and 15 per cent in tourist class, are considerably smaller than the accumulated growth of the price index in the Spanish economy. For their part, the new weekday vouchers grew by 5.5 per cent in 1995 for all types of ticket.

Talgo 200 tariffs also underwent a specific treatment, although in this case the simplification was simply to eliminate the "club" class. Data covering the three routes covered by Talgo units are shown in Tables 14, 15 and 16.

As may be seen, the evolution of tariffs in this case has been quite different, since a distinction was made regarding the "tourist" and "preferential" classes as a whole, submitting the latter to much more significant tariff increases than the former. The smaller increases were registered on the Madrid-Huelva route, tourist class (values between 5.7 per cent and 7.5 per cent) and the largest on the Madrid-Malaga route, preferential class, which showed tariff increases between 17.5 per cent and 19.5 per cent.

Table 14. **Talgo 200 Madrid-Malaga. Tariffs in pesetas**

	Tourist			Preferential		
	Valley	**Plain**	**Peak**	**Valley**	**Plain**	**Peak**
31.01.93	6 000	6 600	6 900	8 400	9 200	9 700
18.03.94	6 400	7 100	7 300	8 700	9 500	9 900
02.01.95	6 600	7 400	7 700	10 000	11 000	11 400
% 93-95	10%	12%	11.5%	19%	19.5%	17.5%

Table 15. **Talgo 200 Madrid-Cadiz. Tariffs in pesetas**

	Tourist			Preferential		
	Valley	**Plain**	**Peak**	**Valley**	**Plain**	**Peak**
26.07.93	7 300	8 000	8 400	10 200	11 100	11 700
18.03.94	7 700	8 500	8 800	10 500	11 400	11 800
02.01.95	8 000	8 900	9 100	11 900	13 400	13 600
% 93-95	9.5%	11.2%	8.3%	16.6%	20.7%	16.2%

Table 16. **Talgo 200 Madrid-Huelva. Tariffs in pesetas**

	Tourist			Preferential		
	Valley	**Plain**	**Peak**	**Valley**	**Plain**	**Peak**
26.07.93	6 900	6 900	8 000	9 700	9 700	11 100
02.01.95	7 300	7 300	8 600	11 100	11 100	12 700
% 93-95	5.7%	5.7%	7.5%	14.4%	14.4%	14.4%

6.2. Air transport

The evolution of prices in tourist class corresponding to air services from Madrid to each one of the Andalucian airports (we continue to include data from Granada for purposes of comparison) is shown in Table 17. As may be seen, the operating companies (in this case Iberia and Aviaco) have imposed, throughout the period, tariff increases of between 31.5 and 33 per cent on the connections to Malaga and Cadiz, while the Madrid-Seville route, which in 1992 cost almost the same as Madrid-Granada, has followed a much less marked series of increases, in agreement with the evolution of railroad tariffs which, certainly, must have been the constant point of reference, so that global increases barely reached 20 per cent, which is significantly similar to the average increase in AVE tariffs, tourist class, for the same period.

Table 17. **Air transport. Tariffs in pesetas**

| | 1992 | 1993 | 1994 | 1995 | | | % 92-95 |
				Jan	May	Nov	
MADRID-SEVILLE	11 675	12 660	13 233	13 450	13 450	13 950	19.8
MADRID-MALAGA	12 525	13 700	14 767	15 850	16 200	16 550	32
MADRID-GRANADA	11 575	12 650	13 100	14 900	14 900	15 350	33
MADRID-CADIZ (JEREZ)	12 775	13 950	14 500	16 200	16 200	16 700	31.4

6.3. Bus

As has been indicated above, annual increases in tariffs for road passengers are set by the Administration, upon the request of the operating companies, from the year after awarding the licence, and thus their evolution throughout the period is not especially significant; we have, in any case, believed it interesting to unite, in one single chart, data corresponding to 1995 tariffs for the main lines under study (Table 18). As may be observed there is a considerable difference between the price per kilometre on the Madrid-Ciudad Real line and the price on the remaining lines. This difference is related to the innovations introduced by the Administration for awarding of new licences, put into practice after publication of the Enabling Act for Road Transport.

Table 18. **Buses: Tariffs in pesetas, 1995**

	Tariff	Ptas/km
MADRID-SEVILLE (520 km)	2 560	4.92
MADRID-CADIZ (663 km)	2 905	4.38
MADRID-CORDOBA (400 km)	1 490	3.72
MADRID-MALAGA (544 km)	2 660	4.88
MADRID-C.REAL (190 km)	1 525	8.02
MADRID-GRANADA (434 km)	1 815	4.18

7. ANALYSIS OF THE INDUCTION EFFECT

7.1. Opinion of AVE users

As stated above, an interpretation of the concept of induced demand is especially difficult to pinpoint, in particular if the subject under analysis is, as with AVE, a totally new infrastructure and not complementary to one already in service.

It seems clear that in such a situation the easiest aspect to detect in the conduct of a potential user would be the lack of disposition to travel by a means of transport other than the one in use. Once this is established, and taking into account all necessary precautions concerning surveys carried out among passengers, where the request is for their preferences and not for their acts, we believe it is especially interesting to provide information on the results of the successive surveys which the Department of Surveys of RENFE has been carrying out among passengers since a few months after the AVE began operations.

The questions which the user should answer are, with very small variations, as follows:

1. If the AVE were not available, would you have taken this trip?
2. If so, what means of travel would you have chosen?

Surveys have been carried out on five occasions since 1992 and available results show a difference, as we shall see, between "long-distance", "shuttle" and "Talgo 200" users. Data drawn in the first survey (Table 19) show that 18.7 per cent of users would not have made the trip were it not for the AVE. We note that the survey was carried out at a time when AVE services had been running practically for a year, that is once all anomalous effects had disappeared, due both to the novelty of the inauguration and the Seville Expo celebrations.

Table 19. **Induction. AVE passengers**

If the AVE were not available, would you have taken this trip?	Mar 93 %	Nov 93 %	Jul 94 %	Nov 94 %	Oct 95 %
No	18.7	12.0	13.4	16.1	11.7
Yes	80.2	87.7	85.7	83.4	87.8
N/A	1.2	0.3	0.8	0.5	0.5

The percentage decreases significantly, to 12 per cent in the 1993 survey and, in following years, fluctuates between a maximum of 16.1 per cent in November 1994 and a minimum of 11.7 per cent in October 1995.

The shuttles have specific considerations and very differentiated nuances. Indeed, the first survey dating from June 1993 was completed eight months after beginning to provide the service (possibly excessively early), where results show that 28.7 per cent of users only travel because of the AVE. This percentage remains practically stable in the second survey, which coincides with that for "long distance", but drops considerably over the next few years, reaching relatively similar but slightly higher percentages (between 13.9 per cent and 18.5 per cent) than those of Madrid-Seville passengers (Table 20).

Table 20. **Induction. Shuttles**

If the Shuttle were not available, would you have taken this trip?	Jun 93 %	Nov 93 %	Aug 94 %	Nov 94 %	Oct 95 %
No	28.7	27.6	13.9	16.1	18.5
Yes	70	72.2	85.9	83.4	80.7
N/A	1.3	0.2	0.2	0.5	0.7

Finally, Table 21 shows how passengers in Talgo 200 express a less decided preference for high speed, as is natural since they are users of "improved" and not completely "new" services. The first June 1993 survey, at the time when services began, shows a result according to which 15 out of every 100 passengers would not have travelled were it not for the AVE. On the contrary, the 1994 and 1995 surveys show very modest results and probably more in accordance with reality, with a level of induced travellers between 3 per cent and 6.9 per cent.

Table 21. **Induction. Talgo 200**

If theTalgo 200 were not available, would you have taken this trip?	Jun 93 %	Dec 93 %	Apr 95 %	Aug 95 %
No	15	3	6.9	6.36
Yes	82.9	95.5	91.0	92.87
N/A	2.1	1.5	2	0.77

It should be noted that in all surveys the percentage of refusals to respond is extremely low which means that, whether or not the response is sincere, the user has, in general, an established opinion.

Answers to the second question were equally interesting: what means of travel would you use if not the AVE? In this case, data resulting from the 1994 survey show the following results:

- For the Madrid-Seville route, 520 km by road in spite of the expressway, 48.9 per cent of users willing to travel would have used the aeroplane versus only 7.6 per cent who would have driven or 6 per cent who prefer the bus.
- Shuttle users who prefer the private car account for 54.7 per cent (there is no airport in Ciudad Real) and 20.3 per cent prefer the bus, while Talgo 200 users prefer the aeroplane (25.6 per cent), private car (19.6 per cent) and the bus (12.3 per cent).
- Concerning the possibility of using a conventional railroad or train, although for Madrid-Seville passengers it is only the third choice, shuttle users consider it second and Talgo 200 users consider it first, which is fairly logical if, as we said above, the Talgo 200 is, for the user, a substantial improvement but not a different product from the conventional train.

Leaving numerical data aside for a moment, it seems evident that the effects of induction, both in terms of an increase in number of trips per user and of a decision to travel by those who otherwise would not do so, must be detected on the Madrid-Cordoba-Seville connection (because the considerable decrease in travel times allows for a return trip within the same day, which eliminates lodging expenses), as well as on the shuttles. On the other hand, the Cordoba airport has practically no commercial function, which would be an additional justification. Regarding the shuttles, besides the circumstance mentioned above, there must be and is proof that two complementary circumstances are present. First, the increase in the number of residents of Ciudad Real and Puertollano, attracted by less expensive housing, which allows for the development of all or part of the professional activities in Madrid, especially for the liberal professions. The second element is a massive flow of university students who, were it not for the AVE, would be forced to make significant monthly expenditures, particularly on lodging, to attend university in Madrid. For students and professionals, travel time in the AVE's comfortable seating may even provide an occasion for study or work. It must be remembered that for Ciudad Real or Puertollano travel times are under one hour.

This reflection is more solidly based if we study information relative to a different aspect of the induction effect, that is, the increase in frequency of number of trips by service users.

In this case, the successive surveys completed by RENFE have shown results featured in Table 22. As may be seen, the most significant datum is the high percentage of users who account for more than four weekly trips, which in April 1993 was already 23 per cent. This percentage tended to decrease in the period May-November 1994 (which matches, although not completely, tariff evolution) to recover later and reach maximum values in the September 1995 survey.

Table 22. **Induction. Frequency of travel. Shuttles**

PERCENTAGES	Apr 93	Jun 94	Nov 94	Sep 95
4 journeys or more per week	26.9	29	19.1	30
2 journeys per week	8.3	11.4	11.4	8.5
2 journeys per fortnight	14.7	14.6	21.2	13.1
2 journeys per month	12.8	18.6	16.3	15.7
2 journeys per quarter	9	8.8	12.5	13.9
Less than 2 journeys/quarter	13.5	5.7	7.6	11
First-time journey	14.7	10.4	10.7	8.1

The second type of frequency (two weekly trips) remains relatively stable (between 8.3 per cent and 11.4 per cent) throughout the period, and it is the third category (two trips every two weeks) which seems to absorb the decrease registered at the end of 1994. This indicates a transfer effect to the immediately lower group which is not, however, carried on to the fourth stage.

For the Talgo 200 (Table 23), all frequency categories range between relatively stable margins, although it is true that, if we were to remark on any given effect, this should be the systematic decrease in percentage of users who make more than four weekly trips, in exchange for a relatively similar increase in the number of those who make one weekly return trip.

Concerning long-distance travel (Table 24), 1993 data show 33.7 per cent of passengers travelling for the first time, which gives a very good idea of the attraction held by AVE over potential users. This percentage held, in October 1995, at the relatively high level of 20 per cent. Users of the two first categories, who accounted for 9.6 per cent in March 1993, reached 19.8 per cent in 1995.

Table 23. **Induction. Frequency of travel. Talgo 200**

PERCENTAGES	Jun 94	Nov 94	Sep 95
4 journeys or more per week	4.6	3.7	1.3
2 journeys per week	2.6	5.6	5.8
2 journeys per fortnight	10.8	10.1	9
2 journeys per month	15.5	12.9	15.2
2 journeys per quarter	23.8	23.5	23.6
Less than 2 journeys/quarter	24.2	24.4	26.1
First-time journey	18.3	18.1	19.3

Table 24. **Induction. Frequency of travel. AVE (long-distance)**

PERCENTAGES	Apr 93	Jun 94	Nov 94	Oct 95
4 journeys or more per week	5	5.6	6.9	7.9
2 journeys per week	4.6	11.8	8.7	11.9
2 journeys per fortnight	7.4	9.8	11.1	11.8
2 journeys per month	9.4	18.3	15.4	14.4
2 journeys per quarter	16.9	18.8	14.5	15.6
Less than 2 journeys/quarter	23.1	16.2	21	18.2
First-time journey	33.7	18.6	22.2	20

The Madrid-Cordoba-Seville line is, in general, more difficult to analyse. Growth data (Diagrams 8 and 9) both appear somewhat erratic and, particularly, in the case of Seville it could be thought that, in principle, the predominant effect is a transference in reference to the aeroplane. In this sense it should be observed that 1994 -- a stable year for the Madrid-Seville AVE service -- coincides with a 5.6 per cent increase in air passengers, while in 1995, AVE traffic grew by 10.8 per cent, while the number of air transport passengers decreased by 3.6 per cent.

In any case, if we compare absolute values reflecting number of passengers per mode of transport, it is clear that the reason for the increase responds to model transference to a very small degree. Intrinsic causes remaining for analysis are, respectively, supply, tariffs and running times.

7.2. Supply and induction

In the search for convincing interpretations for the traffic slowdown in 1994 and the recovery over 1995 on the Madrid-Seville route (the AVE network's most important), RENFE officials looked to supply tables. Indeed, immediately after the end of Expo 92, the company readjusted scheduling in 56 weekly trains each way as they forecast, correctly as it turned out, a strong recession in demand. These values were modified upward twice in the first semester of 1993, with a considerable increase in monthly traffic over the previous month, although there was as yet no way of comparing with previous situations. A new downward adjustment took place in September 1993, with effects felt (in the shape of limited demand increase) the following month. The scenario lasted until September 1994 with the most negative consequences appearing in the period April-August of that year, resulting in a considerable drop in the number of passengers, which accounts for the stagnation registered for the whole year. Finally, increases in the number of trains implemented in September 1994 and September 1995 caused a sustained growth of demand which had an effect, without exception, throughout the year.

This interpretation, perfectly plausible, is justified in the fact that if the operating company tries to bring the level of occupancy to a maximum, the potential client is sometimes too limited when deciding on the mode of travel (impossibility of selecting class, time, smoking/non smoking sections, etc.). This fact dissuades some travellers, benefiting the aeroplane, which captures part of the trips lost by AVE.

We could now mention that, regarding the train, there is an induced demand, resulting more from certain characteristics of the service provided than from the existence of the infrastructure. Travelling times would certainly not be included among these characteristics. Proof of the trust placed among AVE management in this approach is the fact that since 24 March 1996, the company forecast shows 90 trains each way on the Madrid-Seville route.

Air service has followed a policy of supply which differs significantly from that described immediately above for the AVE, where the trend was, in principle, to adjust the number of available seats to market conditions.

Table 8 shows precisely the evolution of this strategy throughout the period. 1992 shows a top 125 weekly Madrid-Seville flights. In 1993, a year when demand covered was reduced by nearly two-thirds, the range of weekly flights available was between 57 and 45. In 1994, which registered the highest number of passengers in the previous three-year period, the operating company improved supply to a maximum by varying the number of weekly flights between 42 maximum and 15 minimum. In 1995, on the contrary, the decision is to provide a constant supply of 31 flights/week, which resulted in a loss of some 10 000 passengers for the year (-3.6 per cent).

The evolution of the Madrid-Malaga service is, though less marked, quite comparable to the Madrid-Seville variant. As shown in Table 8, the final 1995 result is a constant supply, adjusted downward along the year for all services. The case of Granada is an exception and results from demand generated by the preparations for the World Skiing Championships.

In a word, faced with the impossibility of competing with the decided increase in supply by the railroad company and given the probable high cost of adjusting supply to market demand, the airlines decided to opt for a conservative policy that consisted in providing a more rigid and reduced supply. In view of the improvement of occupation indices and the probable reduction in cost/passenger-km (the inverse of what must be taking place in the AVE), it must be agreed that the policy is adequate.

7.3. Tariffs and induction

Concerning tariffs, and specifically their periodic increases, it is impossible to detect any globally dissuasive or inductive effect defined with sufficient clarity. A comparison of traffic and tariff tables seems to indicate that users of all modes generally submit without resistance to tariff increases, which normally take place at the same time of the year and which, according to the operating companies, are linked to similar general increases in price indices, which, in most cases, is not true.

The clearest proof of this lack of correlation is shown by comparing the evolution of the increase in long-distance passengers in the "club", "preferential" and "tourist" classes (Table 25) with the corresponding evolution in tariffs for these same classes as described in Table 12.

Table 25. **Long-distance AVE**
Evolution in total passengers by type of ticket

	CLUB	PREFERENTIAL	TOURIST
1992	78 291	270 964	827 217
1993	96 134	412 302	1 366 831
1994	92 853	430 269	1 413 581
1995	96 350	470 525	1 520 960
% 93-95	0 %	14.0 %	11.3 %

One further precision: surveys carried out among AVE passengers (the latest in October 1995) show that 42 per cent of long-distance users consider tariffs reasonable, while only 7 per cent believe them to be too high. Percentage levels of "acceptance" reach 44 per cent on the shuttles and 54 per cent on Talgo 200.

There is, however, a significant exception to the description provided and that is the shuttles, routes where passengers tend to behave as users of inter-city trains. Diagram 6 shows how the intense growth on the Madrid-Ciudad Real route over the first months of 1994 is cut in April of that year as a result of an increase in tariffs (10 per cent) in all tourist-class tickets. This decrease in the number of passengers holds precisely until September 1994, when a new weekday voucher was put on the market which, although not a substantial reduction in price per trip, was more in tune with users' wishes. This qualitative aspect, rather than the quantitative, should be emphasized when analysing the relation between traffic increases and tariff policies in the case under study.

7.4. Shorter times and induction

Information regarding running times for the main connections in the corridor and for the various modes are shown in Table 26. Data included refer strictly to travel times, without taking into consideration times of access, waiting and dispersion which, as is well known, in the case of air transport can be considerable, and where, as a whole, total time spent in travelling is greater by a factor of three than real travel time in the entirety of connections under analysis. This circumstance is less frequent in other modes, especially in users' perceptions.

Table 26. **Travel times**

	Bus	Conventional train	AVE/ Talgo 200	Air	Car without motorway	Car with motorway
Madrid-Seville	6h	6h	2h30	0h55	6h30	4h45
Madrid-Cordoba	4h15	5h	1h40		5h	3h35
Madrid-Cadiz	7h45	7h40	5h10	0h55	7h45	6h
Madrid-Malaga	6h30	7h20	4h40	1h	6h50	5h
Madrid-Ciudad Real	2h30	2h55	0h48		2h25	2h
Madrid-Puertollano	3h45	3h42	1h05		2h55	2h30
Puertollano-Ciudad Real	0h45	0h47	0h17		0h30	0h30
Madrid-Huelva	7h15	5h	7h30		7h50	5h35

A comparison of data in general corroborates observations made throughout this presentation so as to interpret the new configuration of traffic in the corridor. If there is anything to remark it is, on the one hand, the relationship between the reduction in running times on road routes and increases in AADT in the census stations analysed above and, on the other hand, the effects on conventional railroad services as a result of the AVE service.

It is evident that such outstanding time differences could only result in the disappearance, sooner or later, of conventional railroad services. This has practically been the case. RENFE currently only provides a single night train per day each way on the Madrid-Seville-Cadiz-Algeciras route, while intercity services practically disappeared in 1993.

The evolution of railroad traffic using conventional trains on that route for the period 1991-1995 is shown in Diagram 15. The diagram shows, rather than a drastic reduction in the number of passengers on conventional trains, the impressive quantitative jump for rail traffic as a whole from the 356 000 passengers who travelled by railroad between Madrid and Seville in 1991 and the more than 1 400 000 in 1995.

Diagram 15. **Conventional train Madrid-Seville. Passengers transported**

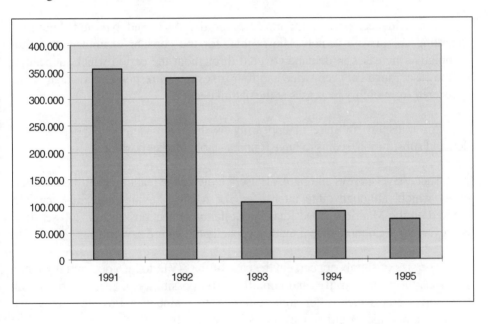

8. CONCLUSIONS

The fundamental aim of this paper has been to identify the factors which, in our opinion, have to date had the most significant effect on the generation of new traffic within the framework of infrastructures that give access from Madrid to the main cities in Andalucia.

We have tried to consider induction both as the generation of trips by new users and as an increase in the frequency of trips by habitual passengers.

Compared with the data, generally quite precise, which concern high-speed rail and its competition with air transport, data relating to roads have in some way been indirect as a result of the lack of systematic origin-destination surveys in this sector.

The evidence, precise in the cases of the AVE and bus and "intuitive" regarding the private vehicle, shows that, for the corridor examined, there are cumulative increases in demand covered throughout the period which, depending on the case, range between twice and four times the corresponding average values registered for mobility increases at the national level.

Air transport, in spite of appearing as the main victim in the process of demand substitution, seems to have found a stable market position.

Successive surveys among AVE users indicate the magnitude of the inductive effect which, although quite intense on the Madrid-Seville route, is especially marked on the Madrid-Ciudad Real-Puertollano connections. Talgo 200 services, however, show no more than a modest capacity to capture new traffic.

The size of supply appears, in the case of the AVE, to be a determining factor when capturing new traffic and conditions the possibility of reacting by the air transport sector which, after some attempts to maintain a flexible supply, has decided to provide a rigid, downward-adjusted supply.

On the contrary, tariffs do not appear to be a significant factor in any of the modes or connections, at least if we analyse tariffs and their increases in quantitative terms. In qualitative terms, a very diversified supply of tariffs may appear to have been the cause for considerable increments in demand for some specific connections.

One section of this paper has dealt with a retrospective analysis of the opening of the first Madrid-Seville-Cadiz line, an experience which lies far back in time but which bears an interesting relationship with what has been studied in the text. We could establish an analogy whereby the AVE would play the role of a new mode capable of dominating the market, and the aeroplane the obsolete mode now incapable of competing in the new situation. However, our intention was wider: we have tried to warn of the risk of possible "mirages" caused by the presence of a new mode of operation or a new means of transport on the market.

BIBLIOGRAPHY

Wais San Martin, F. (1967), *Historia General de los Ferrocarriles Españoles*, Editora Nacional.

Artola, M. (1978), *Los Ferrocarriles en España: 1844-1943*, Servicio de Estudios del Banco de España.

Hills, Peter J. (1996), "What is Induced Traffic?", in: *Transportation*, V. 23.

Goodwin, Phil B. (1996), "Empirical Evidence on Induced Traffic. A review and synthesis", in: *Transportation*, V. 23.

Inglada Lopez de Sabando, V. (1994), "Análisis empírico del impacto del AVE sobre la demanda de transporte en el corredor Madrid-Sevilla", in: *Estudios de Transportes y Comunicaciones*, No. 62.

Bonnafous, A. (1987), "The regional impact of the TGV", in: *Transportation*, V. 14.

Nash, C.A. (1991), "The case for high-speed rail", in: *Investigaciones Económicas,* V. 15.

Owen, A.D. and Philips G.D.A. (1987), "The characteristics of railway passenger demand", in: *Journal of Transport Economics and Policy*, V. 21.
Madrazo, S. (1991), *La edad de oro de las diligencias*, Nerea.

RENFE (1993), *Estudio del producto AVE: El viaje en AVE*, April-December.

RENFE (1993), *Estudio de producto Talgo 200*, July-December.

RENFE (1994), *Estudio de producto AVE. Larga distancia, Lanzadera y Talgo 200*, July-November.

RENFE (1995), *Estudio de producto AVE: Larga distancia, Lanzadera y Talgo 200*, April.

FRANCE

François PLASSARD
École Nationale des Travaux Publics de l'État
Vaulx-en-Velin
France

SUMMARY

Vaulx-en-Velin, June 1996

113

INTRODUCTION

Given the steady increase in traffic around the globe, whatever the mode of transport, one cannot help but speculate as to the factors which have sparked such growth. Is this ever-increasing mobility of both people and goods an unavoidable consequence of the yearnings for freedom which lie deeply embedded in all individuals, or does it in fact have clearly identifiable causes, in which case something could theoretically be done to influence it?

At first glance, it would seem to be one of the characteristics of a certain way of life -- a form of mobility which has arisen from industrial societies and is spreading gradually, but seemingly irreversibly, to all countries as they enter the community of market economies. If so, it would be difficult to separate mobility from the infrastructure which shapes it.

At the same time, however, it must be noted that it has been the policy of all industrialised countries to develop transport infrastructure with the dual objectives of maintaining adequate fluidity in high-traffic areas and, for land-use planning purposes, of opening up access to less industrialised regions. Here, one might well wonder about the consequences of such investment and whether it is not conducive to a degree of mobility which is getting increasingly out of control.

To answer this question, one must first specify the nature of **mobility** and any ways in which it might tie in with the development of infrastructure. A number of studies and research into mobility trends provide a clearer picture of the **impact of infrastructure** on those trends. Lastly, how the growth of mobility relates to new infrastructure leads to the more fundamental issue of **transport systems**, inasmuch as mobility involves overall travel behaviour and thus the way in which space is organised.

1. MOBILITY AND INFRASTRUCTURE

As was once done for the consequences of transport infrastructure on regional development[1], it would be tempting to try to establish a simple causal relationship between the development of infrastructure and increased mobility. Indeed, the available data show clearly that, in most countries, the two series are ascending and a strong correlation can be demonstrated.

But it necessary to go beyond this rather simplistic view for at least two reasons:

-- The concept of mobility is too vague and can give rise to interpretations which are thoroughly contradictory;
-- It is necessary to try to uncover any intermediate factors which might explain how the development of transport infrastructure relates to increased mobility.

1.1. The distinction between traffic and mobility

Most of the statistics currently available relate to traffic rather than mobility, and yet a clear distinction has to be made between the two. While traffic refers to the use of infrastructure, mobility refers to the behaviour of individuals. More importantly, stable levels of traffic can conceal shifting patterns of mobility, just as traffic can increase despite highly stable mobility.

Infrastructure **traffic** is defined as the number of units (vehicles, people, tonnes, etc.) which use the infrastructure in a given unit of time, such as 50 000 vehicles per day on a motorway.

Mobility, on the other hand, may be defined as the number of trips a person makes in the course of a day (or a year, etc.). It is a concept based on the notion of trips: a trip is generally defined as the sum total of successive journeys (which may involve more than one mode of transport) needed to carry out a given activity. These definitions show clearly that, in the realm of city transport, for example, the figures reported by public transport authorities (number of trips) cannot always be used to assess individual mobility.

The apparent simplicity of the term masks formidable questions of definition and measurement but, above all, it is not possible to grasp the relationships between transport infrastructure and mobility simply in terms of cause and effect.

1.2. Ruling out a simple causal relationship

All that can be observed is that, in the industrialised world, statistical series on traffic or mobility, as well as series relating to infrastructure (in terms of investment outlays or useful life), are both ascendant. The example of lorry traffic on the motorways is particularly significant and provides a good illustration of how the issue ought to be approached.

In France, there has been a sharp growth in the volume of lorry traffic as the motorway system has developed. Can it be inferred from this that the motorways were the cause of the increased traffic? Unquestionably, development of the motorway system has altered the behaviour of consignors and carriers alike. Consignors, factoring into their corporate strategies the effects of the improved traffic conditions brought about by the opening of new motorway segments, have gradually changed their ways: they have specialised their production units and ensured the coherence of their production systems through greater flows of goods; they have significantly reduced inventories in order to operate on a just-in-time basis. This prompts three remarks:

1. The greater ease of traffic afforded by motorways has altered the balance among the various production factors and businesses have, quite naturally, made increased use of the cheapest of these factors, i.e. transport;
2. It is not so much the existence of motorways which has altered mobility patterns as the transformation of the production system brought about by lower transport costs; in all probability, it is the low cost of motorway road haulage services which has been responsible for growth in goods traffic on this type of infrastructure;
3. The growth of lorry traffic on the motorways does not necessarily correspond to an overall increase in goods traffic, since a large part of that growth stems from a modal transfer from rail to road.

Ruling out any kind of direct relationship between infrastructure growth and increased mobility, it would nonetheless be possible, as a number of authors have suggested, to deduce a relationship in which infrastructure acts as a constraint on transport.

117

Figure 1 a) below shows that rising mobility can, in fact, be considered a long-term trend shaped mainly by outside factors and that infrastructure has only a limited influence. Moving from period ① to period ②, it would seem reasonable to believe that the creation of infrastructure is behind the sharp increase in mobility. Actually, mobility was low in period ① because infrastructure was inadequate in relation to the desired level of mobility. Between period ② and period ③, the increase in mobility is less than the new infrastructure would suggest, and by period ④ no additional mobility would appear to be generated by infrastructure.

Figure 1. **Traffic, mobility and infrastructure capacity**

a) increasing mobility

b) infinite mobility

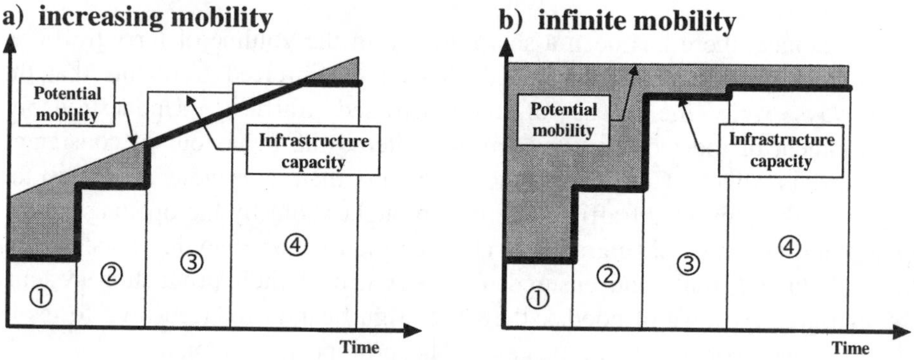

In contrast, if potential mobility is assumed to be infinite, as portrayed in Figure 1 b), it is infrastructure capacity which defines the limits of mobility. In this case, increased mobility and greater infrastructure capacity are equivalent.

1.3. Relationships underlying the models

Even if they generally deal more with traffic than with mobility, the way forecasting models are designed can shed light on the relationships which can be established between infrastructure and increased mobility. Whatever their mathematical structure, whether they are aggregative or disaggregative, all models distinguish a generation function and a resistance function.

In its simplest form, the gravity distribution model used for forecasting traffic T between two places i and j can be expressed as:

$$T_{ij} = \frac{M_i^\alpha \, M_j^\beta}{C_{ij}^\gamma}$$

where the numerator includes traffic generation variables and the denominator, variables of spatial resistance.

In none of the major models is infrastructure represented by a traffic-generation variable, but resistance factors take the cost of spatial movement into account in a variety of ways.

1.3.1. The determinants of mobility

As shown by Tables 1 and 2 below, it is primarily wealth indicators which best explain increasing mobility, whether it be national wealth (in the case of freight) or household income (for passenger transport). Price levels of the various modes of transport come into play when determining real household income and computing the relative prices of those modes.

Table 1. **Freight models**[2]

Mode	Source	Variables used
Road	Forecasting Directorate (66-90)	• Traded GDP
Road	OEST (85-90)	• Industrial production • Road haulage prices
Rail	SNCF (62-80)	• Demand for industrial goods
Rail	Forecasting Directorate (66-90)	• Traded GDP

Table 2. **Passenger transport models**[3]

Mode	Source and reference years	Variables used
Traffic on national road system (journeys)	OEST (71-80)	• Household consumption • Fuel prices
Road traffic of households (passenger cars)	OEST (75-89)	• Gross Domestic Product • Fuel prices
SNCF (main network)	OEST (70-90)	• Household consumption • SNCF fares • Fuel prices

These various forecasting models do refer to infrastructure, but primarily call attention to the risk of saturation which can arise from the potential gap between the capacity of the road and motorway systems and the foreseeable demand for travel[4]. They incorporate the relationship between infrastructure and trends in the demand for travel in the same way as the one depicted in Figure 1 b).

1.3.2. The resistance function

All traffic forecasting models incorporate a spatial resistance function which expresses the (economic) cost and (psychological) difficulty inherent in spatial movement. In the earliest models, this function was based only on the cost of transport, but over time it grew increasingly complex, expanding to encompass transit time, the difficulties and the frequency of public transport. Later on, in our discussion of the Lyons/Saint Étienne regional model (subsection 2.3.2), we shall be able to consider a specific example of how overall cost is computed.

It would therefore seem to be more because of the economic or perceived cost of accessing it that new infrastructure has an influence on mobility. Opening a toll-free motorway would make possible new travel which was previously precluded by excessive journey times. The changing costs of moving through space prompt consignors and households to make new trade-offs between mobility and immobility and among the various possible forms of mobility.

2. EXPERIMENTAL ROUTES

Of all forms of transport infrastructure, **motorways** are the one for which there is sufficient hindsight to assess how they have altered mobility. But it is probably **high-speed rail** which has most sharply brought back into focus the links between new infrastructure and mobility, insofar as the first French TGV service gave rise to considerable changes in mobility. Nor can one fail to mention the consequences of new **urban transport** infrastructure, and the example of Lyons suggests a number of qualified conclusions.

2.1. The example of the French TGV

The first service to operate in France -- the high-speed rail link between Paris and Lyons -- brought about some major changes in the forms of mobility. Even so, recent research into the impact of the subsequent *TGV Atlantique* services prompts questions as to whether that might have been an exceptional situation.

2.1.1. The Lyons-Paris link

Let it simply be recalled that, between 1981 and 1983, the introduction of high-speed rail services between Paris and Lyons cut travel time from four hours to only two for an almost identical price. This considerable change in accessibility vastly altered mobility, yet along with the sharp increase came a veritable transformation of the forms of mobility. Lastly, it can be seen that this growth in mobility was of limited duration.

A considerable increase

The effects on traffic are by now well known. Between 1980 and 1984, overall rail traffic between Paris and south-eastern France rose from 12 to 18 million passengers, with business travel experiencing the sharpest growth. According to figures from joint surveys[5], total traffic between Lyons and Greater Paris on an average weekday rose by 160 per cent between 1980 and 1984, whereas the corresponding increase in business travel was 200 per cent; growth in travel for personal reasons was therefore limited to just under 80 per cent. This substantial growth in traffic was attributable to the new high-speed service.

The figures from LET[6] surveys on business travel between Paris and the Rhône-Alpes region are broadly similar: the number of business trips by train rose by 150 per cent between 1980 and 1985 -- by 125 per cent for trips out of Paris and by 175 per cent for travel originating in the Rhône-Alpes region. To provide a rough idea of the proportions involved, it can be estimated that 36 per cent of business trips in 1985 corresponded to induced travel, 27 per cent to shifts from travel by air or by car and 37 per cent to travel which was already carried out by rail in 1980.

The induced traffic which came to light was the result of an increase in two parameters: individual mobility and the number of persons who travelled. Looking only at business travel, we can attempt to apportion the additional traffic induced by each factor:

Table 3. **Number of annual business trips per capita between Lyons and Paris**

	Plane	**Train**	**Car**	**Total**
1980	6.9	5.9	1.7	14.5
1985	4.3	12.9	2.0	19.2

Even if these figures should be taken only as a rough guide, they nonetheless show that the rise in individual mobility far exceeded growth in the number of travellers: while trips rose by 56 per cent overall, individual mobility was up by 34 per cent and the combined number of air and rail passengers by 16 per cent. It would therefore appear that the changes attributable to high-speed rail stemmed far more from the mobility factor than from the number of customers: people accustomed to travelling travelled more, but comparatively few people who had not travelled previously began to do so.

In addition, the numbers in Table 4 below show that the changes in mobility varied widely depending on the direction of travel. Growth in traffic originating in Paris was due more to a greater number of customers, whereas the predominant factor in the growth of traffic originating in the Rhône-Alpes region was mobility.

Table 4. **Increase in traffic between 1980 and 1985**

	Daily mobility	Travellers	Total
Ex-Paris	4%	16%	21%
Ex-Rhône-Alpes	42%	30%	85%
TOTAL	34%	16%	56%

A new dimension -- spatial polarisation -- must therefore be factored into the relationships between mobility and infrastructure. Traffic growth associated with new infrastructure can have differing impacts on the towns and regions served.

Another way to travel

The introduction of new high-speed rail services not only triggered a sharp rise in mobility, it also altered travel behaviour by causing train passengers to adopt the practices of air travellers.

Before TGVs started running between Lyons and Paris, only 25 per cent of train travel between the two regions took place without a night away from home, versus nearly 60 per cent for travel by air. High-speed rail caused airline customers to transfer their travel behaviour to the trains since, in 1985, 62 per cent of return trips by TGV were completed in a single day. This would suggest that there had been a formidable, pent-up demand for short trips but that the cost of air travel had made them economically unacceptable to many businesses. From this standpoint, TGVs can be seen as veritable 'planes on rails.'

Even so, one cannot help but question the economic efficiency of these new travel patterns. Studies on the consequences of high-speed rail have shown that certain business travellers on the TGV, instead of making a single trip between Lyons and Paris to meet with two or three different contacts, were now making two or three trips involving just one contact; trips have been getting shorter and shorter and easier to arrange. As a result, it is not possible to associate this sharp growth in travel with high economic efficiency of mobility. On the other hand, the TGV has made greater flexibility possible.

Hidden behind the clearly identifiable phenomenon of rising traffic and, in most instances, the mobility which goes with it, are less easily detectable changes in the forms of mobility and thus in the societal effectiveness of travel.

An effect with a limited time frame

The sharp rise in mobility following the introduction of the TGV had a limited time frame. After a number of years, mobility began to increase at its previous pace, as if the fading novelty factor brought a return to normal mobility trends.

Figure 2. **Types of TGV traffic trends**
(in SNCF forecasting models)

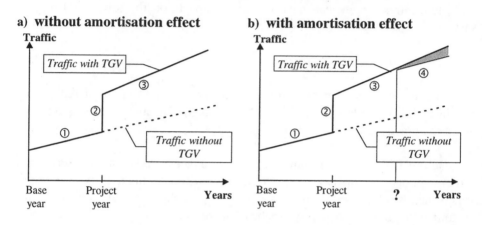

This phenomenon, which the SNCF factored into the traffic forecasts it needed for its cost/benefit analysis of high-speed rail projects, may be represented by means of Figure 2. In Figure 2 a) (above left), the SNCF differentiates between three phases:

-- Phase ① corresponds to "normal" traffic growth before the new infrastructure is introduced;
-- Phase ② corresponds to the traffic induced by the new infrastructure;
-- Phase ③ marks a return to growth which is steady, but slightly less robust than before the new infrastructure was introduced.

The observations which have been made since the *TGV Sud-Est* service began would seem to indicate that, after a few years, traffic tends to revert to a growth rate identical to the one which prevailed prior to introduction. A Phase ④ should therefore be added, as shown in Figure 2 b) above. Is this an effect of saturation or of recession? A waning of interest in rail travel? None of the answers to these questions would appear to be determining factors, but all have their relevance, as the consequences of the *TGV Atlantique*'s introduction have shown.

2.1.2. The TGV Atlantique

In 1989, before the *TGV Atlantique* was introduced, and again in 1993, four years later, the *Laboratoire d'Économie des Transports* (LET) conducted a series of surveys under conditions which were identical to those of the studies carried out some ten years earlier for the *TGV Sud-Est*. The findings of these surveys[7] shed valuable light on traffic trends for the three modes of transport -- road, rail and air.

Here, the effects on mobility are far less clear-cut than for the Paris-Lyons service: under the combined impact of recession and the tarnished image of rail transport, train traffic diminished by 11 per cent for business trips between 1989 and 1993. It can be seen, then, that new infrastructure does not necessarily induce a rise in mobility. But closer analysis yields a better understanding of how mobility is affected by high-speed rail.

The authors of the report differentiate between three travel zones on the basis of their respective distance from Paris:

1. Local zone (200-250 km);
2. Medium-haul zone (between 300 and 600 km);
3. Long-haul zone (over 600 km).

The authors also make the following remarks:

1. In the long-haul zone, air travel is strengthening its monopoly, and trains are becoming marginalised;
2. In the local zone, traffic has fallen off drastically (by 24 to 37 per cent, depending on the town) because of the economic downturn;
3. It is in the medium-haul zone that the effects of high-speed rail were felt the most, and those effects warrant a closer look.

One reason for this third point is that, within the medium-haul zone itself, the impact of high-speed rail varies considerably with distance, as shown in Table 5 below and the accompanying Figure 3.

Table 5. **Modal shares before and after introduction of the** *TGV Atlantique*
-- Professional journeys on working days --

	1989			1993		
	air	rail	road	air	rail	road
under 350 km	1	51%	48%	0	56%	44%
350-450 km	16%	39%	46%	4%	61%	31%
over 450 km	31%	47%	22%	36%	50%	14%

This clearly shows that air's share rises regularly as distances increase. That of road decreases, but as from a certain intermediary distance, the train occupies a fairly significant place. After the introduction of the TGV service, a general progression in rail's market share can be seen. But this is particularly marked over a distance of 350-450 km, where the two other competing modes see their market penetration diminish.

These surveys therefore give vital clues as to the journey distances for which high-speed rail is likely to alter mobility patterns and thus market shares. Beyond 400 km, TGVs are no longer competitive with planes and, as they are today, their advantage for trips of under 150 km or so is scant.

Figure 3. **Modal shares according to distance**

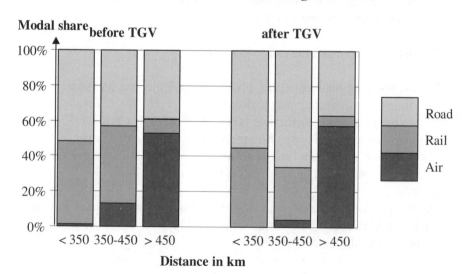

This example of a new high-speed service shows that an investment of this sort does not necessarily engender an overall increase in mobility. It can, however, with traffic remaining constant, cause shifts in mobility patterns which are limited to certain types of travel, and it can redistribute traffic among modes.

2.2. The motorway system

While it is clear that a new high-speed rail service triggers an extremely sharp rise in mobility, at least for the first few years after its introduction, what is the impact of new motorways? As motorways are built and gradually opened to the public, does this too cause mobility to rise? It is plain to see that motorway traffic has grown rapidly throughout Europe, yet much of this growth stems from an increase in the number of cars on the road, which in turn is correlated with rising income.

The statistics published in France by the Ministry of Transport point to a positive elasticity of traffic with respect to the length of the motorway system; but, above all, they suggest that saturation takes place once that system has exceeded a certain critical size.

Each year, the Ministry of Transport calculates a traffic index which keeps the motorway system constant: to obtain the index for year t as compared with year t-1, traffic growth between t-1 and t is reduced by the amount of traffic over new stretches of motorway opened over the course of t-1. Because of this method of calculation, the index reflects traffic trends arising from the establishment of an increasingly complete motorway system.

Figure 4 below shows that the road traffic index has risen at an average rate of 2.1 per cent per year, as the road system has remained stable. This is undoubtedly a reflection of increased mobility due to the rising income of the population as a whole. In contrast, the index of motorway traffic has risen much more sharply, averaging 4.9 per cent annual growth, suggesting that expansion of the motorway system has been a definite factor.

Figure 4. Indices of road and motorway traffic in France[8]
(base 100 = 1970)

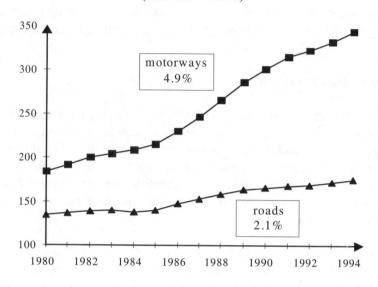

Letting I be the index of motorway traffic and L the length of the motorway system, the average elasticity e of the traffic index with respect to this length can be estimated at 1.42, where:

$$I_t = A\,L_t^e$$

However, as can be seen from the two graphs in Figure 5 below, to compute only an average value (using linear regression) conceals changes in elasticity as the motorway system develops. The regression carried out with the aid of a logistic curve would seem to correspond much more closely to the statistical reality.

Figure 5. Elasticity of use of the French motorway system with respect to its length

Linear model

Logistic model

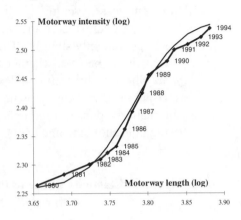

Everything would suggest that the motorway system could be analysed in life-cycle terms, just like any consumer product. Fifteen years were examined. Between 1980 and 1985, the system was extended from 4 500 to 5 500 kilometres, yet elasticity during that period averaged only 0.6. In contrast, the following thousand kilometres, which were opened between 1985 and 1990, seem to have been of great use to motorway users, since elasticity surged to 2.9. Lastly, the final thousand kilometres caused mobility to increase at roughly the same pace as the system's extension, since elasticity was essentially equal to 1.

Even if these figures have to be handled cautiously, inasmuch as longer and, above all, older series would be needed to confirm the hypotheses put forward, there is reason to ask whether this trend does not illustrate the club goods theory, whereby the utility of belonging to or being in a system depends on the number of persons or locations which can be contacted. Several phases in the life cycle of the motorway system can be distinguished, as shown in Figure 6 below.

1. During the first phase, the number of towns linked to the system was insufficient to generate heavy use. This period corresponds to the system's **learning** phase (e<1);

129

2. In the second phase, the opening of new stretches of motorway created a genuine network which considerably increased the number of possible destinations. Elasticity is very high. This is the **rapid development** phase (e>1);

3. In recent years, even though just as many kilometres of new stretches have been opened as in the previous phase, the quality of the system has improved only slightly. This is the **maturity** phase (e=1);

4. It remains to be seen whether the fourth phase will take place in the years ahead: the traffic index can be expected to level off in the **decline** phase. Any growth in traffic would then be merely an automatic response to the opening of new stretches of motorway and rising household income (e<1).

Figure 6. **Elasticity of use of the French motorway system with respect to its length**

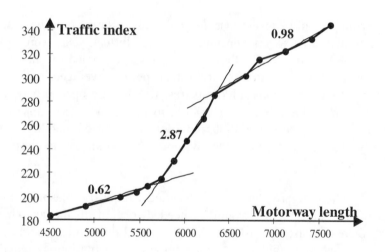

It may therefore be hypothesised that the relationship between the introduction of new infrastructure and increased mobility differs according to each transport system's particular stage of development.

2.3. Two traffic models for urban and regional transport

The examples to be drawn from major nationwide rail and motorway systems would seem to confirm the existence of a relationship between a system's growth and increased mobility. In the case of urban and regional transport, however, the relationship would seem far less clear-cut.

2.3.1. The forecast for mass transit traffic in Lyons

LET's recent research into mass transit in Greater Lyons[9] provided the basis for a model to simulate mobility. This model "explains" urban mobility (in terms of per-capita trips, designated M) by means of two variables:

1. An indicator of supply (the number of per-capita passenger-kilometres on offer, designated O);
2. A price indicator (the average price of a trip, per passenger, designated P).

This leads to the following equation: $M = O^{0.82} * P^{-1.52}$ ($r^2 = 0.88$).

Figure 7. **Mobility and the supply of mass transit in Greater Lyons**

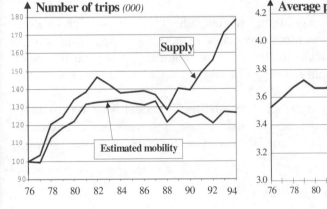
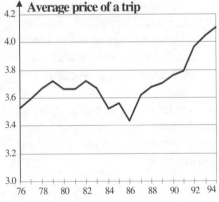

The above figure shows that mobility initially mirrored improvements in supply, which corresponded to the opening of the first metro line. Thereafter, both mobility and supply deteriorated. Lastly, the opening of Line D of the metro considerably improved supply but failed to stop the steady decline in mobility.

This divergence in trends between supply and mobility, beginning in 1988, can be explained by a continuous rise in mass transit fares. Given the very high price elasticity of this form of mobility (1.52), traffic could only have diminished. It therefore emerges clearly that, to explain the relationship between mobility trends and the creation of new infrastructure, all aspects of the transport on offer need to be taken into consideration. This conclusion is further supported by the example of regional travel between Lyons and Saint Étienne, France.

2.3.2. The Lyons/Saint Étienne regional model

Because of the saturation of the motorway which connects Lyons and Saint Étienne, two cities in the Rhône-Alpes some sixty kilometres apart, regional and national authorities have tried to explore various ways in which the situation could be improved:

1. Improving the existing motorway is impossible inasmuch as zoning restrictions preclude construction of a third lane;
2. One solution would be to build a second motorway which would run parallel to the first;
3. An alternative would be to upgrade the rail service, thereby encouraging some motorway users to take the train; this solution would avoid having to build a new motorway, since traffic on the existing one would fall off sufficiently.

Using existing traffic data, a multimodal traffic model was constructed to simulate the consequences of the various possible improvements[10]. The model was a bimodal one (rail and road) which can be summarised in the following two equations:

1. A traffic generation equation:

$$T_{ij} = K*(R_iP_i*R_jP_j)^{0.5}*c_{ij}^{-2.18}*[(P_i-P_j)/(p_i+P_j)]^{-0.5} \quad ;$$

2. A modal split equation:

$$T_f/T_r = K'*(t_f/t_r)^{-2.14}*(R/Rm)^{3.0}*(F_{ij}/T_{ij})^{0.34} \,,$$

where:

T_{ij} = traffic between areas i and j;
K and K' = constants;
R_i and P_i = income (revenue) and population of area i, respectively;
c_{ij} = the combined overall cost of road and rail;
T_f and T_r = rail and road traffic, respectively;
t_f and t_r = travel time by rail and by road, respectively;
R = household income (revenue) of populations P_i and P_j;
Rm = mean income (revenue) for all links;
F_{ij} = frequency of trains between i and j.

Figure 8. Effects of changes in passenger car travel time on traffic between Lyons and Saint Étienne

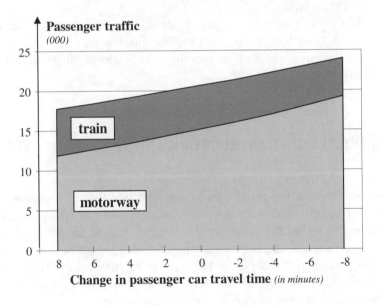

It is not our intention to present all of the findings of this study, but it is worth considering one of its conclusions, which is illustrated in Figure 8 above, as a basis for further reflection.

If, by making various capital investments, travel time on the motorway can be cut by a number of minutes, then motorway traffic will increase substantially. The main impact of this improvement, however, will be to erode the relative advantages of the railway, which will thus lose some of its customers. The study shows that increasing the frequency of rail services not only increases railway custom but also, in a symmetrical manner, prompts a large number of motorway users to switch over to the train.

2.4. Conclusion

This lengthy discussion of the relationships between new infrastructure and mobility leads us to five conclusions:

1. In most of the examples analysed, it is possible to show a statistical correlation between improved facilities and increased mobility;
2. The improvement of the facilities on offer is more important than the infrastructure itself;
3. The influence of other variables, such as price and income, can be a deciding factor;
4. The consequences of infrastructure can trigger substantial variations in mobility with regard to other modes of transport;
5. Quantitative changes in mobility can conceal shifts in patterns of mobility.

3. MOBILITY, INFRASTRUCTURE AND TRANSPORT SYSTEMS

The above examples prompt us to consider that the relationships between new infrastructure and mobility are many and complex. Transport infrastructure, whether for travel by road or rail, has no inherent significance. Its efficiency in terms of shifting mobility depends on all of the conditions in which it operates, i.e. access and usage costs, degree of availability and technical effectiveness in terms of travel speed. It is the combination of these parameters which correlates mobility with infrastructure.

But we cannot conclude with this simple quantitative relationship, since three questions underlie all of the above analysis:

1. Do not the relationships between new infrastructure and induced mobility have more to do with the **transport system** as a whole than with the particular infrastructure under consideration?
2. Underneath the quantitative changes in mobility, are **new patterns** of mobility emerging -- patterns which will ultimately have far-reaching consequences?
3. Is it not the case that new transport infrastructure induces **new ways of organising space,** which themselves will generate new forms of mobility?

3.1. An all-encompassing transport system

While it would seem difficult to challenge the fact that new infrastructure has some impact on mobility, it has to be added that the changes involved are not always positive and that they can affect the entire transport system.

Indeed, any change in the supply of transport constitutes a change in the broader entity which is the overall transport system. For users, a mode of transport, a particular component of infrastructure or any given service is just an element which enables them to meet their own objectives in terms of travel or freight. Any changes, as the example of the French TGV so clearly shows, alter the relative advantages of each mode; not only do they (in some cases) generate induced traffic, they can also trigger modal transfers. From this standpoint, any improvement to the transport system causes a relative deterioration of all other elements of the system which have not been changed.

There is hardly any other possible explanation for the virtual monopoly which road hauliers now enjoy in respect of freight: improvements to vehicles and development of the motorway system have given them features which other means of transport are unable to provide. What this means is that no attempt to influence mobility -- to maintain a sustainable growth rate, for example -- can be limited to a single mode or a single component of transport infrastructure; it must incorporate the entire transport system.

Current research shows that it is increasingly difficult to separate the levels which transport specialists used to differentiate. A mode is no longer an autonomous transport system but just one link in a far wider transport chain; and it is no longer possible to disregard interactions among the various types of transport composing that chain. Today, no decisionmaker can afford to disregard the relationships which have been taking root between regional transport and urban transport; and, to a considerable extent, the vehement

135

opposition which was directed against construction of a new high-speed rail line between Lyons and the Mediterranean coast stemmed from the fact that the project failed to take regional transport into account.

All of the current models for forecasting traffic attempt to incorporate this multiplicity of modes and transport systems, in order to achieve greater efficiency. But the effectiveness of intermodal transfer models is still limited if competition among more than two modes is to be taken into account.

3.2. New forms of mobility

Driven by technological progress, all transport systems have evolved towards greater speed, safety and capacity. Infrastructure -- increasingly specialised and tailored to certain types of vehicles -- has played a role in that evolutionary process; and it is all of these improvements which have caused mobility patterns to shift.

The emergence of new suburban areas now seems inextricably linked to the development of means of urban transport (trains, tramways and, subsequently, urban motorways). It is these new travel options, specially tailored to an urban environment, which have given rise to the daily commuting which characterises our contemporary urban societies.

A common feature of all the new infrastructure currently being introduced (motorways and high-speed rail services) is that it has been designed to cut transit time significantly. Because of this, it gives rise to types of travel which were hitherto impossible. Just-in-time logistics may have been spawned by a new organisation of production, but it could never have emerged if businesses did not have quick, reliable and inexpensive means of transport at their disposal.

Improvements to the road and motorway system have facilitated increased travel. Whether it be in the form of weekend excursions, splitting annual leave into a number of different trips, or holidays which are farther afield, more numerous and of shorter duration, a veritable explosion in mobility has been taking place.

As we saw with regard to business travel, high-speed rail has extended a type of travel which was once the exclusive province of the airlines. Improved transport conditions, engendered by the development of infrastructure, give rise to mass migrations, concentrated over a small number of days and, in all likelihood, saturation and congestion alone will be able to alter these patterns.

3.3. Transport infrastructure and the organisation of space

To understand how the development of transport infrastructure can affect mobility, it is necessary to explore the new modes of spatial organisation which this infrastructure brings about and upon which, at the same time, it is based. The existence of new travel options enables new trade-offs between location and mobility and is conducive to the concentration of particular activities in certain areas.

3.3.1. *New trade-offs between location and mobility*

The primary objective of most models to determine where activities should be located is to minimise travel costs, which encompass not only price but also lost time and the inherent risk of travel. For this reason, any change in the conditions of transport would be expected to create new location options. As it happens, however, improvements which make transport easier have a tendency to discourage relocation, even from economically aberrant sites, inasmuch as the drawbacks of a poor location can be offset by relatively inexpensive travel. By facilitating such travel, new infrastructure makes it possible to keep activities in locations which would otherwise become untenable. This is why shifting travel patterns generally correspond, in spatial terms, to an absence of relocation: people commute and activities stay put.

In addition, businesses have set up production systems which are based on a spatial scattering of functions. To reap the benefits of low taxes or cheap labour, companies are prompted to manage increasingly complex and numerous flows of goods and information. Whereas one might think that enhanced ease of transport would make it possible for businesses to relocate to areas which had previously been served poorly, what is in fact taking place is a growing concentration in the large metropolitan areas: in order to cope with recession and the vicissitudes of economic activity, businesses are adopting risk-minimisation strategies in terms of location, employment and products. For such firms, major metropolitan areas increase the number of available options, even if it means increasing the amount of travel which is vital to their business.

Enhanced accessibility also means that location decisions which will have to be made sooner or later can be put off: by affording more time, this greater accessibility makes for more rational decisions by enabling firms to wait until situations currently in flux have stabilized. It is for this reason that a number of Rhône-Alpes firms developing international sales strategies, for which a Paris connection is vital, have agreed to remain temporarily in Lyons while waiting to see how their foreign markets develop. High-speed rail has made transitional situations bearable and has even, in a few extreme cases, enabled them to become permanent.

This holds true for business locations, and it also holds true for where people live. Households, faced with the problems of juggling with the many sites at which their various members are engaged in activities, as well as with the high price of urban housing, increasingly take quality-of-life considerations into account when choosing acceptable solutions, which more often than not makes it necessary to travel more often and over greater distances. Job market trends are reinforcing this preference for a stable home. Certain managers whose professional circumstances are in the midst of change keep the same home, because of the spouse's employment, the children's schooling and, in some cases, the difficulty in finding another suitable home for their family. Given the precariousness of employment and the need to take jobs in far-off places, it is the family home which provides the territorial anchor for fairly extended periods of time, until circumstances stabilize.

Under the circumstances, new transport infrastructure which makes high speed possible is less a factor determining location than one which makes it possible to postpone inevitable relocation for longer. For a growing number of executives, high-speed rail has made it possible to live in Lyons and work in the Paris area, or *vice versa*. As transport becomes easier and easier, increasingly vast labour market areas have been taking shape and assuming travel patterns previously found only in urban areas, thus warranting their labels as "urban regions".

3.3.2.   *Geographical concentration of activities and people*

Location is an issue not only for activities and for people, but also for infrastructure itself. The way space is being organised in Europe reveals two major trends in the selection of transport infrastructure.

1.   There is a growing accumulation of transport infrastructure, some of which combines a number of different modes, in areas of high population density. The goal is to relieve congestion and maintain the viability of these large metropolitan areas, which risk being asphyxiated by creeping immobilisation. To cite just one example, Greater Paris has seen a succession of ring roads being built farther and farther from the centre of town and, in the most heavily concentrated area, increasingly rapid and extensive transport systems have been springing up;

2.   At the same time, however, infrastructure is being constructed in sparsely populated areas to further land-use planning objectives and help achieve interregional equilibrium.

Such decisions have an impact -- in the long term at least -- on spatial organisation and, for this reason, on mobility trends. Consequently, mobility tends to rise more quickly in the case of primary services between major cities, aggravating problems of saturation. The increased mobility attributable to new transport infrastructure will be far greater if the infrastructure in question connects two very large metropolitan areas than if its intended purpose is to lessen the isolation of an area which has been partially drained of its population. Traffic models (discussed in Chapter 2, "Experimental Routes") have clearly taken this phenomenon into account by identifying traffic generation factors and factors of spatial resistance.

By making an overall contribution to the polarisation of space around a number of major centres, transport infrastructure reduces the number of primary traffic generation areas and makes those areas more concentrated. Such infrastructure also -- this time indirectly, via the location decisions of activities and people -- gives rise to new travel.

What this means is that to explore the relationships between traffic infrastructure and mobility leads inevitably to land-use planning policies.

3.3.3.   *Mobility as a societal value*

It would not be possible to conclude this discussion of mobility without evoking its role in representations of space or its place in the value system which underlies western societies.

It is probably because mobility and, undoubtedly, speed are considered pillars of societal organisation that transport infrastructure is made use of immediately, as soon as it opens. Any impediment to a person's freedom to travel is now deemed an infringement of individual liberties. Moreover, it is likely to be years before increasingly widespread restrictions on the use of automobiles are considered a normal means of regulating society.

These observations lead to the conclusion that what is behind the societal and spatial transformations which follow the construction of major transport infrastructure is a change in the value society places upon time -- a change which legitimises, first, the design and, later, the use of faster means of transport. The conflict between the French authorities and associations for the defence of the Rhône Valley and Provence substantiates this interpretation: a certain kind of quality of life for some means putting a low societal value on time, whereas the priority which others attach to economic efficiency corresponds to a much higher estimation of the value of time. When seen in this light, the conflict is no longer only, or even chiefly, a matter of routing, but of two conceptions of societal space and thus of time.

Recession, by bringing the idleness spawned by joblessness back to the fore, is calling these values into question. The way in which work fits into the equation is changing fast, in that employment can no longer ensure an acceptable division of income or social integration. Society may also begin to have second thoughts about the value of economic efficiency and thus of time saved; if the importance of these concepts were to diminish in relation to other values, such as the quality of time spent engaged in various activities, it would be likely to trigger a quest for new societal relationships and new patterns of mobility.

It emerges that the relationships which have been brought to light between transport infrastructure and mobility are the result of a necessarily temporary societal trade-off between immobility and mobility, between extension of the territory of a social group and the resultant cost thereof -- the cost of going through space. In all probability, then, far greater importance will have to be attached to relationships between representations of time and representations of space, as well as to relationships between spatial patterns, if we are to gain a thorough understanding of the transformations which infrastructure-induced mobility both brings about and reflects.

CONCLUSION

After this brief survey, which is in no way intended to be exhaustive, three conclusions emerge from the discussion: the relationship between infrastructure and induced mobility, which is the central issue, cannot be a simple one; in assessing that relationship, there is a need to differentiate among highly diverse situations; and the nature of the issue changes with the time frame.

1. While it can be readily agreed that the mobility induced by transport infrastructure is no simple matter of cause and effect, it is more delicate to grasp the full complexity of the relationship. First, it is necessary to analyse the efficiency of the transport system as a whole;

the second stage is to introduce spatial specifics; a third and final phase entails analysis of the societal behaviour which underlies decisions to build infrastructure and mobility patterns alike.

2. The range of research on which this paper is based -- both the modelling work and studies of a more qualitative nature -- suggests that distinctions need to be drawn between highly diverse situations. Major infrastructure systems (rail, road or air) undoubtedly induce a measure of additional mobility; yet, at the same time, they concentrate travel over a number of major routes, which ultimately results in spatial reorganisation. Here, price premiums are not significant and would not appear to curtail mobility. At the urban level, however, and with regard to mass transit in particular, changes in the prices users must pay have a far greater impact on mobility than improvements to transport facilities.

3. Lastly, all of the attempts to assess the relationship between infrastructure and mobility using the concept of elasticity have done so over relatively short periods. They provide a good understanding of a number of short-term adjustments, but they fail to anticipate shifts in behaviour over longer time frames. To grasp these shifts in behaviour, even if they are partially detectable from broad trends in mobility, would undoubtedly entail other analysis of societal transformations.

NOTES

1. See, for example (1992), "High-Speed Transport and Regional Development", report for *ECMT Round Table 94, Regional Policy, Transport Networks and Communications*, Paris, November.

2. Excerpt from (1992), *Transports 2010*, Commissariat Général du Plan and Documentation Française, June, p. 167.

3. Excerpt from (1992), *Transports 2010*, Commissariat Général du Plan and Documentation Française, June, p. 168.

4. (1992), *Transports 2010*, Commissariat Général du Plan and Documentation Française, June, p. 281.

5. Observatoire Économique et Statistique des Transports (OEST) and the Ministry for Infrastructure, Housing and Land-Use Development, Paris.

6. Laboratoire d'Économie des Transports, Lyons.

7. Olivier Klein, Gérard Claisse and Pascal Pochet (1996), *Un TGV entre récession et concurrence modale, évolution de la mobilité et mise en service du TGV Atlantique*, Research Report, LET, June, 380 pages.

8. The data used to plot this graph, as well as the following two, are taken from the Statistical Yearbook published annually by the OEST.

9. Eric Tabourin (1995), *Mobilité urbaine*, Laboratoire d'Économie des Transports, Lyons. The model was adjusted to series of data covering the years 1976 to 1994.

10. METRAM, ITEP, LET (1992), *Étude de l'amélioration de la liaison Lyon-Saint Étienne*, Lyons, February.

UNITED KINGDOM

P.B. GOODWIN
ESCR Transport Studies Unit
University College London
London
United Kingdom

The work reported here includes contributions made by the author as a member of the UK Standing Advisory Committee on Trunk Road Assessment (SACTRA, 1994) and summaries of the contributions of other Committee members and colleagues as cited in the text. Additional work was carried out as part of the research programme of the ESRC Transport Studies Unit, formerly part of the University of Oxford and now at University College London.

Judgements on economic and policy implications are the responsibility of the author and only represent the views of SACTRA where direct quotations are given.

EXTRA TRAFFIC INDUCED BY ROAD CONSTRUCTION: EMPIRICAL EVIDENCE, ECONOMIC EFFECTS AND POLICY IMPLICATIONS

SUMMARY

London, June 1996

146

ABSTRACT

The balance of theoretical and empirical evidence indicates that additional traffic is induced by the provision of extra road capacity, due to a range of different behavioural responses.

The amount of extra traffic will vary according to the specific circumstances, size of scheme, existing traffic congestion, geographical and economic conditions and availability of alternatives. In UK conditions, an average result for an average scheme may be of the order of 10 per cent extra traffic in the short run and 20 per cent in the longer run, with a range of 0-20 per cent in the short run and 0-40 per cent in the longer run.

The extra traffic enjoys some benefits itself (hence increasing the calculated benefit/cost ratio of the road) but also erodes the benefit to other road users by shortening the period of relief from congestion (hence reducing the benefit/cost ratio). The net effect depends substantially on the level of congestion. Because of the non-linear nature of the relationship between traffic volume and speed, induced traffic reduces the overall value for money of a road scheme when conditions are more congested. Induced traffic also increases environmental damage. Therefore omission of induced traffic will always result in an overestimate of the environmental benefits of new capacity and usually result in an overestimate of the congestion benefits.

These effects take place over several years. Research to monitor the effects of new road capacity cannot come to meaningful conclusions by observing only first-year effects. Evaluation procedures need to use dynamic concepts allowing for the speed of adjustment, not only a description of a final equilibrium.

The policy consequences which follow depend on wider strategic issues, especially the pace of traffic growth due to factors other than new capacity. Currently, transport policy gives importance to environmental impacts, the need to ensure value for money from public funds and the need to protect economic benefits from erosion by congestion: in these circumstances, induced traffic reduces the effectiveness of a road-construction based transport strategy and gives additional emphasis to the importance of applying efficient methods of managing and reducing the growth in traffic.

1. INTRODUCTION

For over twenty years, the UK Department of Transport used a procedure for road planning firmly based on the assumption that new road capacity did not lead to any increase in the total volume of traffic. After some years of controversy, several consultants' studies and a two-year investigation by a technical committee established by the Department, this assumption was abandoned in 1994. Now, it is recommended practice to make allowance for extra generated or induced traffic in most schemes of any substance.

This paper summarises the historical treatment of this issue, the empirical evidence cited and the arguments about its interpretation, the consequences for economic evaluation of road schemes and the effects on understanding the limitations of road construction as the core of a sustainable transport strategy.

2. HISTORY OF AN ARGUMENT

2.1. Acceptance, 1930s-1960s

Bressey and Lutyens (1938) reported that the Great West Road in London:

"...as soon as it opened, carried 4½ times more vehicles than the old route was carrying; no diminution, however, occurred in the flow of traffic on the old route and from that day to this, the number of vehicles on both routes has steadily increased.... . These figures serve to exemplify the remarkable manner in which new roads create new traffic."

Faster traffic growth on improved and less congested roads than on congested roads is a ubiquitous observation. The argument that this is connected to induced traffic, although somewhat informal in character, shows an unbroken intellectual continuity for nearly sixty years after Bressey and Lutyens' comment. In the post-war years, the most influential research was carried out at the Road Research Laboratory, initially by Glanville and Smeed (1958). Their work showed that traffic growth on roads which were already congested was much slower than traffic growth on roads which were less congested. They concluded:

"That the absence of adequate roads is likely to affect to some extent the amount of traffic is illustrated also by the fact that the rate of increase of traffic using the roads of central London is much less than on the outskirts... . Traffic on a new road consists of three elements: that attracted from other roads; that due to the natural growth in traffic; and the generated traffic which would not have existed but for the presence of the new road."

At that time, no quantified estimate was made of the amount of generated traffic. But research was put in hand and the Road Research Laboratory (1965) published results of modelling using a form of gravity model to explain the amount of travel between zones, with the form:

$$\Delta t_{ij} \cong t_{ij} \; \frac{n\Delta z_{ij}}{z_{ij}}$$

They reported:

"Empirical studies of flows between towns have usually shown that if the deterrence factor is assumed to be Z_{ij}^{-n}, then n lies between 2 and 3.5. Applying this to the approximate formula suggests that the percentage increase in traffic is 2 to 3.5 times the percentage decrease in journey time."

Academics also shared this approach. An influential textbook, Foster (1963) -- at that time at Oxford University, but shortly after to play a leading role in developing the evaluation procedures of the Ministry of Transport -- wrote:

"We have the experience of Los Angeles. Some of the most congested roads in California are expressways built recently to relieve congestion. Build a new expressway and it attracts new traffic on to the roads which later tends to offset the initial decongestion. The effects of this second round of 'generated' traffic, as it is often called, must be taken into account in working out the return on road investment."

149

So by the mid-1960s, a combination of common sense, experience of the effects of large schemes and modelling results was sufficient to persuade the Ministry of Transport (1968) to give official guidance that traffic generation should be allowed for in forecasting the effects of a new road. The following quotation shows the advice at that time:

"Traffic Generation

Traffic is also increased because reduced journey times generate journeys which would not otherwise have been made. It is not necessary to allow for generated traffic on small schemes, where the effect on overall journey times is likely to be small, but for larger schemes, or small schemes which are part of a larger plan, some allowance should be made. The amount of generated traffic is related to the saving in journey times between the principal places of origin and destination and the allowance for generated traffic should be about twice the percentage decrease in total journey time for each pair of origins and destinations... . Generated traffic on large schemes has often amounted to between 5 per cent and 25 per cent over and above the normal forecast traffic level. It may be larger in exceptional cases, for example, where a new bridge produces drastically shortened journey times. Traffic is also likely to be generated by a new route which avoids or replaces a toll route.

"Influence of other road improvements

It may at times be necessary to consider the effects of other schemes in the vicinity which are likely to be carried out within the design period... . If a motorway, or other major road is to be built, it may draw off traffic and reduce demand on the existing road to a level which reduces the need for new roadworks. But the relief of an existing road may also attract generated traffic to that road. Once again, a reliable estimate of the change in traffic patterns is dependent upon an origin and destination survey and by a reassignment of traffic based on estimated reductions in journey times on the motorway or other roads. If no direct information is available it will be necessary to base predictions on experience from other similar schemes.

"In some circumstances, motorway feeder roads, for example, traffic will be increased by the presence of the motorway and estimates of increased traffic can be made using the same technique."

2.2. Rejection, 1970s-1990s

However, within the five years or so following publication of this guidance there was a change in practice. The Ministry of Transport adopted the view that extra road capacity, in general, did not influence the volume of traffic except in a few very special circumstances like new estuary crossings and that allowance would only be made for such traffic if there was new, convincing, empirical evidence in its favour. The reasons for this change are not fully known to the author and seem not to have been published. Two suggestions which have been made to explain the change are as follows:

a) In the late 1960s and early 1970s, the Ministry of Transport developed its formal cost-benefit appraisal system for roads, COBA, with the intention that it should include allowance for generated traffic. (Certainly, its basic logic was consistent with that intention.) However, the early versions did not make such allowance, for reasons primarily of convenience and the longer this lasted the more resistance built up to changing what was seen as a "tried and tested" procedure.

b) An alternative suggestion notes that during evaluation of some controversial road proposals in London at this period, benefits were calculated for traffic generated by the road. Opponents of the scheme argued that this unfairly weighted in favour of the proposal, these benefits being accrued by people who, in a sense, did not yet exist and recalculations were carried out excluding them from the assessment. This practice was interpreted as "conservative" (i.e. it was assumed to lead to an underestimate of benefits -- which is not strictly true, but was thought to be at the time) and became favoured by the Treasury, perhaps as a counter to what was sometimes regarded as over-optimistic calculation of benefits and became entrenched in practice as a result.

Neither of these reasons was based on new evidence and indeed no important publication is known to the author from that period which cast empirical doubt on the previous practice. But for whatever reason, not only the practice changed but also the argument used to justify it.

Not a few people and institutions were uncomfortable with the new approach, which led to some two decades of a continual argument, notably in connection with major road schemes supported by the Government but opposed by a local authority or a local campaigning group of residents. These opponents often sought to challenge the validity of official traffic forecasts at public enquiries into proposed new roads. Such challenges were rarely argued out by reference to scientific evidence: the question became one of whether any opponent was legally *entitled* to challenge the figures. One important case, *Bushell and Brunt v. Secretary of State for Transport and the Environment, 1980,* was taken to the House of Lords (in its capacity as the highest legal court), with a ruling that the forecasts could not be challenged at inquiries.

2.3. Review of traffic growth on the M25

Construction of the M25 has played a particularly important role in generating renewed public interest in the question of induced traffic, because it rapidly became clear that the amount of traffic using the road on almost every section was much greater than had been predicted. Public comment on this was perhaps typified by the Sunday Times (28.8.1988) which described the M25 as a "Transport Fiasco" and "Obsolete before it opened" and quoted Paul Channon, Secretary of State for Transport, as saying that motorways have been victims of their own success -- precisely because they are so fast and convenient, drivers use them more. There was a strong public perception that the M25 had attracted a great deal of extra traffic, beyond that which could be accounted for merely by changes of routes. The Sunday Times graphic (Figure 1) provided a powerful visual image of the contrast between expectation and reality and was subsequently updated and used in several official technical interventions in the argument, e.g. by the National Audit Office and by SACTRA (1994).

The Department of Transport commissioned consultants to review the M25 experience and the general conclusions are summarised as follows [following closely the language of the Department's internal report, as summarised in SACTRA (1994)]:

a)   Traffic that uses a new road may be described as falling within the following categories: reassigned, redistributed, modal transfer, development traffic, generated traffic, change in time of travel. The relative importance of each of these categories on the M25 is unknown.

b)   The majority of **reassignment** effects of a new road are typically assumed to occur within the first three to six months following its completion. The M25 was completed by November 1986 and the majority of reassignment effects are therefore assumed to have occurred by early 1987. Traffic speeds in outer London are continuing to fall. It

Figure 1. **Media coverage of M25 traffic**

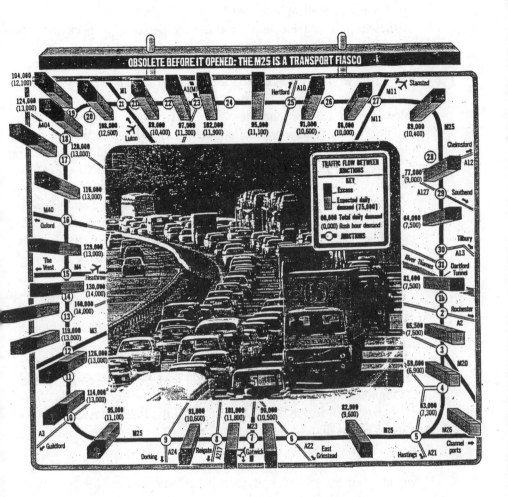

Source: Sunday Times, 28.8.1988.

is possible, therefore, that general increases in traffic levels are disproportionately being attracted to the M25 even after the original take up of reassignment. Where the M25 exhibits peak-hour congestion, then at these times and locations traffic may be routeing back to routes originally relieved by the M25.

c) The absolute volume of **redistributed** traffic is unknown and in general is a matter of judgement. In the context of the M25, it is noted that the population of London and the South East contains a large number of people who are relatively mobile in where they live and work; massive increases in house prices resulted in a large number of individuals living in outlying towns; the motorway network in the South East exhibits strong peak and tidal traffic flows commonly associated with urban commuter flow patterns; and there is evidence that redistribution can happen very quickly, or even anticipate the opening of a new facility. For these reasons, it may be assumed that redistributed traffic has been an important element in recent trends in traffic growth on the M25.

d) The **mode transfer** of individuals from public transport to road would not obviously appear to be a major feature of the traffic characteristics of the M25 in its function as an interurban route and bypass to London. However, it also has another function, catering for movements between outlying areas of London and the region. Given the radial nature of the rail network, certain of these trips would have been via central London. On completion of the M25, such trips may now be accomplished more easily by car. It follows that it is likely that the M25 has promoted some transfer from rail to road.

e) The M25 has promoted significant pressure to develop land within its vicinity, but the majority of such developments have yet to come to fruition. **Development traffic** is likely to be of limited importance in explaining recent traffic but, if they come to fruition, development traffic is likely to be an important feature of future trends.

f) Some other examples are given of schemes which seem to have **generated** new leisure trips: outings from Greater Manchester to Blackpool on completion of the M6/M54, or from Avon to Dartmoor on completion of the southern section of the M5. No information or argument was given on the possible importance of this for the M25.

g)   On certain sections of the M25, where congestion is present in the peak hours, there has been some **spreading of the peak**. Of major importance is that if peak spreading has occurred then the reverse may also occur, following improvements in capacity.

h)   Traffic growth on major radial routes outside the M25 has often been greater than growth on the same radial routes inside the M25, suggesting that "much" of the traffic on the M25 is made up of the reassignment of existing, particularly radial, movements.

Thus, this review tended to confirm, due to lack of convincing evidence, the then practice. Other reviews did not have the same emphasis. Pells (1989) cited 78 published and unpublished studies, theoretical discussions, modelling exercises and traffic counts. There was a wide range of results, with estimated induced traffic (defined very broadly, that is, all extra traffic other than reassignment) ranging from 0 per cent to 76 per cent of observed increases in traffic flows. There was evidence that trip retiming could be important and weak evidence on the relative importance of redistribution, modal change, generated trips (each of which could represent 2 per cent to 10 per cent of traffic) and land-use effects.

In a literature review of the effects of changing levels of congestion, Hawthorne and Paulley (1991) found reference to choice of route, departure time including flexitime, mode shifts including ridesharing and public transport, trip frequency, complex intra-household adjustments in travel and activity patterns and changes in the willingness to own cars. One review which came to the opposite conclusion was by Howard Humphreys and Partners (1993), who suggested that reassignment is the only response for which there is evidence and that all the observed increases in traffic on improved roads could be accounted for by drivers making very long detours to use them. (In terms of environmental impact, the distinction is not very important, though it makes a substantial difference to understanding and assessing the outcome.)

3. THE SACTRA APPROACH

SACTRA (Standing Advisory Committee on Trunk Road Assessment) is a committee appointed by the Secretary of State for Transport, but consisting of outside experts and independent of the management and policy of the Department of Transport. It was asked to consider the conflicting evidence and make recommendations for any changes that might be necessary. The following sections follow the approach taken by the Committee.

3.1. Definitions

There is a danger that the problem of induced traffic can be defined too narrowly, because of the "categories of thought" which are encouraged in the well-established travel demand models. For example, the English phrase "generated traffic" (often used as a synonym for induced traffic) becomes confused with "generated trips". In other cases, it is assumed that the behavioural responses allowed in the conventional four-stage model (generation, distribution, mode-choice, assignment) are the *only* behavioural responses that are possible and in this case it is common to define induced traffic as consisting of the first three of those four, but excluding reassignment.

However, it is axiomatic that travel is rarely an end in itself. People make journeys to carry out the everyday obligations of personal and social life and to engage in work and leisure activities that bring them economic or other benefits. Private companies and public institutions engage in the movement of goods and the provision of services which bring them financial gain or carry out their statutory responsibilities. A very few journeys may be made simply for the pleasure of the journey itself. It is conceivable that a new or improved road might stimulate some sightseers to inspect its design or views, but in general what really *generates* travel are the patterns and locations of residence, workplaces, sources of materials and supplies, shops, hospitals, leisure facilities and so on -- in other words, better access between land uses permits a greater level of social and individual activity which is travel-dependent. Indeed, better access in itself allows for land-use locations to change, for new land uses and for land-use patterns to evolve.

Therefore, the Committee took a very much broader view: induced traffic is defined as including *any* of the individual or system responses which can result in the volume of traffic with an improvement being greater than the volume of traffic without that improvement. This will include the four responses mentioned above (also assignment, if an improvement encourages some traffic to make a detour to obtain the benefits of a faster journey). It can also include the behavioural responses which are not normally included in traffic models -- for example, time-shifting, consolidation of trips. It also includes the longer-term changes in land use and regional development which can result from an important road, even when that is not its prime function.

3.2. By what processes might road improvements induce more traffic?

If traffic arises because of the sum total of social and individual activities and the evolving land-use patterns that influence their location, then in order for this to happen, many millions of decisions and choices have to be made. Policies and plans are formulated which determine the broad patterns of land use and of economic development and define environmental sensitivities. Companies are formed, others go out of business. Public agencies change their workload and priorities. Individuals form and reform into households, obtain and lose employment, develop tastes and preferences. The general state of the economy will determine how much money people have and therefore influence the number and size of cars that people buy. Petrol prices may change as a result of national policy or international developments. Changes in electronics may change the balance of the time spent in in-home and out-of-home leisure.

So the question may be redefined. Given that all these choices and decisions are continually being made mainly for other reasons, might the provision of extra road capacity, to some extent, *change* the decisions which individuals and agencies make, in such a way that there is an alteration to the total volume of traffic? It is helpful to list the main ways in which this could, in principle, occur. These are responses connected with:

-- the total volume of activities;
-- the location of activities;
-- the timing of activities;
-- the mode of transport used;
-- the co-ordination of different individuals;
-- the route chosen;
-- the effects of other responses.

Responses connected with the total volume of activities

Consider a large road scheme which provides a ring road around one town and then substantially reduces the time it takes to travel to the centre of another, improving the links with motorways to many other destinations on the way. What might happen as a result? It is often hoped that a new road will actually give a

157

boost to the area it serves, encouraging developments in the local economy, either by the reduced cost of production and distribution of local companies, or by symbolic and psychological factors connected with confidence and commitment. If the number of jobs increases overall, then clearly there would be an increase in the number of work trips, deliveries and so on.

The same would occur if there are some activities requiring a certain catchment population to make them viable at all, for example, an Olympic standard swimming pool: each of the towns on its own might not have been able to support this but, with access from both, a facility half-way might become possible. If so, then, of course, people will travel to use it.

At a narrower, more personal level, it may be that the improved speed makes it possible to fit in some small, additional activity which previously was not possible -- to go home for lunch, or to visit a friend on the way home.

Responses connected with the location of activities

The same political process also influences changes in the closely related question of the location of activities. Even before the new road is completed, the more alert companies and individuals may realise that there is advantage to be gained from moving, to make use of the opportunities for better communications. A retail firm could apply for planning permission for a new, out-of-town superstore close to one of the new intersections, instead of a town-centre location which they had been considering. A Health Authority may judge that this creates the opportunity for replacing some small, local hospitals by a new, regional hospital with good road access (having, perhaps, weighed in the balance that not all its users would find this convenient). Individuals may calculate that a journey to work which was previously impractical would soon be rather efficient and buy property or apply for jobs which would previously have been ruled out. They might consider, though, that this move would probably require the household to have two cars instead of the one that they have at the moment.

In this case, though, the decisions could be taken before the road opens, they would have ramifications afterwards. Thus, out-of-town shopping centres tend to rely on a higher level of car use by the customers and different patterns of lorry deliveries by the suppliers, than town-centre shops. This could increase suburban traffic levels, but reduce town centre traffic. In the first town, the ring road may help to make work journeys from one suburb to another and these are often by car.

In the second town, road access to the town centre is improved, which may tempt more drivers to do their shopping there, but this would be subject to the availability of parking space.

The responses may not only be economic in character, but also political: if, for example, the town centre in the bypassed town starts to get less trade, the shops might become less attractive and compete by making a merit of their lower traffic levels, engaging in large-scale pedestrianisation and urban improvement and winning shoppers back on an improved public transport network. On the other hand, the traffic levels in the centre of the second town may become excessive and there may be a political response by measures of traffic restraint, parking control and so on.

All these decisions are rather big and important ones and although some responses might be quite quick, it is unrealistic to assume that everything would settle down very quickly. Other companies and individuals will take much longer to see the new opportunities (and may even be too late to make use of them). New residents moving into the towns for other reasons entirely will start to build up their patterns of working and living which take on board the new road and the consequent effects on patterns of land use and the local economy, as given features of their new homes.

So, given that it is the pattern of land use and activities that causes traffic to occur, we would want to take account of any alteration in these patterns which is stimulated by the changes in ease of movement from one place to another.

Responses connected with the timing of activities

A new road is, of course, available on a 24-hour basis, but people always use it more at some times of the day than others. It may be that (because of the way that human beings arrange their lives) people generally prefer to carry out many of their out-of-home activities by leaving home at a comfortable time in the morning and getting back in the early evening. Before the road was improved, traffic congestion might have been so bad that it was an unattractive proposition to do this and those people who had a choice decided instead to leave home at a "second-best" time -- earlier or later than they would have preferred. With the improved road, they can revert to a more convenient time.

More indirectly, there is an evident pattern (not necessarily to do with transport) for large, out-of-town shops, garden centres, etc. to adopt different conventions on opening hours and days of the week than has been traditional. If the developments referred to above actually occur, there would be some shift in the daily or weekly balance of peak period and off-peak traffic.

Responses connected with the method of transport used

Quite apart from the structural changes discussed above, people will continue to make some -- perhaps many -- trips from the same origin to the same destination for the same purpose at the same time of day as before. However, it may be that the improved road now makes it practical for some people to travel by car or coach instead of the train they used previously. Alternatively (if, say, the improvement has been implemented with incorporation of bus priority measures and park-and-ride facilities), it may be that the new balance of advantage lies more with buses that previously had been made very unreliable by congestion. In that case, there might be some people who would find it useful to make some journeys by bus instead of car or rail.

Responses connected with the co-ordination of different individuals

There are a number of types of journey where the needs of more than one individual have to be taken into account, for example, complex round-trips to take the children to school and then call in at the shops on the way to work, or arrangements to share car use among employees at the same workplace. In these cases -- which are often quite tricky to organise -- new road facilities might just tip the balance between the practical and impractical: this could result in an increase in the number of people sharing cars (resulting in less traffic) or the possibility of fitting in more journeys using the same car (resulting in more traffic).

Responses connected with the route chosen

There are very often several different routes that can be chosen for a given journey and it will nearly always be the case that an improved road changes the balance of advantage of one route over another, so more people will find it convenient to use the improved route. The effect of this could go in either direction: if the improved route is straighter and more direct, then the miles travelled by the cars using it will go down. On the other hand, it may be that the improved road is so fast that it is worthwhile going some distance out of your way to use it and, in this case, the journey time will go down but the total miles travelled will go up, and there would be an increase in traffic on the feeder roads leading to the new route.

Responses connected with the effects of the other responses

It is part of the everyday experience of modern life that, in general, where there is an increase in the amount of traffic, it tends, after a certain point, to go slower. This means that if any or all of the above responses become important they start to influence the conditions on the improved (and other) roads and, therefore, change the conditions within which the decisions are being made. If many people desert the alternative, unimproved route, it may become more attractive and other people now find its speeds fast enough to open new opportunities for them. If too many new activities are encouraged by the improved road, then travel on it will not be so fast and, after a while, some of them may be put off again. There is a continual process of feedback and it may be many years before all these interacting decisions settle down -- or, indeed, this may never happen.

Thus a consideration, in broad, qualitative terms, of the processes known to be part of modern living establishes that it is *possible* for sensible, ordinary decisions to result in extra traffic to be induced by provision of extra road capacity. However, if this occurs it is likely to be marked by quite complex processes, with responses which will start immediately, or even before, the improvement is completed, but which will take quite a long time to be completed.

3.3. Empirical evidence

3.3.1. *Differential growth rates*

The earliest evidence had taken the form of observation of differential growth rates. Later evidence of this character has been cited by the Institution of Highways and Transportation (SACTRA, 1994, Figure 2) and by Mogridge *et al.* (1987), whose analysis of data for London extended Glanville and Smeed's approach. Growth in traffic at the outer London boundary cordon still approximately kept pace with the average increase in car ownership, at 2.3 per cent per year. However, the growth rate at the inner London cordon was 0.8 per cent a year and in central London was 0.4 per cent a year.

Nationally, traffic growth rates have also been slowest where congestion is worst and fastest where existing capacity is still spare, or new capacity is provided. From 1980 to 1990, measured traffic on major roads in built-up areas grew by 20 per cent, on major roads in non-built-up areas by 58 per cent and on motorways by 73 per cent.

Of itself, observation that traffic has grown more where there is spare capacity for it to do so, does not prove that the provision of capacity caused the growth. However, from the late 1950s to 1990, the amount of traffic on trunk roads in the UK increased overall by a factor of eight. During this period, about 3 000 km of motorways were constructed. Present trunk road traffic patterns in time and space could not have been fitted onto the 1950 road network. In such circumstances, it is logically necessary to assume that some degree of suppression will occur. If, then, an increase in capacity is provided, it is equally logical to assume that the otherwise suppressed traffic will appear.

3.3.2. *Evidence inferred from econometric and survey studies of travel demand*

In this section, evidence is reviewed that does not directly address the issue of induced traffic, but is itself well-established and which can be combined to make indirect, but powerful, inferences. Four apparently separate strands are included, namely, evidence on the effects of money costs of car use, motorway capacity, travel time budgets and the value of time.

The cost of car use

It is well established that out-of-pocket money costs of travel have some effect on the amount of traffic. A literature review by Goodwin (1992) cited 13 studies in which the effect of fuel price on fuel consumption had been calculated (with a short-term elasticity of around -0.25 to -0.3 and a long-term elasticity of -0.7 to -0.8); 11 studies in which the effect of fuel price on traffic levels had been calculated (with results of -0.16 for a short-term effect and about -0.3 for a long-term effect and other studies, not specifying the time period, showing results of about -0.5). A review of Australian evidence by Luk and Hepburn (1993) cited 28 studies and came to the conclusion that the long-term elasticity of traffic levels with respect to fuel costs was -0.1 in the short run and -0.26 in the long run. Oum *et al.* (1992) report seven studies of automobile usage with respect to fuel price, giving elasticities in the range -0.09 to -0.52. Halcrow Fox *et al.* (1993) assess a short-term price elasticity for car use in the London region of -0.16 and a long-term value of -0.31 as likely values from a "review of reviews". They also found a range of values for different journey purposes of -0.05 to -0.87 from a stated preference experiment. Virley (1993) gives a short-run effect of fuel prices on fuel consumption of -0.09 and a long-run effect of -0.46.

Taking these results as a whole, we can say with some confidence that, at the aggregate level, there is some effect of the money costs of car travel on the volume of traffic, with an elasticity somewhere in the range -0.1 to -0.5.

Motorway capacity

Williams and Lawlor (1992) analysed the relative strength of different factors behind the growth in motorway traffic over the period 1978-1988 and suggested that a 10 per cent increase in motorway length led to about a 1 per cent increase in motorway traffic. A more recent study by the Centre for Economics and Business Research (1994) used an elasticity-based approach, embedded in a macro-economic model relating transport and economic factors, to assess the extent of generated traffic associated with a roads expenditure 50 per cent higher or lower than the current programme. The Executive Summary of that report summarises the conclusions as follows:

"*A 50 per cent increase over present plans...would increase road usage by only 0.77 per cent. A 50 per cent cut would reduce road use by only 1.1 per cent.*"

This finding was interpreted by the report's sponsors (the British Road Federation) as indicating that induced traffic was negligible. However, a closer reading of the calculations indicates that the 50 per cent increase in spending is estimated to provide, by 2010, a 7 per cent increase in trunk road capacity and it is this 7 per cent extra road capacity which generates the extra 0.77 per cent of traffic. At average levels, this implies an elasticity of traffic with respect to capacity of 0.11 (i.e. 0.77/7), very similar to the Williams and Lawlor work.

Travel time budgets

Many researchers, reviewed by Gunn (1981), have found that the total amount of time spent travelling is, on average, rather similar for people living in different countries, or in areas of very different characteristics and travel opportunities. Downes and Emmerson (1983) concluded that faster travel speeds generally encourage more travel to be made and when extra use of time savings in other locations is included, travellers spend all of the potential time saving from

163

higher travel speeds on further travel. Examination of the conclusions of 13 authors in the field in a special issue of the journal, *Transportation Research*, January 1981, does not show strong support for the idea that travel time budgets are absolutely stable (which would imply that all travel time savings were ploughed back into more travel). But, all the evidence was consistent with the weaker proposition that some of the time saved would be re-used in this way. Not all of this would necessarily appear on, or close to, the improved road itself. Stokes (1994) suggested an increase from 1952 to 1992 in the total amount of time spent travelling, from 49 minutes to 63 minutes, with an average increase of 29 minutes per person in car travel being partly offset by a reduction of 15 minutes in other modes.

Value of time

Empirical studies of the trade-off between money and time costs of travel constitute a very large genre of transport research. The current procedures used in the UK are based on a study carried out by the MVA Consultancy together with the transport groups at the Universities of Leeds and Oxford (1987), which also cited about a hundred other references in the field. The study found values of in-vehicle time (at mid-1985 prices) of 3.5 to 5.0 pence per minute for an average car user. At 1993 prices, this is equivalent to a representative value of time for car users of about six pence per minute.

Synthesis of the econometric research findings

There is a logical connection among the above results, which has a direct bearing on the question of induced traffic. First, we connect price elasticities and the value of time.

If we know what effect increases in fuel price would have on traffic levels and if we know the equivalent values to vehicle users of changes in fuel price and changes in travel time, then we can calculate what effect travel time changes would have on traffic levels. Thus:

$$D = f(G)$$

and $$G = M + vT$$

where D is demand, G is generalised cost of travel, M is money cost (fuel price), T is travel time and v is value of time. The demand elasticities with respect to money E_m and time E_t are:

$$E_m = \partial D/\partial M.M/D$$

$$E_t = \partial D/\partial T.T/D$$

The elasticities are proportional to the relative importance of money and time, as follows:

$$E_m/E_t = M/Vt$$

so $\quad E_t = E_m.Vt/M$

Assume: -0.15 as the elasticity with respect to fuel price; 6 pence per minute as the value of time; average time spent travelling by car per day as 25 minutes; and spending per person per day on fuel costs as 50 pence. Then:

$$E_t = -0.15 \times 6 \times 25/50$$

$$= -0.45$$

Thus, a speed change saving 10 per cent of journey time would cause a 4.5 per cent increase in traffic volume. In practice, we would expect the numbers to vary by journey purpose, area, mode, speed of travel, type of person and many other factors. It is important not to exaggerate the degree of precision involved in the calculations.

A particular aspect of importance in considering how sensitive the result is to the assumptions made is that the -0.15 fuel cost elasticity is usually treated as a short-term effect (that is, within the first year). As described above, there is substantial evidence that the longer-term effect is significantly greater than this. If we take the estimated longer-term elasticity to be of the order of -0.3, for example, the implied journey time elasticity would be nearly -1.0. A 10 per cent change in speed would then lead to a longer-term change in traffic volume of nearly 10 per cent. In congested conditions, where time is a large proportion of the generalised cost of journeys, the implied travel time elasticity will be greater and, in uncongested conditions, smaller.

With these caveats, we note that, in round terms, reasonably well-established research on petrol price and on values of time suggests an overall average short-term elasticity of traffic with respect to travel time of about -0.5 and a longer-term elasticity of the order of -1.0.

165

These figures in turn have implications for travel time budgets and for sensitivity to road capacity, which can be compared for consistency with the other strands of research cited above. Thus the interpretation of the results for the short term suggests that about half of the time saved by speed increases would be spent on additional travel. This is consistent with the results of some of the time budget studies. The interpretation of the results for the longer term suggest that most or all of the time saved would be spent on additional travel. This is equivalent to the hypothesis of a constant time outlay on travel and is close to the results of Downes and Emmerson (1983) cited above.

The differential pattern of short- and long-term effects is consistent with the differences between effects on petrol consumption, car use, car ownership and land use if we assume that car-use responses are likely to be swifter than car-ownership and land-use responses; these assumptions seem plausible and themselves supported by some evidence.

Overall, therefore, the average elasticity of traffic with respect to travel time in the range -0.5 (short) to -1.0 (long) seems broadly consistent with just about all the disparate evidence.

If then the CEBR (1994) study is representative of the relationship between road expenditure and road capacity, then the elasticities would imply a short-term level of induced traffic of around 10 per cent of base flow and a longer-term level of about 20 per cent. This is extraordinarily close to the practice recommended by the Ministry of Transport (1968) as noted above. In the nature of averages, this must imply that some specific schemes will be less and others more: a *prima facie* expectation might be that specific schemes will have 0 per cent to 20 per cent induced traffic in the short run and 0 to 40 per cent, say, in the longer run, with the higher figures in areas of greatest prior congestion.

So, from the econometric work, we have both general supporting evidence and a hypothesis on the scale of effect we might expect to observe in other research based on direct measurement of traffic counts. The induced traffic hypothesis suggests that we might look for increased traffic in the order of 10 to 20 per cent of flows, with a range of 0 to 40 per cent. The "no induced traffic" hypothesis is that any extra traffic on improved roads will be balanced by an approximately equal reduction on non-improved alternatives, thus directly addressing the feasibility of obtaining environmental relief in some areas by extra road capacity to divert the traffic.

3.3.3. Comparisons of forecast and observed traffic growth on improved roads

Forecasts of the traffic levels expected on an improved road are routinely made as part of the planning and evaluation of each scheme. Suppose we make the complimentary assumption that the models and assumptions used for such forecasts are correct in every respect except for the omission of induced traffic. Then, if induced traffic is important, there will be a systematic tendency for forecasts to underestimate actual traffic levels, the shortfall on these assumptions being a direct measure of the amount of induced traffic. This is the "purest" example in the research of a putative unexpected effect, since the expectations themselves are entirely clear, which is not always the case in other policy areas.

As noted above, the difference between expectation and outcome lay behind the pivotal role played by construction of an orbital motorway around London, the M25, in generating renewed public interest in the question of induced traffic, because it rapidly became clear that the amount of traffic using the road on almost every section was much greater than had been predicted. By 1992, the total volume of traffic on the M25 was 55 per cent higher than the design year forecasts would have implied.

However, it would be unwarranted to attribute all of this 55 per cent to induced traffic, since some may be due to other errors in the forecasts. The various sections opened between 1980 and 1986, so that there had been six years of full operation and up to 12 years for some sections. Observed traffic growth in other comparable areas, but which had not had such an increase in capacity, in this period was at a rate of between 1 per cent and 3 per cent a year and, if one assumes that this is what would have happened without the motorway, some 30 to 45 per cent of the traffic is still unexplained. Given the suggestion above that some schemes might be found in which induced traffic was at this order of magnitude -- and the observation that large, urban, congested conditions would be where one might expect the greatest effects -- the M25 may be treated as reasonably strong supporting evidence.

Department of Transport monitoring of forecasts and observed traffic

The Department operates a monitoring system to compare observed traffic flows on recently-opened schemes with the forecasts which had been made at order-publication stage. The system was first set up in 1981 and we have been provided with the results of the analysis carried out since then. The first report in this series to be published was the sixth, entitled "Comparison of forecast and

167

observed traffic on trunk road schemes" (Department of Transport, 1993). It analysed the new schemes which had become available during the year, together with the accumulated results of the schemes which had been monitored since the start of the work.

The Department of Transport's view is that if induced traffic were important, but had been wrongly ignored at the time of making the forecasts, there would be a general tendency for observed traffic to be higher than the forecasts, i.e. the forecasts would be underestimates. The Department's general conclusion in the sixth report (as in previous ones) was that:

"There is no evidence of such an effect."

This line of work seems to have been an influential piece of evidence in persuading the Department that induced traffic as a result of trunk road schemes is not of general significance. Reports by the Department of its latest published analysis (Harris, 1993) continue to make the same general argument, which may be summarised as follows:

-- The mean result for all schemes studied is that flows were underestimated by 12 per cent;
-- Forecasts for all the schemes were made using the 1980 or 1984 National Road Traffic Forecasts as part of their basic input data;
-- The 1980 and 1984 NRTFs failed to anticipate the high economic growth rates of the mid-eighties and therefore underestimated the growth in national traffic levels, by an average factor of 16 per cent;
-- Therefore the discrepancy between forecasts and observed traffic for specific schemes have to be corrected for the error in the national forecasts before any inference about induced traffic may be drawn. Once this is done, there is no systematic evidence of the existence of induced traffic.

SACTRA discussed this methodology and inference with the Department of Transport in some detail, as a result of which it was agreed that:

"...the Scheme Forecast Monitoring System was established in 1981 to provide information on the accuracy or otherwise of the Department's traffic modelling and forecasts for individual trunk road schemes. It was not specifically designed to examine the issue of induced traffic and this limits the scope of the analyses which can be applied."

Even so, the monitoring system did produce a substantial amount of information both about errors in forecasting the results of individual schemes (which were not published) and errors for groups of schemes. SACTRA (1994) gives detailed figures for 151 schemes which had been studied in this way. Table 1 summarises the overall results for each category of scheme. Table 2 gives comparable information for the alternative routes, sometimes called "relieved routes" for 85 of these, separately provided by the Department of Transport and published in Goodwin (1996).

Table 1. **Comparison of forecast and observed traffic flows
on 151 improved roads**

Class of scheme	Forecast traffic flow (veh/day)	Observed traffic flow (veh/day)	Extra traffic over forecast	Number of schemes
Urban	244 603	258 520	+5.7%	9
Rural	714 215	809 154	+13.3%	61
On-line and junction improvements	731 120	864 966	+18.3%	27
Motorway	356 222	380 050	+6.7%	11
Bypasses	586 910	593 239	+1.1%	43
Total	2 633 070	2 905 929	+10.4%	151

Table 2. **Comparison of forecast and observed traffic flows
on 85 "relieved routes"**

Class of scheme	Forecast traffic flow (veh/day)	Observed traffic flow (veh/day)	Extra traffic over forecast	Number of schemes
Urban	145 668	146 712	+0.7%	5
Rural	130 956	156 661	+19.6%	39
On-line and junction improvements	n.a.	n.a.	n.a.	n.a.
Motorway	155 367	177 298	+14.1%	7
Bypasses	251 620	315 027	+25.2%	34
Total	683 611	795 698	+16.4%	85

Two particularly important features may be noted.

First, it is notable that the underestimates are greater for the alternative routes than for the improved roads themselves. Observed traffic levels on 39 rural roads which had been relieved by trunk road schemes were nearly 20 per cent higher than forecast. The roads which bypasses had been intended to relieve showed traffic levels 25 per cent higher than forecast, even though the forecasts for the bypasses themselves were (on average) reasonably good[1]. As a whole, the discrepancy for the improved roads was a little over 10 per cent, but for the relieved roads over 16 per cent.

Secondly, the results bear an interesting relationship to the work by the Centre for Economics and Business Research (1994) referred to above, which indicated that there was an elasticity of traffic levels with respect to road capacity of 0.11, interpreted mainly as a first year effect. If then all other aspects of a forecast were correct except for omission of induced traffic and if all induced traffic appeared on the improved road, then, for an average scheme, we would expect the traffic levels to be 11 per cent higher than forecast.

Table 1 shows that the unpredicted traffic in the first year, over and above the forecast, was 10.4 per cent. On the face of it, this could be interpreted as a level of induced traffic entirely in accordance with expectations. Taking only those schemes for which we have counts on both the improved and the relieved roads, the additional unforecast traffic was about 16 per cent, which gives a greater figure than the CEBR results, because extra traffic is appearing over more of the network. But in both cases, the expectation of 10 to 20 per cent induced traffic appears supported by the counts.

The main weakness of this analysis is that it depends on assuming that the forecasts were perfect in all respects other than the omission of induced traffic, which is not credible. The DoT and SACTRA failed to reach agreement on the interpretation of this caveat, as reported by SACTRA (1994). What we can say, however, is that, for whatever reason, there was more traffic than expected and that this was greater on the relieved roads than on the improved ones.

The analysis above relies on comparing actual outcomes with forecasts. Even if no forecasts are made, or they are ignored, it is still possible to look at the growth of traffic on improved roads, provided that the counts include both the improved road and other roads in the same corridor. The induced traffic hypothesis suggests that:

i) the overall traffic growth in the corridor will be higher than some appropriate control corridor or than average growth rates;
ii) the discrepancy will increase over time; and
iii) the reduction in traffic on the relieved roads, if any, will be less than increased traffic on the improved roads.

The following sections describe the results of "before and after" studies which were submitted as evidence to SACTRA, together with some others drawn from literature reviews.

In interpreting these figures, two important points should be noted. First of all, in the simplest case where there is only a short period between before and after counts, if there was no induced traffic we would expect to see increases in flow on the improved sections matched by equivalent reductions in flow on the relieved roads. Secondly, where longer periods of time have elapsed between the before and after counts, some degree of traffic growth may be expected for other reasons. Any explicit adjustment for this would rely on a judgement about how much traffic growth "would have been expected for other reasons", which is tantamount to prejudging how much can be attributed to induced traffic. However, taking the road system as a whole, traffic growth is in the range of 2 to 5 per cent per year.

a)   Barnstaple Bypass

The A39 Barnstaple Bypass opened in July 1989. Devon County Council provided traffic counts on the river screenline at Barnstaple, which is at the northern end of the North Devon Link Road. Table 3 shows the results.

Table 3. **Barnstaple Bypass A39T (2-way AADT flows, pcu/day)**

	1986	1988	1991	1992	Predicted Growth to 1998 (Low - High)
A361 Braunton Road	13 700	15 200	16 200	16 100	-
Old A39	26 100	28 200	31 000	30 000	(27 000 - 30 000)
New Bypass	-	-	10 600	10 900	(3 700 - 9 900)
A39+Bypass	26 100	28 200	41 600	40 900	(30 700 - 39 900)

In this case, soon after opening, the flows were already greater than the flows predicted for 1998, which included general traffic growth. It is not apparent that the traffic on the bypass was matched by a corresponding reduction in traffic on the A39, which has held rather steady. There was some local feeling, based on experience and anecdotal evidence, that new trips are being made on the road and that this is already starting to influence land-use patterns in and around the area.

The Department of Transport adjusted the figures to take some account of general growth which would have happened with or without the scheme and to apply the NRTF correction as discussed above. Taking these adjustments at face value, their effect is to reduce, but not eliminate, the underprediction. On five screenlines, the one with the lowest observed flows was overpredicted (Bideford Bridge, +15 per cent) and the other four had an underprediction even after making the adjustments (West of Barnstaple -16 per cent; River Taw -8 per cent; East of Barnstaple -28 per cent; North Devon Link Road -21 per cent). The Department of Transport concluded:

"On the basis of the information available, we cannot say whether this underprediction represents reassignment from further afield, local economic effects, or induced traffic. However, a residual underprediction of this magnitude is not exceptional when compared with the degree of variation in the forecasting results for other schemes."

b) Pells' Literature Review: Results for M62, York Northern Bypass and
    Severn Bridge

-- M62

Pells quotes results of a study by Judge (1983) in which the generated (including redistributed) traffic on the M62 is calculated by comparing the actual flows with what might have happened, based on the Department of Transport's traffic index for rural roads. This showed a rather slow build-up of estimated induced traffic to a maximum five years after opening, by which it was estimated to account for 18.8 per cent of the flow on the M62. These results were controversial at the time and the Committee cannot be sure that the definition of "generated" traffic is fully in accord with induced traffic as defined here.

The Department of Transport has suggested to us that the additional traffic is believed to be due to a small amount of redistribution, plus reassignment over a wider area, though in this case the screenline was some 40 miles long. If this is the case then, clearly, monitoring studies will have to be designed to cover a very large area indeed.

-- York Northern Bypass

This study was carried out in 1988, using roadside interviews. On average, drivers were found to be making eight more trips per three-month period after the bypass opened than they did before. Table 4 shows the estimated breakdown into different classes of response. It is notable that there was a large proportion of retimed trips.

Table 4. **Results of roadside interviews of drivers
using York Northern Bypass (1988)**

Classification of trips	Number of trips	Per cent
Reassigned	348	89.9
Redistributed	22	5.7
Modal diversion	10	2.6
Re-timed: all	115	29.7
earlier	104	26.9
later	11	2.8
Generated	46	11.9

The Department of Transport argues that the number of extra trips reported should be treated with caution, as drivers making trips more frequently for other reasons would be surveyed and those who have stopped making trips would not. This is undoubtedly true. In any case,the study was a small pilot exercise, of interest mainly because of the attempt (very rare in the other studies reported) to distinguish the various sources of change. The importance of reassignment and trip-retiming is evident.

-- Severn Bridge

Pells reports a survey by Cleary and Thomas (1973), undertaken a year after the opening of the original bridge. It was estimated that 56 per cent of the traffic using the bridge had been reassigned and 44 per cent "generated", which again may not have been defined in the same way as our induced traffic. Nevertheless, the result is striking and it suggests that a similar (or more detailed) study of the behavioural responses to the opening of the second Severn Bridge -- currently under construction -- would be most instructive.

c)   London Trunk Road Schemes

Greater London Council Studies of Six Schemes in London

A substantial amount of research on the existence or otherwise of induced traffic was undertaken, initially by the Greater London Council and subsequently (after abolition) taken forward by the same authors in various other capacities. Work was carried out by Purnell (1985), by Beardwood and Elliott (1986) and others. Six schemes were reported; namely, Westway, the M11, the M3/A316, the North Circular Road, the Blackwall Tunnels and their approaches and a section of the M25.

The main method used in these analyses was to carry out screenline counts of traffic using, as far as possible, the entire corridor of the improved road, both before and after the improvement and during the following several years. The proposition is that if all the observed traffic using the improved road were due to changes in the route chosen by a fixed volume of traffic, then the increased traffic flow on the improved link should be matched by equivalent reductions in traffic flows on alternative routes in the same corridor. A summary of five of the studies follows.

-- **Westway (M40)**

Table 5 shows the 1970, 24-hour counted flows on Westway, compared with the Finchley Road corridor, chosen as a control.

Table 5. Westway (M40) traffic flows, 1970 (vehicles per day)

	Before (May)	After (Sept.)	Change
Westway	-	46 900	+46 900
Other roads[1]	123 500	94 100	-29 400
Total Westway corridor	123 500	141 000	+17 500
Total Finchley Rd. corridor	127 200	129 200	+2 000

(1) Notting Hill Gate, Moscow Road, Dawson Place, Westbourne Grove, Talbot Road, St. Stephens Gardens, Harrow Road.

The authors point out that the total traffic on Westway was greater than the reductions in traffic on all the alternative roads and that in five months, traffic in the Westway corridor as a whole increased by 14 per cent, whereas in the Finchley Road corridor traffic only increased by 2 per cent. They suggest that it is probable that a significant proportion of the additional 17 500 vehicles per day should be counted as "generated" (in our terminology, induced). It is noted that the screenline may not be perfect and that there may be some more distantly reassigned trips from north of Harrow Road. However, it is notable that there were only small changes on the Harrow Road itself during the whole period of the analysis, so the authors did not expect any significant extra reassignment.

Using the same form of analysis, they note that the discrepancy between increases in traffic on the new road compared with smaller reductions in traffic on the alternative roads is greater for inbound peak period trips, amounting to 47.5 per cent of the Westway flow.

Figure 2 shows the results of a similar exercise continued over the subsequent 14 years, compared with both the Finchley Road corridor and the old Brompton Road corridor.

It may be seen that traffic growth on the Westway corridor continued steeply for some five years after opening, by comparison with the much more stable traffic levels on the other corridors. In a subsequent submission, Elliott has suggested that (on admittedly somewhat arbitrary assumptions about the level of "natural" growth) nearly two-thirds of the traffic on Westway might be counted as induced.

Figure 2. Traffic growth recorded on Westway, Finchley Road and Old Brompton Road corridors

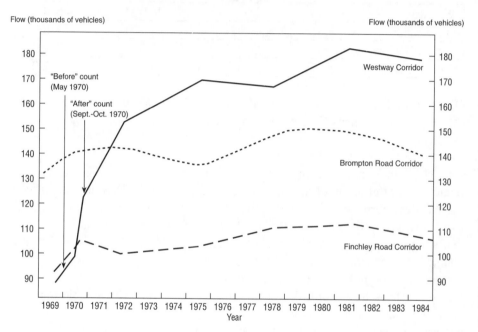

Source: Purnell (1985).

The Department of Transport commissioned a separate assessment of these figures from consultants Howard Humphreys and Partners, as part of preparation for evidence at a 1993 Public Inquiry on the A406 North Circular Road -- Popes Lane to Western Avenue Improvement Scheme. The consultants took note of the underestimate and suggested that the additional traffic induced by Westway could be due to wider area reassignment, modal transfer and possibly trip redistribution, though the effect was obscured by the length of the screenline and construction work which affected the before counts.

-- M11 near Epping

Counts were carried out at three-year intervals at the GLC boundary, of traffic using the M11 corridor between London and, on completion, Cambridge. Table 6 summarises the results.

Table 6. Traffic counts (M11 Corridor) 24-hour, two-way flow (vehicles per day)

	1974	1977	1980	1983	Change 1974 to 1983
M11	0	22 987	34 682	53 104	+53 104
Other roads[1]	100 556	83 327	93 288	85 253	-15 303
Total corridor	10 0556	106 314	127 970	138 357	+37 801

(1)   A104, A121, Loughton Way, A113, Lambourne Road, A1112.

Here, the authors suggest that, over the nine-year period, 29 per cent of the observed M11 flows could be accounted for by reassignment (i.e. 15 303 out of 53 104), though the remainder consists of both induced traffic and general traffic growth. Their chosen control, the A23 London-Brighton corridor, showed traffic growth of 29 per cent in the same period as the M11 corridor showed 38 per cent. For peak-period inbound flows only, the M11 corridor showed increases of 56 per cent, whilst the A23 corridor showed 33 per cent. The M11 itself showed a growth of 130 per cent in the period of approximately six years after opening. The authors contend that a significant proportion of this extra traffic is induced. Some additional evidence on rail travel in the corridor was also provided and it was suggested that this indicated a possible increase in road traffic at the expense of rail.

The Department of Transport suggested, based on the assessment by Howard Humphreys & Partners, that:

"The reported growth on the M11 itself is regarded as more indicative of wide area reassignment and modal transfer than generated trips."

-- A316 near Sunbury

The A316 was not a completely new road, but a conversion from dual 2-lane to dual 3-lane shortly after the M3 was opened from Camberly to Sunbury in 1975-1976. Counts were taken at the GLC boundary. Table 7 summarises the results. Traffic flow in the corridor as a whole increased by 84 per cent, while in their chosen control corridor (M4/A4) traffic increased over the same period by 66 per cent. For peak inbound flows only, traffic on the A316 corridor increased by 107 per cent, but by 41 per cent on the control M4 corridor. The A316 itself showed a growth of 160 per cent from before the M3 was opened (1974) until 1983.

Table 7. **Traffic counts (A316 corridor), 24-hour, two-way flows (veh/day)**

	1971	1974	1977	1980	1983	Change 1971 to 1983
A316	17 384	21 312	44 005	52 394	55 229	+37 845
Other roads[1]	35 472	38 743	42 780	41 923	42 184	+6 712
Total corridor	52 856	60 055	86 785	94 317	97 413	+44 557

(1)   Staines Road East, Vicarage Road, Chertsey Road.

-- Blackwall Tunnels and Approaches

This study concerned the duplication of the Blackwall Tunnels in 1968-1969 and improvement of the approach routes either side of the Thames, using Thames screenline counts, cordon counts and roadside interviews. Table 8 shows the short-term changes from 1968 to 1969 and Table 9 shows the longer-term changes in the period 1962-1982.

Table 8. Traffic counts (Lower Thames screenline), 12-hour, two-way flows, veh/day

	Before (1968)	After (1969)	Change 1968 to 1969
Blackwall Tunnels	22 741	32 194	+9 453
Other bridges/tunnels[1]	50 422	51 751	+1 329
Total screenline	73 163	83 945	+10 782

(1)   Tower Bridge, Rotherhithe Tunnel, Dartford Tunnel.

Table 9. Traffic counts (Lower Thames screenline), 24-hour, two-way flows, veh/day

	1962	1972	1982	Change 1962 to 1982
Blackwall Tunnels	21 000	51 000	72 000	+51 000
Other bridges/tunnels[1]	45 000	82 000	95 000	+50 000
Total screenline	66 000	133 000	167 000	+101 000

(1)   Tower Bridge, Rotherhithe Tunnel, Dartford Tunnel (+41 000 out of the +50 000).

From 1962 to 1982, there was a 153 per cent overall growth in traffic across the screenline, or 91 per cent if the Dartford Tunnel is excluded -- it is included only from 1972.   A control screenline, consisting of the five bridges from Richmond to Hammersmith, showed a growth of 64 per cent in the same period. The morning peak flows (two-way) showed a growth of 106 per cent/50 per cent with and without Dartford included in the original screenline and an 8 per cent growth in the Richmond-Hammersmith screenline.

The Department of Transport suggested to us that the screenline used was very limited and excluded London, Southwark, Blackfriars and Waterloo Bridges, all of which serve the A2 corridor.   This point would be very relevant if those other bridges showed traffic reductions during the period.   The Department comments:

"The reported growth could possibly show trip redistribution and retiming of trips which would be consistent with Departmental advice for estuarial crossings."

-- **M25 (River Lea screenline)**

Table 10 shows data collected by the GLC and Hertfordshire County Council on roads north and south of the M25 at the River Lea screenline.

Table 10. **Traffic counts M25/River Lee screenline, 12-hour, two-way flows, veh/day**

	Before (Nov. 83)	**After (Feb.-Mar. 84)**	**Change 1983 to 1984**
M25 (A10-A121)		40 487	+40 487
Other roads[1]	199 576	176 476	-23 100
Total screenline	199 576	216 963	+17 387

(1) A414, B181, Essex Road, B194, A121, A110, A406, A503, A102.

Over the very short period concerned, the authors suggest that the reductions in traffic on alternative routes was equivalent to 57 per cent of the observed flows on the M25. If this percentage is assumed to be reassigned traffic, the remainder could be treated as induced.

The Department of Transport suggested:

"This section of the M25 created a continuous length of motorway from the A1(M) to the Dartford Tunnel giving a major opportunity for wide area reassignment, as acknowledged by Pells. It would provide a similar opportunity for trip redistribution."

This comment raises an important issue of principle about "scheme" versus "strategic" assessment and monitoring. The suggestion is that in this case (because other schemes had already been completed) it was this one scheme which unlocked the accumulated potential of the other, previous schemes. It would seem wrong to attribute all the effects on the scheme which happened to be last in line and this underpins the central importance the Committee attaches to strategic assessment of whole corridors or regions.

Discussion

In examination of these results and their interpretation as evidence of induced traffic, five different sorts of criticisms were discussed by SACTRA.

First, it is extremely difficult to be sure that any cordon or screenline observations are absolutely complete (because of rat-runs) and that a big enough area is covered. This is because there is no limit, in principle, though of course there is in practice, to the distance that a small proportion of traffic may reassign. Therefore, there is always some probability that a proportion of the traffic has escaped the net. No retrospective assessment has been made of the extent of this potential source of error. There may well have been other roads, not included in the traffic surveys, which did indeed experience a reduction in their traffic levels.

Secondly, we have to consider the role of "control" corridors and screenlines. In principle, these should be very similar to the improved road in every respect, except that no improvement is made. In practice, this is almost impossible to achieve. In these studies, for example, the control M4/A4 corridor is very close to the A316 and the river crossings in the Upper and Lower parts of the Thames are influenced by very different road conditions and geographical circumstances.

Thirdly, as mentioned above, there is a "cleft stick" concerning the time-period of study. Over a very short period, we can discount the problem of general traffic growth, but a full range of behavioural response could not yet have been completed. With a longer time period, we would expect to have seen a fuller response, but many other things will also have changed in the meantime and it will not be possible, with certainty, to distinguish "growth due to inducement" from "growth due to other factors".

Fourthly, at best, these analyses indicate that induced traffic may exist. They are not able to give a deeper understanding of the relative importance of different components, such as the balance between trip rate changes, redistribution, mode shift, retiming and reassignment. Also, like the Department of Transport counts discussed above, they are not able to distinguish induced traffic from long-distance, reassigned traffic.

Fifthly, urban areas in general (and London in particular) may not be relevant to interurban schemes.

Nevertheless, there do seem to be three recurrent elements in the studies, which should be taken seriously as evidence of induced traffic. They are considerable "unexplained" growth in almost all cases; traffic growth greater than average in the improved corridors; and greater peak period growth on the improved roads. These are discussed below.

-- *Unexplained growth:* Increases in traffic on the improved roads are consistently greater than reductions (if any) in traffic on alternative routes. Taking the three studies where there was only a short time interval between the before and after counts [Westway, Blackwall Tunnels, M25 (A10-A121)], the net measured increase in traffic in the corridor as a whole ranged from 9 per cent to 14 per cent of the total before flow in the corridor and from 33 per cent to 37 per cent of the measured after flow on the new section. This cannot be explained by general traffic growth and there has been no suggestion that counting or screenline errors would be of this order of magnitude.

-- *Greater overall growth:* Increases in traffic in the corridors as a whole have been greater than both traffic growth generally and growth in the corridors selected as controls. Taking three sets of results for which longer time period of counts were given, the growth after the immediate increase on opening the improved section amounted to 93 per cent in 14 years for Westway, 131 per cent in six years for the M11 and 178 per cent in nine years on the A316. This sort of growth is not easy to explain by general income related trends and reinforces the general discussion of differential growth.

-- *Greater peak period growth:* Peak period growth rates in the improved sections have been notably high, which is not characteristic of traffic growth generally. This suggests that when extra capacity is provided there is a reversal of peak-spreading, consistent with both a suppression effect due to congestion and an induced traffic consequence when that is released.

d)   Rochester Way Relief Road

A study of the Rochester Way Relief Road was carried out by Youness and Crow of Imperial College London, supported by the British Road Federation and the Rees Jeffreys Road Fund. The report of this study was submitted to SACTRA by several different agencies, drawing special attention to the conclusions of the authors that:

"...there is no evidence at all to show that the road has induced or generated a great deal more traffic within the corridor...the increase in traffic has been no more than might have been expected had the road not been built (about two per cent per annum)."

Tables 11, 12 and 13 show traffic counts on three screenlines, representing the western and eastern boundaries of the Rochester Way Relief Road corridor and transverse (i.e. north-south) movements across the corridor, respectively.

Table 11. **Traffic counts, western screenline,**
Rochester Way Relief Road (A2), 18-hour, 2-way flow, pcu/day

	1978	**1990**	**Change (1978 to 1990)**
RWRR (West)	-	68 400	+68 400
Other roads[1]	87 200	41 739	-45 461
Total	87 200	110 139	+22 939

(1) Shooters Hill Road, Corelli Road, Woolacombe Road, Rochester Way, Dover Patrol Slip Road, Kidbrooke Park Road.
Source : Youness (1990), Table 3.1.

Table 12. **Traffic counts, eastern screenline,**
Rochester Way Relief Road (A2), 18-hour, 2-way flow, pcu/day

	1978	**1990**	**Change**
RWRR (East)	-	60 400	+60 400
Other roads[1]	144 300	118 000	-26 300
Total	144 300	178 400	+34 100

(1) Shooters Hill Road, Rochester Way, Bexley Road, Footscray Road, Sidcup Road.
Source: Youness (1990), Table 3.2.

In both the above tables, it is clear that there has been a significant reduction in the traffic on other roads covered by the screenlines, amounting to about half the measured increase on the Relief Road itself. (This is similar to the results of

Purnell, Beardwood and Elliott referred to above, although the authors do not draw the same conclusions.) The third table records the north-south traffic crossing the Relief Road. The increase of 30 per cent of movements is substantial.

Table 13. **Traffic counts in roads crossing the**
Rochester Way Relief Road (A2), 18-hour, 2-way flow, veh/day

	1978	1990	Change
Transverse roads[1]	77 700	100 700	+23 000

(1) Kidbrooke Park Road, Westhorne Avenue, Well Hall Road, Westmount Road, Glenesk Road (the only one to show a reduction), Reifield Road.

Source: Youness (1990), Table 3.3.

Discussion

The basic methodology of this study was similar to that of the GLC studies discussed above and the same caveats and cautions apply. However, discussion of this report also revealed an additional important influence on interpretation, namely, the policy context in which the scheme was conceived and built. The authors themselves make a very important caveat, namely that:

"The forces suppressing growth in radial movements, such as inner London congestion and parking controls, have remained unchanged and unaffected by the new road."

The specific circumstances of this road scheme were that new radial capacity was produced which could not be used for much increased traffic, due to "downstream" constraints. As a matter of local policy, grade separation and the retiming of traffic signals therefore allocated additional effective capacity to transverse movements. When investigating whether there has been induced traffic, therefore, it is necessary to look at both the radial and the transverse movements. The evidence seemed to be that there was indeed an increase in transverse movements, over and above that accounted for by reassignment.

The implication of this seems to be that if other factors, whether policy or physical constraints, are preventing the growth of traffic, then there may be little induced traffic and intended speed increases can be achieved, in the improved section if not elsewhere. This is an important point not only for forecasting, but also for the policy assumptions on which the forecasting is based. If induced traffic is foreseen, but is prevented by deliberate policy measures or capacity restraint elsewhere in the network, then clearly the geographical area over which the forecast must be made has to be considerably wider than the scheme itself. As one of the authors also comments, current plans for a further upgrading of the Blackwall crossing (one of the capacity constraints) "could well release an element of suppressed traffic" which had not previously been apparent.

Overall, the pattern of changes shown in this study is similar to those shown in the GLC studies. This study is often thought to be one of the more persuasive pieces of evidence against the existence of important induced traffic effects, since this is how it is often quoted. Tables 11 to 13 above do not seem to support this interpretation.

Following discussion of these results, SACTRA commissioned one of the authors of the study, Mr Geoffrey Crow, to update the work. Of particular relevance are his conclusions that:

"This review of the changes in traffic flows following the opening of the Rochester Way Relief Road, which has included new data for the period since 1990, has shown that there may possibly be some evidence of an element of induced traffic after all...

"What is clear from the figures is that there has been no substantial increase in the traffic flows within the corridor as a result of the construction of the RWRR. This applies particularly to the traffic flows during the peak periods, but then this is hardly surprising, as the Relief Road was deliberately planned to have limited capacity. This was to be sufficient for all the traffic which would be diverted onto it from other routes at the time of opening, but gave no allowance for any future growth. As a result of this, the majority of growth during the peak hours has occurred on other roads within the corridor (to the detriment of the local environments). Had the local authority been able to take more effective measures to limit growth on these other roads, then doubtless the overall growth would have been even smaller...

"A significant growth in traffic resulting from a generated or induced effect might thus have been expected outside the peak. That this has not occurred is most probably due to other capacity constraints on the onward routes at the western end of the corridor."

Thus, analyses of traffic counts were carried out, by the Greater London Council, of five road schemes in London and by Imperial College London, with support from the British Road Federation, of an additional scheme. They show certain features in common, especially that traffic increases on the sections with extra effective capacity have been greater than the reductions (if any) on other roads for which relief was expected. Although it is not possible to quantify with confidence the relative contributions of different behavioural responses, the analyses did not identify reductions in traffic using other roads amounting to more than about half of the observed increase in traffic using the improved road. Furthermore, there was strong evidence of a shift towards the peak period. The results are consistent with the expectation that, in urban areas where there are many alternative destinations modes and activities, induced traffic may be an appreciable consequence of major road building schemes. Its extent, however, will be influenced by availability of capacity on surrounding and downstream roads and by the effectiveness of any prevailing policies of traffic restraint.

e)   Schemes in the Greater Manchester Area

The Greater Manchester Transportation Unit reported a number of experiences drawn from their monitoring programme. Two in particular are discussed here, the Leigh Bypass (A579) and the M66.

--   **Leigh Bypass (A579)**

Table 14 shows the results of traffic counts carried out before and after the opening of the Leigh Bypass (Atherleigh Way). In this case the reduction in traffic on the bypassed road through Leigh town centre was less than the traffic on the scheme (i.e. the overall amount of traffic on a screenline increased with the scheme). Traffic using the section of the old road up to the start of the bypass increased by 37 per cent.

Table 14. **Traffic counts on the Leigh Bypass (A579),**
pcu/day (07.30-18.00)

	Before (Nov. 85)	After (Nov. 86)	Change 1985 to 1986
Leigh Bypass[1]		4 320	+4 320
Bypassed sections of road[1]	8 465	5 880	-2 585
Total screenline	8 465	10 200	+1 735

(1) Mean of two sections, St Helens Rd/Atherleigh Way to Kirkhall Lane and from there to Lovers Lane, by the old and new routes.

Source: Castle & Lawrence (1987), Table 2.

The Department of Transport commented that data was not provided from parallel routes A578 and A573 (5 and 1 km to the West) and suggested:

"Our examination of the data has identified that the major post opening increases in traffic occurred within the first six months, which would be more consistent with reassignment than other forms of induced traffic."

This suggestion (though based on an assumption about the time-scales of effects for which no evidence is provided) is nevertheless important, as it implies that counts carried out shortly after a scheme opens are less likely to find induced traffic even if it is important.

-- **Manchester Outer Ring Road (M66)**

Traffic counts were carried out, separately for east-west and north-south movements, before and after the opening of the Manchester Outer Ring Road (M66) linking the M63 at Portwood to the M67 at Denton. Tables 15 and 16 show the results.

Table 15. Traffic counts across east-west screenline
Manchester Outer Ring Road (M66), 12-hour, two-way flows, pcu/day

	Before (1988)	After (1989)	Change 1988 to 1989
M66		30 750	+30 750
Other roads[1]	64 426	48 671	-15 755
Total screenline	64 426	79 421	+14 995

(1)   B6167, Windmill Lane, A6017, A560, Werneth Low Road.
Source: Pizzigallo & Mayoh (1989), Table 2.

Table 16. Traffic counts on roads crossing
Manchester Outer Relief Road (M66), 12-hour, 2-way flows, pcu/day

	Before (1988)	After (1989)	Change 1988 to 1989
M66 (slips)		15 661	+15 661
Other roads[1]	134 767	139 001	+4 234
Total	134 767	154 662	+19 895

(1)   A635, B6390, M67, A57, Windmill Lane, Lingard Lane, A560, A626.
Source :   Pizzigallo & Mayoh (1989), Table 1.

These tables show an increase in total traffic flows in the corridor of the improvement of about 23 per cent, with reductions on alternative routes totalling about half the flow on the new section and an increase in transverse movements. This shows a remarkable similarity to the case of the Rochester Way Relief Road in London. The Committee noted that, in both cases, the pattern of extra traffic could be consistent either with induced traffic, or with reassigned traffic but over a very wide area. It is not easy to distinguish these effects without survey data over a sufficient area and of appropriate detail.

The Department of Transport commented that the screenlines excluded the A6 and A34 north-south routes, on which there was a significant reduction in peak-hour traffic flows and suggested that, if these were included, nearly all the traffic on the M66 would seem to be reassigned.

Thus, consideration of a radial relief road and an outer orbital route in the Manchester area showed broadly the same pattern as the London studies, namely that: reductions in flows on the roads relieved were less than the increases in flow on the improved roads; additional traffic may be seen in transverse movements, over and above those on the improved corridor itself; and there is a marked effect on the time of day at which journeys were made.

f)   Amsterdam Orbital Motorway

In September 1990, the Zeeburger Tunnel, being the final part of the Amsterdam Orbital Motorway, was opened. Hague Consulting Group participated in a study for The Netherlands' Ministry of Roads, based on traffic counts and telephone surveys five months before and two months after the opening. Table 17 shows the results of the traffic counts, about which further discussion is given by Kroes *et al.* (1996).

Table 17. **Traffic counts across the North Sea Canal, Amsterdam, 24-hour flows, veh/day**

	Before (April 1990)	After (November 1990)	Change (April to November)
Zeeburger Tunnel	-	57 700	+57 700
Other routes	294 200	259 600	-34 600
Total crossing	294 200	317 300	+23 100

The authors adjust the results to allow for seasonal effects and for an "autonomous growth" in traffic averaging 3.5 per cent over the period, which reduces the overall increase in traffic attributed to the Tunnel from 8.0 per cent to 4.5 per cent, when expressed as a percentage of total flows, or from 40 per cent to 22.7 per cent, when expressed as a percentage of the flows using the Tunnel itself. This seems to suggest that there has been a reduction in traffic of about 45 000 vehicles on the other routes to compare with the increase of 57 700 using the Tunnel. Without this growth assumption, a reduction of only 34 600 vehicles on the other routes has actually been observed.

The above figures relate to 24-hour measured traffic flows. The study included also a telephone survey of drivers carried out five months before and two months after the opening. The main findings were that:

189

-- 30 per cent of drivers reported that they had changed their departure times significantly, giving a 16 per cent increase in trips timed in the morning peak;

-- 25 per cent of drivers changed their route;

-- Only 1 per cent to 3 per cent of drivers changed their mode of travel, accounted for mainly by a small reduction in the number of car-pools; and

-- The increase in traffic across the waterway was only slightly higher than that in the country as a whole. It was concluded that the survey gave no evidence of significant induced growth on a 24-hour basis.

Given that the "after" survey was only two months after opening, it is clear that more substantial changes in behaviour, if any, would not be apparent by then. On this, the authors comment, "Other effects are expected in the longer run and monitoring continues". It is notable that there had been such a large shift in the time of day at which journeys were made, so soon after opening. Indeed, this seems to have been a more important consequence of the Tunnel than the change of route. This study in Amsterdam has indicated, like the British ones, that an appreciable proportion of traffic flow on the improved link is not matched by an equivalent reduction on other routes. A very short-term survey suggested that the most important behavioural response after reassignment was a shift in the times at which journeys are made.

Summary of findings from traffic counts

A short summary of the results for the UK schemes is shown in Table 18.

Table 18. Summary of studies of specific schemes

Scheme	Interval	Result
Barnstaple Bypass	3 years	Corridor flows +48 per cent. After "NRTF correction", extra traffic +39 per cent on some specific links, about 20 per cent overall
M62	5 years	Flow +19 per cent after correction by index for rural roads
York Northern Bypass	ambiguous timescale	Redistribution, modal diversion and new trips 20% of interviewed drivers
Severn Bridge	1 year	Authors suggest 44% induced traffic
London Schemes:		
Westway	4 months	Corridor +14%, Control +2%
M11	10 years	Authors suggest 40%-50% induced traffic
A316	9 years	Corridor +38% (peak 56%), Control +29% (peak 33%)
Blackwall	12 years	Corridor +84% (peak 107%), Control +66% (peak 41%)
	1 year	Screenline +15%
M25/Lea	20 years	Screenline +91% (peak 50%), Control +64% (peak 8%)
	4 months	Corridor +9%
Rochester Way	2 years	Corridor West +26%, East +24%, Transverse +30%
Leigh Bypass	1 year	Screenline +20%
Manchester Ring	1 year	East-West +23%, North-South +15%

Induced traffic must be heavily dependent on the context, size and location of the scheme, but theoretical calculations based on literature reviews give an average value for the elasticity of traffic volume with respect to travel time of about -0.5 in the short term and up to -1.0 in the long term. This is consistent with an expectation that an average road improvement, for which the traffic growth due to all other factors is forecast correctly, will see an additional 10 per cent of base traffic in the short term and 20 per cent in the long term.

Examination of the size of errors in traffic forecasts for improved roads and observations of traffic growth on those roads, both subject to caveats, nevertheless give results which are of similar orders of magnitude. Those are average figures and, in the nature of averages, must be subject to variation in individual values -- a range from zero to double the average is not inconsistent with any of the indirect or direct results. There are five important conclusions.

Unexpected short-term growth

For 151 Department of Transport schemes, traffic flows were, on average, 10.4 per cent higher than forecast a year after opening and 85 of these observed flows on the alternative routes were, on average, 16.4 per cent higher than forecast. Taking the seven studies where there was only a short time interval between the "before" and "after" counts [Westway, Blackwall Tunnels, M25 (A10-A121), York, Severn, Leigh, M66], the net measured increase in traffic in the corridor as a whole ranged from 9 per cent to 44 per cent of the total before flow in the corridor, with an unweighted mean of 20 per cent. (It is likely that the schemes which were subject to such close study were selected and cited because there was a greater than average concern about induced traffic.)

Greater unexpected longer-term overall growth

Increases in traffic in the corridors as a whole have been greater than both traffic growth generally and growth in the corridors selected as controls. For six sets of results for which longer periods of counts were given (Barnstaple, M62, Rochester Way, Westway, M11, A316) the growth ranged from 20 per cent to 178 per cent, with an unweighted mean of 77 per cent. This sort of growth is not easy to explain away by general income-related trends.

Greater peak period growth

Peak period growth rates in the improved sections have been notably high, which is not characteristic of traffic growth generally. This suggests that, when extra capacity is provided, there is a reversal of peak-spreading, consistent with both a suppression effect due to congestion and an induced traffic consequence when that is released.

Limited relief to alternative routes

Increases in traffic counted on improved roads have, in general, not been offset by equivalent reductions in traffic counted on the unimproved alternative routes either in the short or long run.

Sensitivity to policy context

In the one case where the study had taken account of the transport policy context in the surrounding area, it was strongly argued that this had an effect on the quantity and location of the induced traffic.

Finally, we note SACTRA's conclusions about the location and importance of induced traffic:

"We conclude, therefore, that both economic logic and modelling studies demonstrated convincingly that the Net Present Value of a scheme can be sensitive to the treatment of induced traffic. This matter is of profound importance to the value for money assessment of the Road Programme.

"We consider that induced traffic is of greatest importance in the following circumstances:

-- *where the network is operating or is expected to operate close to capacity;*
-- *where the elasticity of demand with respect to travel costs is high;*
-- *where the implementation of a scheme causes large changes in travel costs.*

"This suggests that the categories of road where appraisal needs to be most careful are roads in and around urban areas, estuary crossing schemes and strategic capacity-enhancing interurban schemes (including motorway widening). We accept that the last category is included on the grounds of logic rather than modelling evidence. Indeed this is an important gap in understanding which needs to be filled."

The report was submitted to the Secretary of State for Transport in May 1994 and on 19 december 1994 the Government responded with an announcement that, on the balance of evidence, the Department of Transport accepted that "there is likely to be a significant proportion of schemes where there is a real possibility of extra traffic" and stated that "For national road schemes in preparation, the likely significance of induced traffic will be assessed in every case."

4. GENERATED TRAFFIC AND THE EVALUATION OF BENEFIT

It is important to emphasize that all classes of induced traffic receive some benefit, either in the form of reduced costs or of greater opportunities. It is wrong to treat some classes of induced traffic as being "true" benefit and others as being of lower order. However, it is also the case that nearly all induced traffic will tend to impose some additional environmental costs of some form and *some* of the induced traffic imposes additional external costs of delays to other traffic. Thus, the effect of induced traffic on the overall economic contribution of a road improvement will be quite different in congested and uncongested conditions, may be different when the road is near a city or in the countryside and will usually be different if there is a different proportion of long-distance to short-distance traffic, or private to freight traffic.

This section summarises the SACTRA argument on the effects of including induced traffic on the economic appraisal of roads schemes, as outlined by Mackie (1996) and Coombe (1996), both essentially based on the use of equilibrium analysis and the next section develops the critique further by using a dynamic approach suggested by Dargay and Goodwin (1994).

4.1. Equilibrium analysis

Mackie (1996) uses the four SACTRA diagrams, shown below.

Figure 3. **Equilibrium user benefits**

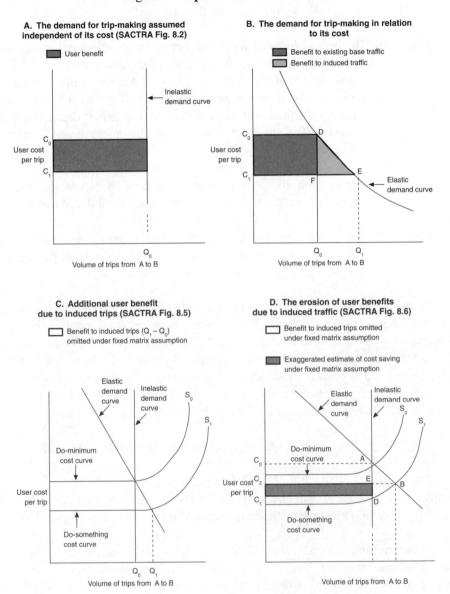

A. The demand for trip-making assumed independent of its cost (SACTRA Fig. 8.2)

■ User benefit

Inelastic demand curve

C_0
User cost per trip
C_1

Q_0
Volume of trips from A to B

B. The demand for trip-making in relation to its cost

■ Benefit to existing base traffic
■ Benefit to induced traffic

C_0
User cost per trip
C_1

D
E
F
Elastic demand curve

Q_0 Q_1
Volume of trips from A to B

C. Additional user benefit due to induced trips (SACTRA Fig. 8.5)

☐ Benefit to induced trips $(Q_1 - Q_0)$ omitted under fixed matrix assumption

Elastic demand curve
Inelastic demand curve
S_0
S_1

Do-minimum cost curve

User cost per trip

Do-something cost curve

Q_0 Q_1
Volume of trips from A to B

D. The erosion of user benefits due to induced traffic (SACTRA Fig. 8.6)

☐ Benefit to induced trips omitted under fixed matrix assumption

■ Exaggerated estimate of cost saving under fixed matrix assumption

Elastic demand curve
Inelastic demand curve
S_0
S_1

Do-minimum cost curve
C_0
C_2
User cost per trip
C_1

A
E
B
D

Do-something cost curve

Volume of trips from A to B

In each case, the calculated benefit uses the principle of consumer surplus, i.e. the extra benefit enjoyed by the consumer over and above the outlay (in time and money) he has to pay. The figures demonstrate the following effects:

195

Figure 3A: If there is no induced traffic, each road user enjoys the full value of the cost saving made by the new road.

Figure 3B: If there is induced traffic, the existing travellers enjoy the full value of the cost reduction, but the new travellers (i.e. the induced traffic) receive a lower consumer surplus benefit because, for some of them, the trip itself brings a benefit less than the original cost, as proved by their previous decision not to travel. This reduced benefit may be approximated by the "rule-of-a-half".

Figure 3C: Comparing the assumptions in A and B, some benefit is therefore omitted if no allowance is made for induced traffic.

Figure 3D: However, the induced traffic also causes some increased congestion and prevents the existing travellers from getting all the cost savings they would have expected.

In this figure, the aggregate benefit to travellers between A and B due to the fall in cost per trip is C_0DEC_1. This benefit may be considered in its two components -- the benefit to the base trips (Q_0) of C_0DFC_1 and the benefit to the $(Q_1 - Q_0)$ trips induced by the fall in costs depicted by area DEF. Provided the cost change is not too large, it is reasonable to assume the demand curve is linear over the relevant range. In that case, the average induced trip receives a benefit equal to half the cost change. Hence, the total user benefits may be written as:

$$(C_0 - C_1) Q_0 + \tfrac{1}{2}(C_0 - C_1) (Q_1 - Q_0) = \tfrac{1}{2}(C_0 - C_1) (Q_0 + Q_1).$$

This is the so-called "rule-of-a-half" formula. It can be extended to deal with complex networks, more than one mode and many origin-destination pairs. It was the basic evaluation tool used in the land-use/transportation studies of the 1970s.

Thus, omitting induced traffic causes two errors: an underestimate of benefit and an underestimate of loss. The crucial question is therefore what are the relative sizes of these two? Coombe (1996) summarises the results of theoretical and modelling work by Williams and others and shows that, in conditions of congestion, the effect of induced traffic slowing down everybody else is greater than the extra benefit it enjoys itself. This arises as an inevitable consequence of the non-linear nature of the relationship between the volume of traffic and its speed.

Thus, the omission of induced traffic is only a "conservative" simplification (as defined above) in those circumstances where new roads are built with no great present or future problem of congestion.

4.2. Dynamic analysis

A separate issue arises when the equilibrium analysis is replaced by a dynamic approach, as pursued by Dargay and Goodwin (1994). The following section outlines their argument (which is substantially due to Dargay, not her co-author).

The benefits to travellers in period t from a discrete change in travel costs (whether this is generalised costs usually employed, or the money price or time alone) at time 0, can be measured by the *change in consumer surplus*, measured by the area under the demand curve at time t, $D(t)$, where $D(t) = f_t(c)$. Assuming D is integrable, the change resulting from a change in costs from c to c' is given by:

$$B(t) = \int_{c'}^{c} D(t)\, dc \tag{1}$$

If D is a linear function of costs, this integral is evaluated as:

$$\int_{c'}^{c} D(t)\, dc = -\tfrac{1}{2} [\, f_t\,(c') + f_t\,(c)]\,(c' - c) \tag{2}$$

where $f_t(c')$ is the level of demand in period t, given a change in costs from c to c' in time 0 and $f_t(c) = D(0)$, the level of demand at the initial price, c, which is the same for all t, and given that D(0) is in equilibrium. Although equation (2) is exact only for linear functions, this same formula, known as the "rule-of-a-half" is a reasonably good approximation to the actual integral for marginal changes in c even if D is a non-linear function of c, as used above.

Since demand does not respond instantaneously to changes in costs, we have a series of demand curves, D(t), representing the level of demand in different time horizons from t = 0 to the time of complete adjustment, or equilibrium, t*, following a change in costs in time 0. By definition, consumer surplus B(t), resulting from the change in costs, is then also dynamic and changes over time. The intertemporal profiles of demand and benefits are generally also affected by

197

non-price factors, so that $D(t) = f_t(z,c)$. However, in order to simplify the exposition, we will assume that all other factors remain constant, so that $D(t+i) = D(t) \; \forall \; i$ if c is constant.

$$\varepsilon(t) \; = \; \frac{(D(t) - D(0))}{\Delta C(0)} \; \frac{c}{D(0)} \; = \; \frac{\partial D(t)}{\partial C(0)} \; \frac{c}{D(0)} \; . \tag{3}$$

Here, $\Delta C(0)$ is a change in costs from c to c' occurring at time 0, $D(0)$ is the level of demand at time 0 given the initial price c and $D(t) - D(0)$ is the change in quantity demanded after a time interval t. We would expect this elasticity to grow monotonically with increasing time and approach some asymptotic value ε^*, the long-run elasticity, as $D(t)$ approaches its equilibrium value, D^*. It is possible to have other adjustment patterns, e.g. oscillation, but in most economic situations $|\varepsilon(t)| < |\varepsilon(t+1)|$ for all $t < t^*$ and $\varepsilon < 0$, so that $D(t) < D(t+1)$ for price falls and $D(t) > D(t+1)$ for price rises, assuming that $D(0)$ is in equilibrium. This implies that $B(t) < B(t+1)$ for price falls and $B(t) > B(t+1)$ for price rises. This is shown in Figure 4.

Figure 4. **Over- or underestimation of consumer surplus**

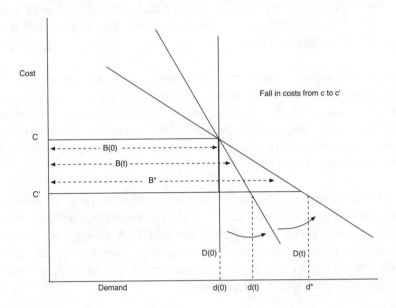

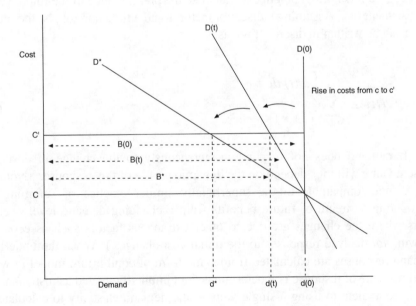

It is interesting to compare this diagram with the apparently similar presentation of Mackie, above. If it is assumed that the total volume of traffic is unaffected by changes in the cost or speed of travel, there is a vertical demand curve similar to that labelled D(0).

Suppose we argue (as is often stated, though with dubious evidence) that changes in route choice are likely to be completed quite rapidly, but that changes in mode or destination choice, or trip frequency, would take longer to apply. If this were true, then the vertical demand curve could be thought to apply, equivalently, to assignment or to short-term effects and the sloping curve to other responses or to longer-term effects.

If established practice changes to include the broader range of behavioural response, then it will in any case involve a shift in emphasis from the vertical to the sloping demand curve. But whereas the SACTRA analysis sought only to replace one implausible equilibrium demand curve by another more sensitive one, a dynamic analysis seeks also to consider the time scale over which short-term responses are converted to longer term ones.

In order to assess the total costs or benefits to travellers of a given change in travel costs, it is normal practice to calculate the present value of the future stream of costs/benefits. Assuming a discount factor, r and a time horizon, N, the present value can be written in discrete time as:

$$PV(B) = \sum_{t=0}^{N} \frac{\int_{c'}^{c} D(t)\, dc}{(1+r)^t}.$$ (4)

If demand does not respond instantaneously to the change in costs, the present value will thus depend on the dynamic profile of this response. (Note that this is not comparable to the superficially similar practice of summing and discounting a stream of future benefits from a changing demand level over the years where the changes are due to other extraneous factors such as economic growth, *not* delayed responses to the initial cost changes.) When the underlying demand responses are calculated from some form of equilibrium model in which the time-scale of response is indeterminate and implicitly treated as instantaneous, this is equivalent to using a single-value static demand elasticity to calculate the consumer surplus, rather than a time-dependent dynamic elasticity, so that $\varepsilon(t) = \varepsilon_s$ $\forall\, t \geq 0$, where ε_s is a constant. This assumption of a static elasticity also implies that $D(t) = D_s$ and thus that $B(t) = B_s \ \forall\, t \geq 0$, so that the (undiscounted) benefit is the same for all t and the PV becomes:

$$PV(B_s) \ = \ B_s \sum_{t=0}^{N} \frac{1}{(1+r)^t} \, . \tag{5}$$

The question that arises is, what happens to the calculation of present value when we erroneously use a static elasticity?

If the source of the static elasticity is a good long-term equilibrium model, then its implied elasticity is sometimes perceived as the long-term asymptote of a dynamic process. On the other hand, if the source is some sort of non-lagged time-series analysis, it is likely that the elasticity will be close to the initial or short-term value of a dynamic elasticity. (Neither of these dynamic interpretations of static elasticities is always valid, because of misspecification bias, but it is convenient to take these as the limiting cases at this stage of the argument.)

It emerges that the nature of the error caused depends on the relationship of the static elasticity to the dynamic elasticity, the speed of adjustment to equilibrium, the discount rate, r and the time horizon, N. In the first example, the long-run elasticity, ε^*, is used instead of the dynamic elasticity. In this case, $|\varepsilon^*| > |\varepsilon(t)| \ \forall t < t^*$. This implies that $D^* > D(t)$ and $B^* > B(t)$ for price falls and $D^* < D(t)$ and $B^* < B(t)$ for price rises. Thus, the benefit to consumers of price decreases is overestimated and the (negative) benefit or loss entailed by price increases is underestimated, as compared with the true situation where initial small responses build up over a period into bigger responses. In the assessment of intertemporal benefits, each term in the summation in the present value calculation is over- or underestimated as shown above, so that the sum of the discounted benefits will include the sum of these errors and thus be over- or underestimated in the same fashion. The slower the speed of adjustment the greater will be the discrepancy. However, as the time horizon increases, N approaches or exceeds t^*, so the error becomes smaller. Also, the higher the discount rate, the less weight to future benefits, which are more nearly accurate, so the error increases.

In the second case, suppose we erroneously use a short-run elasticity, $\varepsilon(1)$, where $|\varepsilon(1)| < |\varepsilon(t)| \ \forall t > 1$, instead of the dynamic elasticities $\varepsilon(t)$. Then for $t > 1$, $D(1) < D(t)$ and $B(1) < B(t)$ for price falls and $D(1) > D(t)$ and $B(1) > B(t)$

for price rises, so the benefit of price decreases is underestimated and the loss of price increases is overestimated. Again each term in (4) with the exception of B(0) and B(1) is over- or underestimated, as is the discounted stream of future benefits. The effects of differences in the speed of adjustment, discount rate and time horizon are the opposite to the case above.

The biases described are not due essentially to the mistake of using an elasticity which is erroneously higher or lower than the true value (although this is important for other reasons). They arise from using a single value, whatever it is, instead of a time-dependent function. However, given that the two limiting cases discussed have opposite patterns of bias, it is interesting to suggest that there is likely to be some notional value of an elasticity -- somewhere between the short-term and long-term value -- whose use as a static elasticity would give the same value for consumer surplus as a full calculation of the path of response over time. This value will be a sort of pivot representing the point of transition from underestimate to overestimate of benefits, which will depend on the intertemporal response pattern, the discount rate and the time horizon chosen.

The change in consumer surplus at time t is thus determined by the initial level of demand, the change in price and the dynamic elasticity, $\varepsilon_{T,RC}$. From this relationship we can calculate the percentage error in the estimated present value of benefits or costs resulting when a static elasticity is incorrectly applied instead of the (correct) dynamic one. For a given discount rate and time horizon, it can be shown that, for this particular model specification, the percentage error will depend only on the elasticity and the direction and magnitude of the relative change in price. In Table 19, an example is given using the estimates of the elasticities for total car traffic with respect to running costs. A discount factor of 8 per cent and a time horizon of 30 years are used for the present value calculation. The errors resulting for cost increases and decreases of from 10 to 50 per cent are shown for two separate cases. The first uses the estimated short-run elasticity, while the second uses the long run.

Table 19. **Percent error in consumer surplus using static instead of dynamic elasticities**

	Percent change in running costs					
	Percent increase			Percent decrease		
Static elasticity	10	20	50	10	20	50
SR -0.4	3	5	12	-3	-6	-18
LR -1.3	-1	-2	-5	1	3	9

The errors in Table 19 are expressed as a percentage of the total change in consumer surplus. For practical purposes, they will usually need to be converted into a percentage of net present value, which will always be greater than the above figures: for the interesting policy decisions where benefits are within 20 per cent of costs, for example, biases of this scale in consumer surplus will normally substantially influence the rate of return and may reverse the decision.

We see that for small changes in price the error is marginal regardless of which elasticity is used. However, the error increases as the price change becomes greater and for large price changes the error is quite substantial. Further, we see that using the short-run elasticity overstates the loss incurred by a price rise, while using the long-run elasticity understates it. For a price fall, the opposite occurs: the short-run elasticity understates the benefits gained while the long-run elasticity overestimates them. However, the effect is only symmetric for rising and falling prices when the price change is marginal. As the percentage change in price becomes larger, the asymmetry increases. In this case, the error is greater for price falls than for price rises. This asymmetry arises because of the non-linear functional form used for the demand function - with a linear demand function such asymmetries would not exist. Also, in this particular case, the error is much greater using the short-run elasticity than the long-run elasticity. Although this need not be the case, it will generally be so unless the chosen time horizon is very short. Finally, as shown earlier, we can find a static elasticity which will yield zero error. In this case, the elasticity is about -1.0.

In accepting SACTRA's advice, the UK Department of Transport (1994) issued a technical guidance note on how this should be done, which includes a table of recommended generalised cost elasticity values. The note says:

"These values represent short-term elasticities and should be used for sensitivity tests of opening year flows. Larger values of up to twice the above should be used for sensitivity tests of design year flows."

The "design year" is usually the fifteenth year after opening. It will be obvious that if the elasticities used for the fifteenth year after opening are around twice that used for one year after opening, all the questions of an adjustment path discussed in this paper become relevant and indeed it would be impossible to calculate a net present value *unless* such a path is assumed.

Thus in accepting the existence of induced traffic, it is necessary to accept the behavioural adjustment process which would bring it about. If this adjustment is not instantaneous -- which may be taken as axiomatic -- then unbiased measures of benefit must be based on the path and pace of a process which takes place over time and it becomes apparent that the "zero induced traffic" assumption led to not one source of bias, but two.

Despite the rather simple models used and the preliminary nature of the results, a few conclusions can be drawn. Most importantly, using static elasticities for transport policy assessment could lead to erroneous estimates of the impact. It could be argued that, for small cost changes, the errors will be small and could be ignored. For large changes, however, the errors can be significant.

We can consider the broad practical implications of this argument. The direction of bias will depend on the specific context of current practice. For example, consider the case of a pricing policy in which the price of road use was increased (by petrol prices or a road pricing scheme), the revenue being used to support public transport. Current assessment of such a policy would be influenced by petrol price elasticities and public transport fares elasticities which, being drawn from unlagged analysis of time series data, are significantly less than empirically estimated longer-term figures. Moving to some form of median elasticities, therefore, would in both cases require an increase in the elasticity assumed.

It may therefore be suggested that the policy bias in some current practice leads to an overestimate of the welfare loss in raising prices (in this example, for road use) and an underestimate of the welfare gain in reducing prices (in this example, for public transport). The static evaluation of consumer surplus changes would therefore seem to make the policy appear less worthwhile than it really is.

On the other hand, some policies are evaluated using transport models, usually calibrated on cross-section data, which claim to give a long-run equilibrium forecast of the effects of the policies under test. This is especially so in the case of evaluation of major infrastructure investments, in which travel time rather than money price is commonly the largest element of benefit. If the model claims are deserved, then the implied elasticities will be those that apply in the long run and will be greater than median values. In this case, the bias is the reverse: the value of reducing costs will be overestimated and the disbenefit of increasing them will be underestimated.

A final and particularly important example, would be the evaluation of a "package" of policies, some of which have short-term effects and others longer-term effects. It would cause distortion if the package as a whole is evaluated in terms of its final equilibrium, without consideration of the different time-scales of the various components.

In summary, therefore, it follows that policies or projects to be compared should be evaluated with explicit treatment of the time-scale of the behavioural response which will apply. The assumption that evaluation can be carried out by reference to an assumed equilibrium will lead to biased choices.

4.3. Rule-of-a-half for reassignment also

Now we raise a possible third source of bias. The former practice may be crudely summarised by saying that reassignment = instantaneous response = vertical demand curve = full value of benefit, as compared with a cartoon alternative of other demand responses = dynamic response = sloping demand curve = rule-of-a-half. Thus Mackie [in relation to Figure 3(a) above] writes:

"In this case, the user benefits of an improvement are simply equal to the change in user (time plus operating) cost...the user benefit is simply the cost difference per trip...multiplied by the fixed volume of trips."

This is directly relevant to the evaluation aspects of the induced traffic argument, because benefits to induced traffic are only given on average half-credit by the "rule-of-a-half" procedure, whereas benefits to reassigned traffic are given full credit. So (quite apart from congestion and speed flow considerations) identification of some of the traffic as induced reduces the value of its benefits.

However, if it were the case that the benefits to reassigned traffic should also be assessed by rule-of-a-half principles, then (a) benefits would be over-valued even for reassigned traffic, which is worrying and (b) the importance of this particular reason for distinguishing traffic as induced or reassigned reduces or disappears, which is comforting.

Consider the hypothetical case of a toll road agency considering the charging level on a road. It is important (a) for the agency, that accurate estimates are made of the revenue which could be raised at different charging levels and (b) for the Department of Transport, that an accurate estimate is made of the consumer surplus changes that result from these different charging levels.

-- Reassignment is the only influence on the market for the charged road; there is no induced traffic or any other response than reassignment;
-- There is a fast, charged route and a slower, free alternative;
-- Neither are congested, so there is no feedback effect of the traffic split on speed;
-- We have the possibility of charging easily, with no hassle or interruptions to traffic and users are fully aware what the charges are.

Now consider progressively increasing the price on the charged route and ask how many travellers will choose the free or charged road at different levels of charge. In other words, what will be the shape of the revealed demand curve on the charged route?

Proposed Answer

Just suppose that it will be a perfectly ordinary, downward-sloping, smooth (or smoothish) curve. The higher the price, the lower the traffic on the charged road. There will be some price that will be so high that nobody will use the road and another price that will be so low that the demand will be virtually the same as if the road was uncharged.

(I am very confident that this will be true in the real world and fairly confident that all but the crudest assignment models would also produce this result. However, I accept that this is not provable in a mind experiment. Readers who believe it to be true are now invited to consider the implications for evaluation. Readers who do not believe it to be generally true are asked to consider the gentler question -- if there were *particular circumstances* where this result might apply, what are the implications for evaluation in those circumstances?)

Now, we consider how to assess the changes in consumer utility that are involved in using the road. The only way we can do this is to consider the area under the demand curve.

For the uncharged road, there is no congestion and everybody who still uses it has the same travel time, so there is no change in their consumer surplus. For the charged road, there is no congestion so no changes in travel time and the only variable influence on consumer surplus is the price charged.

In the case where the curve slopes (i.e. it is not vertical), it will be logically necessary to apply the "rule-of-a-half" or an equivalent procedure which approximates to this area. This reflects the property of utility revealed in the slope of the demand curve itself, namely that the change in benefit for those who change their behaviour to a previously available but rejected alternative is at the margin less than the change in benefit to those who continue with their previous behaviour but at different cost. *Some people do not value the benefit of using the charged road as highly as others and therefore are not prepared to pay as high a price for using it.* (If this were not so, then nobody at all would use the charged road at prices above a certain threshold price level and absolutely everybody would use it at prices below this level. This is the strict interpretation of a vertical demand curve and seems completely implausible.)

This is not new in principle, already being accepted when assessing the consumer surplus changes involved in the cases, for example, of the effects of journey time changes on the choice of mode, or on time of day of travel.

However, if the approach is a) valid for effects of time on mode and time of day choice and b) valid for effects of price on route choice, then it must be valid when considering the effect of travel time changes on route choice, because of the interchangeability of money and time when using the generalised cost framework.

Conclusion

The "full value" assumption is only valid when route choice is not sensitive to different levels of generalised cost on alternative routes. Otherwise, the rule-of-a-half should be used.

5. POLICY IMPLICATIONS OF THE IMBALANCE BETWEEN CAPACITY GROWTH AND TRAFFIC GROWTH

Discussion on the effects of road construction on the total volume of traffic is a pivotal one, because of the centrality of infrastructure provision in the history of transport policy. But although there is general agreement that the question has policy implications, it is by no means agreed exactly what those implications are.

The question is not a new one. Glanville and Smeed (1958) already captured much of the current discussion when they wrote:

"It is sometimes seriously suggested that it is not worthwhile building new roads because generated traffic will be so great that former users will be little better off than before. This is clearly a generalisation that does not stand up to inspection, for there are examples too numerous to mention where this has not occurred and, in any case, added capacity at the same speed is an advantage in itself, although there may be accompanying disadvantages."

However, the context is different in the 1990s from what it was in the 1950s, notably in two respects. First, there is a much greater awareness of those classes of "accompanying disadvantages" that relate to environmental impacts. Secondly, there have been radical changes in the larger strategic question of road policy, namely whether it is possible for capacity expansion to keep up with traffic growth.

Here, it is important to distinguish between the incremental effect of specific schemes and the roads programme as a part of the whole transport strategy. The "induced traffic" argument is crucial to the assessment of the environmental impact (and indeed effect on congestion) of any specific road scheme, or combination of schemes. As discussed above, the evidence on this is substantial and reasonably convincing. But this is not the same issue as the credibility of the road programme as a whole to keep up with traffic growth. On this question, it will be argued that induced traffic is a relevant, but secondary, issue, since the imbalance between capacity growth and traffic growth could, in broad terms, still apply even if there were no induced traffic (though the policy response to that might be different).

These two issues tended to become confused, partly because of the timing of the publication of the Report of the Royal Commission on Environmental Pollution (1994) (which made only passing comments on induced traffic) in October 1994, the SACTRA report on induced traffic (which made only passing comments on the problems of overall transport strategy) in December 1994 and subsequent reductions in the scale of the road programme.

We now move to consider the broader question of the relationship between growth in road traffic and growth in road capacity and how this had changed the nature of the policy argument about road building directly and therefore the context in which all other environmentally friendly policies can be considered.

For all advanced countries, the ratio *traffic levels/size of road network* has grown over time, or in other words traffic growth rates faster than the growth of the road network are a ubiquitous experience. This is not a new phenomenon, though for many years (and in some places still) it was thought to be a temporary problem due to inadequate road budgets or inefficient administrative arrangements for progressing a construction programme.

The recognition that it might be impossible for road capacity to keep pace with unrestrained traffic growth was an important element in the convergence of policies aimed at responding to urban congestion and those aimed at environmental improvements. It was not an accident that this new consensus happened first and most swiftly in towns, especially the small- and medium-sized historic cities, where there is the most obvious dissonance between traffic and the urban environment and a sense of cultural identity and civic pride.

What happened next was that the ideas of traffic moderation that had been born in the towns quickly spilled over into the countryside, where the forecasts of traffic growth are much higher. This had a swift effect. For example, Stokes *et al.* (1992) reported to the UK Countryside Commission that current trends and the Department of Transport forecasts implied traffic growth rates in the countryside of perhaps 300 per cent or 400 per cent over the next thirty years. The Commission (in a response included in the same document) concluded that:

"...demand for road traffic should be managed in such a way that it is consistent with the conservation of the basic countryside resource...the countryside can neither afford nor accommodate the predicted growth in road traffic."

The completion of a new consensus in the towns and the beginnings of one in the countryside, about the unsustainability of projected traffic growth, was described (Goodwin 1994) as "phase 1 of the new realism".

But all this rethinking left the national road network relatively untouched, the subject of great controversy, with neither signs of consensus nor a mechanism that might create one. By about the autumn of 1994 it became possible to argue that there were signs of a next stage in the argument; phase 2 of the new realism.

Throughout the early 1990s, there had been increasingly intense opposition to road schemes from a quite unusual alliance of those with property to defend and those with nearly no property at all, reinforced by technical opposition from some local authorities. While the motives for people to participate in demonstrations are likely to be more personal than technical, there was nevertheless an underlying technical argument. The opponents of each scheme claimed that traffic growth would not be so high if there were better alternatives and that it is wrong to evaluate one road scheme at a time, in isolation from all the others on the same road and that expanded trunk road capacity delivers more traffic onto unexpandable local roads than they can cope with. Those claims, though often intuitive, corresponded with an increasingly respectable line of academic research and professional judgement.

In addition, in the summer of 1994, a new, decisive argument emerged from an unexpected source. This was the report published by the British Road Federation CEBR (1994), which was cited above as the source of a small but useful additional piece of evidence on induced traffic. It had a more important consequence, however, which serves as a reminder that not only policies, but also research reports, can have unexpected effects.

The work made a calculation of what would happen with the then current trunk road programme, of £2 billion a year and what would happen if the trunk road programme was reduced or increased, the increase tested being an extra 50 per cent, to £3 billion a year, from now until the year 2010.

The results, though sensitive to some modelling assumptions which are open to argument, seem robust. They suggested that, with the current trunk road programme, the congestion on the trunk road network as a whole will get worse every year, not better. And *even if £3 billion a year were spent*, though the pace of deterioration would be somewhat less, congestion would still worsen every year. This seemed to confirm what many were beginning to suspect, but which had not been part of the emerging consensus: no realistic trunk road programme can keep pace with forecast traffic growth, on current trends. So the work seemed to establish, almost by accident, that the accepted urban imbalance, between potential demand and possible supply, is true of trunk roads also.

That proposition started to have a traumatic effect on transport policy, highlighted by, but not essentially due to, the induced traffic evidence. The political undercurrent was that it may often be reasonable to ask people to accept some personal sacrifice, or environmental loss, if it will make things better overall. But on current trends and the current programme, things were not going to get better. The sacrifice -- at best -- just slows down the pace at which things get worse.

Thus, on trunk roads and motorways, as in towns, it became necessary to accept that supply of road space is simply not going to expand in line with demand. Therefore, on trunk roads also, not just in town centres, that means demand will have to be moderated to meet supply. This is another and stronger, version of the argument about "unintended consequences" but of a rather different form. Here, the issue was that the basic expectation of the ability of the **strategy** of road construction to keep pace with traffic growth was challenged.

Within this policy context, some new capacity may be provided, but with different criteria. It is not possible to design a new road until it is decided what traffic load to design it for and that now implies a policy choice, not a forecast. Political authorities now have to choose whether to have their traffic engineers design for 80 , 60 or 40 per cent of potential demand. Any of these choices means that each scheme for extra capacity has to be accompanied by an explicit complementary traffic restraint policy which matches the traffic to that capacity. Otherwise, any benefits are rapidly eroded.

This, combined with the results of the induced traffic research, tends to introduce new themes in the focus of road capacity provision, for example, smaller bypasses aimed at diverting through traffic rather than providing for future growth and with closures or restrictions in the bypassed area to ensure that the planned environmental improvements are actually achieved.

The implication would be a move towards a very much greater emphasis on quality of the road system and less on quantity. Expenditure would increase on road maintenance, strength of pavement, design quality and especially on integrated alternatives to road building and expenditure on new capacity would reduce.

This shift of emphasis, which is proceeding at different speeds but with broadly similar features all over Europe, took place in Britain over several years following publication of the Department of Transport National Road Traffic Forecasts in 1989. By 1994, the issue had a very high political profile and this meant that publication of the SACTRA report in late 1994 took place in a highly charged atmosphere. As a result, it was not treated as a technical report of interest mainly to a handful of professionals, but as a major public document. In particular, it was treated as a document with a *political* significance which went beyond its actual content. This is shown in the newspaper reports (see Annex) from the "quality" end of the British press spectrum (and reflected in more dramatic language in the popular papers and with more technical discussion in the specialist journals.) What was notable was that the report was very widely welcomed, both in what it said and in what commentators liked to build on it.

In the course of the discussions described above, it became apparent that new arguments started to appear, changing the nature of the interaction between empirical research, forecasting based on it and the policy conclusions derived from it. Two aspects will be mentioned:

i) the significance of revised forecasts; and
ii) the implications of induced traffic.

Less means more

The long-standing assumption was that -- as far as possible -- the supply of new road capacity should be aimed at providing enough space to cater for forecast demand. It follows that the higher the traffic forecasts, the higher the required capacity provision.

If it is not possible to match road capacity to forecast levels of traffic, then the relationship between forecast and policy changes. The 1989 traffic forecasts represented a transition from self-fulfilling forecasts to self-defeating ones, or a shift from what Owens (1995) called "predict and provide" to a new paradigm of "predict and prevent". In reaction to this is a line of argument which might run: *"The traffic forecasts were technically faulty anyway: traffic growth has been exaggerated. There will not be as much traffic as we have assumed. Therefore it will be possible to provide enough capacity to match it. So we can return to the previous policy."*

With this argument, a lower forecast could justify a bigger road programme than a higher forecast. Some aspects of this approach may be detected in a view which is emerging from some sections of the motor industry, notably the International Organisation of Motor Vehicle Manufacturers, based in Paris. Streit (1995), for example, proposes that in the mature markets of western Europe, car ownership is already nearly at saturation and little further growth is expected, while the network of highways and motorways should be developed to generate prosperity. In general, forecasts of car ownership and use from the motor industry are lower than those emerging from governments and academics and there is consequently less inclination to consider environmental objectives as requiring restrictive action.

Welcoming induced traffic

It is understandable that those opposing road schemes have been eager to accept the evidence for induced traffic and those supporting road schemes have tended to reject that evidence or minimise its scale. But, following acceptance of the SACTRA recommendations, a new argument emerged:

> *"Traffic generated by new roads should be welcomed as a sign of new economic activity, Richard Diment, director of the British Road Federation, told a conference in Taunton last week... "Many people in many parts of the country would love to see some additional traffic on their roads", Diment said, "as it would be a sign that the economy was picking up* [Local Transport Today (30/03/95)].*"*

Foster (1995) pursued a related line, suggesting:

> *"...the right transport answer...to the discovery that there will be too much congestion after a road opens...is to plan a larger road, subject to an overall cost benefit test."*

Both used the phrase; *"there is too little investment, certainly not too much"* and therefore we should expand the road programme further -- to provide enough capacity to match the forecast traffic levels **and** a bit extra to cater for the induced traffic.

The problem with this argument is that this would imply a roads programme well over 100 per cent bigger than in recent years, just for the trunk roads, plus even greater increases on all the surrounding local roads. If one were to assert that this hypothetical case is so far from political reality that it is simply not going to happen, then it must follow that an increasing proportion of the road network will be operating close to capacity, for longer periods of time and these are precisely the conditions where a small volume of induced traffic has the most damaging effects on traffic congestion.

6. CONCLUSION

A demand-led general strategy of road construction does not easily lend itself to become part of the package of sustainable transport policies. Aside from the effects of construction itself, this is for two main reasons:

a) as a general case, new road capacity will be expected to increase the total volume of traffic, hence increase those aspects of environmental damage that are proportional to the volume of traffic and

b) because at a strategic level the main effect of road construction is to influence the pace at which both congestion and environmental damage from traffic get worse, rather than offering potential for it to improve. The conditions under which particular schemes (such as the small bypasses implemented together with traffic reduction measures in the bypassed area) might be environmentally friendly rely heavily on the simultaneous implementation of other transport policies designed to offset or constrain the negative effects.

The magnitude of these effects is dependent on other policies being implemented. In particular, traffic restraint policies (or the same prevailing conditions not derived from deliberate policy) will condition the extent to which induced traffic is a problem and, conversely, achievement of the benefits of new capacity, either on an improved road itself or on alternative routes that a new road is intended to relieve.

There is a strong dynamic process in operation in the evolution of policy thinking resulting from such analysis. Ideas which have emerged in towns become modified and applied in the countryside, or on motorways. Especially during major transitions in thinking, the pace of change may be quite fast and would then be expected to interact with other political constraints, e.g. budgets or imminent elections. In any case, it becomes useless to consider what the policy "is" at any moment in time; one should rather see policy itself as a continually changing set of objectives and priorities.

It is apparent that the process of individuals' responses to new capacity also takes place over time, with indications that traffic patterns in response to a new road are still adapting after several years.

The overall effect of these results is to weaken the case for "road construction to meet demand" as an environmentally friendly or economically efficient policy and, in those cases where it might apply, to place great emphasis on the contingent effects of other policies which are operated at the same time. In particular, there is a warning that construction intended to give relief to over-stressed areas (e.g. in the case of bypasses) is unlikely to be successful unless other policies are in force to prevent the regrowth of traffic in the bypassed area. There are also strong indications that behavioural responses, in the order of five to ten years, have to be taken into account, not just first-year effects.

Thus, the following broad conclusions are suggested.

-- First, the balance of evidence reasonably clearly indicates that additional traffic may be induced by the provision of extra road capacity, as a result of a combination of a wide variety of different behavioural responses.

-- Secondly, the amount of extra traffic will vary according to the specific circumstances, size of scheme, existing traffic congestion, geographical and economic conditions and availability of alternatives. In UK conditions, an average result for an average scheme may be of the order of 10 per cent in the short run and 20 per cent in the longer run, with a range of 0-20 per cent in the short run and 0-40 per cent in the longer run.

-- Thirdly, the extra traffic enjoys some benefits itself (hence increasing the calculated benefit/cost ratio of the road) but also erodes the benefit to other road users (hence reducing it). The net effect depends substantially on the existing and expected level of congestion. Because of the non-linear nature of the relationship between traffic volume and speed, induced traffic reduces the overall value-for money of a road scheme when conditions are more congested.

-- Fourthly, these effects take place over time, with a relevant period of several years for behavioural changes and possibly longer for land-use changes. Research to monitor the effects of new road capacity cannot come to meaningful conclusions by observing only first-year effects; and evaluation procedures need to use dynamic concepts allowing for the speed of adjustment, not only description of a final equilibrium.

-- Fifthly, there is no single, clear-cut relationship between the observation that road construction increases the volume of traffic and the policy consequences that follow from that. This depends on wider strategic issues, including the pace of traffic growth due to factors other than new capacity. The specific circumstances of a transport policy debate in the 1990s give importance to environmental impacts, the need to ensure value for money from public funds and the need to ensure that economic benefits from infrastructure are not eroded by congestion: in these circumstances, recognition of the reality of induced traffic increases doubts about the effectiveness of a road construction-based transport strategy and gives additional emphasis to the importance of applying efficient methods of managing and reducing the growth in traffic.

NOTE

1. Actually, the *range* of error was worse in the case of bypasses than most other schemes, with a ratio of forecast/observed from 0.552 to 2.038, but these errors were roughly symmetrical: the forecasts were poor, but not evidently biased.

BIBLIOGRAPHY

Beardwood, J. and J. Elliott (1986), Roads Generate Traffic. *Proceedings of PTRC Summer Annual Meeting.*

Bressey, C. and E. Lutyens (1938), *Highway Development Survey 1937.* Ministry of Transport, HMSO.

Castle, A. and J. Lawrence (1987), Leigh Bypass: Before and After Studies. Greater Manchester Transportation Unit.

Centre for Economics and Business Research (1994), *Roads and Jobs.* British Road Federation, London.

Cleary, E.J. and R.E. Thomas (1973), *The Economic Consequences of the Severn Bridge and its Associated Motorways.* Bath University Press.

Coombe, D. (1996), Induced traffic: What do transportation models tell us? *Transportation* 23 (1).

Dargay, J.M. and P.B. Goodwin (1994), Evaluation of Consumer Surplus with Dynamic Demand Changes. *Journal of Transport Economics and Policy.* XXIX (2) 179-93.

Department of Transport (1989), *National Road Traffic Forecasts (Great Britain) 1989.* HMSO, London.

Department of Transport (1994), Guidance on induced traffic, HETA Division.

Downes, J.D. and P. Emmerson (1983), *Do Higher Speeds Increase Travel or Save Time?* Transport and Road Research Laboratory, Crowthorne.

Foster, C.D. (1963), *The transport problem*, London, Blackie & Son.

Foster, C.D. (1995), The dangers of nihilism in roads policy, Henry Spurrier Memorial Lecture, Chartered Institute of Transport, March.

Glanville, W.H. and R.J. Smeed (1958), The Basic Requirements for the Roads of Great Britain. ICE Conference on the Highway Needs of Great Britain, 13-15 November 1957, Institution of Civil Engineers, London.

Goodwin, P.B. (1992), A review of new demand elasticities with special reference to short and long run effects of price changes. *Journal of Transport Economics and Policy*, XXVI (2), May.

Goodwin, P.B. (1994), Traffic growth and the dynamics of sustainable transport policies. Linacre Lecture to launch the ESRC transport research centre programme. Working Paper 811. ESRC Transport Studies Unit, University of Oxford.

Goodwin, P.B. (1996), Empirical evidence on induced traffic: A review and synthesis. *Transportation* 23 (1).

Gunn, H.F. (1981), Travel Budgets - a Review of Evidence and Modelling Implications. *Transportation Research* 15A (1).

Halcrow Fox and Associates, Accent Marketing Research and the University of Leeds (1993), *Review and Specification of Model Elasticities.* Department of Transport.

Harris, R.C.E. (1993), Monitoring Department of Transport Traffic Forecasts. *Proceedings of PTRC Summer Annual Meeting.*

Hawthorne, I. and N.J. Paulley (1991), *Adaptive Responses to Congestion: Literature Survey.* Transport and Road Research Laboratory, Crowthorne.

Hills, P.J. (1996), What is induced traffic? *Transportation* 23 (1).

Howard Humphreys and Partners (1993), *A Publication Review of Traffic Generation Studies. Evidence for Inquiry on A406 North Circular Road Popes Lane to Western Avenue Improvement.*

Judge, E.J. (1983), Regional Issues and Transport Infrastructure: Some Reflections on the Lancashire-Yorkshire Motorway, in *Transport Location and Spatial Policy* by Button, K.J. and D. Gillingwater (eds), Gower, Aldershot.

Kroes, E., A. Daly, H. Gunn and T. van der Hoorn (1996), The opening of the Amsterdam Ring Road: a case study on short-term effects of removing a bottleneck, *Transportation* 23 (1).

Luk, J. and S. Hepburn (1993), *New review of Australian travel demand elasticities*. Australian Road Research Board, Victoria.

Mackie, P.J. (1996), Induced traffic and economic appraisal, *Transportation* 23 (1).

Ministry of Transport (1968), *Advisory manual on traffic prediction for rural roads*, London, HMSO.

Mogridge, M.J.H., D.J. Holden, J. Bird and G.C. Terzis (1987), The Downs/Thomson paradox and the transportation planning process, *International Journal of Transport Economics* XIV (3), 283-311.

The MVA Consultancy, Institute for Transport Studies at the University of Leeds and Transport Studies Unit at the University of Oxford (1987), The Value of Travel Time Savings, *Policy Journals,* Newbury.

Oum, T.H., W.G. Waters and J.-S. Yong (1992), Concepts of Price Elasticity of Transport Demand and Recent Empirical Estimates, *Journal of Transport Economics and Policy* XXVI (2).

Owens, S. (1995), From "predict and provide" to "predict and prevent"? Pricing and planning in transport policy, *Transport Policy,* 4 (1).

Pells, S.R. (1989), User Response to New Road Capacity: a Review of the Published Evidence. Working Paper 283, Institute for Transport Studies, Leeds University.

Pizzigallo, P. and J. Mayoh (1989), *Manchester outer ring road Portwood to Denton, a before and after study.* Greater Manchester Transportation Unit.

Purnell, S. (1985), The effect of strategic network changes on traffic flows. PRA Note 4, BP 105, Greater London Council.

Road Research Laboratory (1965), *Research on Road Traffic*, London, HMSO.

Royal Commission on Environmental Pollution (1994), *Eighteenth Report: Transport and the Environment*. HMSO, London.

SACTRA (1994), *Trunk Roads and the Generation of Traffic*, HMSO, London.

Stokes, G. (1994), Travel time budgets and their relevance for forecasting the future amount of travel. European Transport Forum, PTRC, Warwick. Working Paper 802. Transport Studies Unit, University of Oxford.

Stokes, G., P.B. Goodwin and F. Kenny (1992), *Trends in transport and the countryside*. The Countryside Commission, Cheltenham.

Streit, H. (1995), Disaggregate approach to individual mobility demand and the saturation hypothesis, OICA/ECMT Workshop on long-term forecasts of traffic demand, Berlin, May.

Virley, S. (1993), The Effect of Fuel Price Increases on Road Transport CO_2 Emissions. Transport Policy Unit, Department of Transport.

Williams, I. and C. Lawlor (1992), Growth of Traffic on Motorways and Other Trunk Roads. Report by Marcial Echenique & Partners for the TRRL.

Younes, B. (1990), The Operational, Environmental and Economic Impacts of the Rochester Way Relief Road. PhD Thesis, Imperial College, London.

OTHER CONTRIBUTIONS

During the Round Table, several participants submitted written contributions describing the situation in their respective countries. These contributions are reproduced below as complementary information.

GERMANY

Ulrich BLUM
Technische Universität Dresden
Fakultät Wirtschaftswissenschaften
Dresden

WHAT IS INDUCED TRAFFIC?
- A RESTATEMENT -

(1) Transportation is demand derived from other markets. The utility of transport and its transportation consumer surplus (M) relate to the primary goods markets. TCS is identical to the sum of consumer and producer surplus, assuming a competitive equilibrium (CE). In case of market imperfections, TCS will be lower than the sum of surpluses from the primary markets, as parts are extracted as rents by those who profit from these imperfections (Blum, 1997; Jara-Diaz, 1986).

(2) Transport is thus an intermediary input for production by firms or demand by households, or a distinct property of goods in the sense that goods have bundles of properties, i.e. transportation. In the same way as production defines transportation volumes, transportation infrastructure as potential supply may be related to production potentials (Blum, 1982).

(3) Following this view, transportation is a volume (measured in vehicles or vehicle-kilometres, persons or person-kilometres, tons or ton-kilometres) depending on some kind of price. The product of both gives the transportation turnover or -- more economically -- total transaction costs.

(4) Prices are an important factor determining the level of transportation demand. More generally speaking, transportation volume depends on a portfolio of metrics (prices, for instance, general costs) that evaluate distances in terms of geography, especially topography, language differences, legal differences and so forth. Inasmuch as the simple transportation price is a result of price differences in different primary

223

markets, these transportation metrics are outcomes of underlying metrics in the primary markets, i.e. differences in preferences, languages, etc. (Blum, Leibbrand, 1995; Gaudry, Blum, McCallum, 1996).

(5) Induced traffic is the volume of total transportation stemming from changes in any one of the price, activity or performance variables that influence transportation demand and supply. It can only be sensibly derived from the relation of the (secondary) transportation market to the underlying (primary) markets.

(6) Not all changes in price, activity or performance variables lead to (positive or negative) induced transportation. If new traffic can only be identified by means of transportation market separation (i.e. across modes from road to rail, across motives from work to leisure, across firm structures from internal to the firm to external to the firm, assignments from link 1 to link 2), this cannot be considered as induced traffic if it cancels out *in toto*.

(7) The identification of induced traffic is tautological, if it results from an axiomatic system that assumes constant travel time budgets (CTTB). CTTB assume that if only one transportation market exists, aggregate price elasticities must be -1 (with time as a price). In a multi-transportation market setting, it puts constraints on direct and cross-price elasticities (Varian, 1992).

The concept of CTTB furthermore may be challenged for several reasons:

– The price elasticities found in time-series demand models differ considerably from -1; they are in the order of magnitude of -0.3 (Blum, Foos, Gaudry, 1988). In cross-sections, these elasticities are in the order of magnitude of -1.5 to -2.5 (Blum, 1996).

– There is no way to consistently relate changes in individual time budgets to changes of total time budget of a group because of the non-linearity of aggregation. In the example given below, two persons have their trip times changed on a link from period t to period t+1. In the first case, trip time rises by a factor of 1.25, in the latter case it falls by a factor of 16 per cent. Both persons maintain their travel time budget of 50 and 80 respectively because of an elasticity of -1. The total travel time budget, however, has increased. We follow from this little example that the concept of aggregate travel time budgets (and averages from them) lack mathematical rigour.

224

	Period t		Period t+1	
	No. of trips	**Trip time**	**No. of trips**	**Trip time**
Person 1	5	10	4	12.5
Person 2	10	8	16	5
No. of trips, average trip time	15	9	20	8.75
Total time budget	135		175	

- It assumes that time cannot be substituted for other goods; this is in contradiction to empirical findings which show to what extent values of time vary across modes (Gaudry, Mandel, Rothengatter, 1993).

- Moreover, it implies the independence of the transportation market from other goods markets, which is in sharp contradiction to the notion of derived demand.

(8) In fact, induced traffic emerges in two forms (Blum, 1997):

- If the economic and, thus, transportation system are known, rational expectations can be built on the effects of an impulse on the system. Consequently, the change of transportation volume can be foreseen in the "true" model of the economy (or its mathematical approximation) and will, in a deterministic or stochastic way, be included in prices.

- If the effects of the impulse cannot be foreseen because of ignorance (in an economic sense, it is sufficient that the markets are not complete, i.e. information on certain future markets are missing), economic agents will not be able to anticipate them. Consequently, the respective future changes will not be reflected in the present price system, and will constitute an externality. Inasmuch as impulses on the economy, especially the transportation system, lead to a spontaneous rearrangement of the economy inducing these types of externalities, this will be reflected by induced traffic.

The first can be accounted for in models, the latter perhaps through simulations.

BIBLIOGRAPHY

Blum, U. (1992), Effects of Transportation Investments on Regional Growth: a Theoretical and Empirical Investigation, Papers of the Regional Science Association, 49, 169-184.

Blum, U. (1997), External Benefits of Transport, A Spatial View, in: *Measuring the Full Costs and Benefits of Transportation*, Springer, Heidelberg-New York.

Blum, U., M. Gaudry, G. Foos (1988), Aggregate Time Series Gasoline Demand Models: Review of Literature and New Evidence for West Germany, *Transportation Research A* 22, 75-88.

Blum, U. and F. Leibbrand (1995), A Typology of Barriers Applied to Business Trip Data, in: Banister, D., U.R. Capello and P. Nijkamp (Eds.), *European Transport and Communication Networks*, Pion, London, pp. 175-188.

Gaudry, M., U. Blum, J. McCallum (1996), First Gross Measure of Unexploited Single Market Integration Potential, in: Sabine Urban (Ed.), *Europe's Changes -- Economic Efficiency and Social Solidarity,* Gabler, Wiesbaden, 449-460.

Gaudry, M., B. Mandel, W. Rothengatter (1993), A Disaggregate Box-Cox Logit Mode Choice Model of Intercity Passenger Travel in Germany and its Implications for High-Speed Rail and Demand Forecasts, CRT 844L.

Jara-Diaz, S. (1986), On the Relations Between User Benefits and the Economics of Transportation Activities, *Journal of Regional Science,* Vol. 26, No. 2, 379-391.

Varian, H. (1992), *Microeconomic Analysis*, W.W. Norton Co.

FRANCE

Michel HOUÉE and Christian CALZADA
Ministère de l'Équipement, du Logement
des Transports et du Tourisme
Paris

IMPACT ON MOBILITY OF THE NORTHERN-EUROPE HIGH SPEED TRAIN[1]

INTRODUCTION

In order to assess the impact on mobility of the Northern-Europe High-Speed Train network, a panel survey was set up, following a decision taken at an international seminar attended by major stakeholders from the five countries concerned (see *Notes de synthèse de l'OEST, no. 55*, December 1991). The following is a preliminary report on the methods used in the survey and on its findings. These show that the impact of the high-speed train was very uneven in the two areas of residence studied (it was more marked in the Nord-Pas-de-Calais area than in Ile-de-France). The same applied to trip purpose (home-work trips were found to be particularly significant).

1. THE PANEL

The Paris-Lille High-Speed Train (HST) began operating in September 1993. It had been brought into service in two stages, with the opening of the Paris-Arras line in May 1993 and its extension to Lille in September 1993. This marked the start of the development of the Northern-Europe High-Speed Train network that was to link Brussels, Amsterdam, Cologne, London and Paris by the year 2000.

It was against this background that the study was carried out. Its main objectives were to:

--   Obtain a better understanding of mobility behaviour following a major infrastructure development across the full range of trip purposes (both leisure and business trips);
--   Further a multimodal approach to the study of the impact on mobility in order to better identify modal shift effects (particularly from road to rail), induced traffic effects (new passengers or more trips by previous passengers?) and mode combination effects (especially the HST/air interface);
--   Identify, if possible, as well as the impact of high-speed travel, other effects more specific to the Northern-Europe high-speed train, such as "border effects", any incipient high-speed train "network effect" and the effects of eliminating detrimental trip discontinuities within the trip chain.

In order to conduct such a study, a unique method of collecting uniform data was required. A panel survey was designed (see study outline) in order to monitor changes in mobility in the Northern-Europe corridor as the various sections of the high-speed line were brought into service. Since the survey was never expanded to other countries as intended, it was actually conducted only in two regions of France, Nord-Pas-de-Calais and Ile-de-France, beginning in October 1992.

The following analysis treats the first two years of the panel's existence for which data were available as two successive cross-section snapshots, in other words, it analyses two independent samples before and after the opening of the line, giving each separate weightings and extrapolating the data to 10 000 households.

2. TRIPS UP AN AVERAGE 4.6 PER CENT, BUT RESULTS UNEVEN

An increase in trips was observed, for the most part trips originating in the Nord-Pas-de-Calais (NPC) area (+10 per cent), an area that was already generating substantially more trips than the Ile-de-France (IDF) before the advent of the high-speed service; the increase masked a very slight decline for the IDF (-1 per cent) (see Table 1).

**Table 1. Corridor traffic flow by number of trips (separate samples)
Percentage contribution* to growth by place of residence
(in the before/after period)**

Area of residence	IDF %	NPC %	All areas %
Total corridor trip generation	-0.9	10.4	4.6
Rail	-2.8	7.9	2.5
conventional business	-1.8	0.9	-0.5
home-work/study	1.3	6.6	3.9
leisure	-2.4	0.5	-0.9
Road	1.7	2.5	2.1
conventional business	1.0	1.0	1.0
home-work/study	1.4	4.6	3.0
leisure	-0.8	-3.2	1.9
Air	0.2	neg.	neg.
conventional business	0.7	neg.	neg.
home-work/study	-0.1	neg.	neg.
leisure	-0.4	neg.	neg.

Neg.: neglible.
*   Component-specific contribution to aggregate growth (t), weighted by the component's share in the aggregate (t-1).

Rail's share of corridor[2] traffic generated in the NPC area rose by +30 per cent, due mainly to a substantial increase in the number of home-work/study trips (+43 per cent), which was attributable to a significant rise in trip frequency by a small number of users. There was an accompanying decline in trips for leisure purposes in both generating areas.

In terms of corridor traffic distribution by trip origin/destination (Figure 1), the most significant increase in the number of individual trips[2] i.e. by individual household members) was in flows from the NPC area to the IDF area (maximum take-up effect, +8.5 per cent). The doubling of NPC/London flows, not nearly so significant, was attributable to fare cuts by ferry companies in 1994 in anticipation of the opening of the Channel Tunnel.

Figure 1. **Percentage contribution to the growth in corridor flows by trip origin/destination area (per 100 trips by individual household members)**

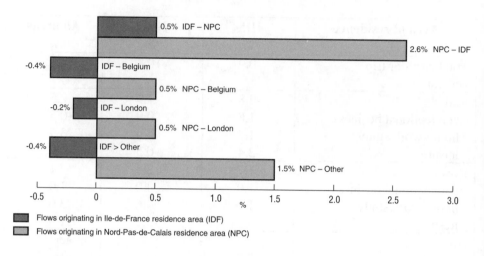

Flows originating in Ile-de-France residence area (IDF)
Flows originating in Nord-Pas-de-Calais residence area (NPC)

3. TRAFFIC ON IDF/NPC LEG, UP AN AVERAGE 5 PER CENT

Turning now to just the IDF/NPC leg[2], there was an overall increase of 5 per cent in trips (all origins) and a much higher increase in trips originating in the NPC area (+8.5 per cent).

There was a marked increase in train travel in the NPC (which was already high) after the opening of the high-speed line (+34 per cent). This was paralleled by a slight decline in road traffic (-8 per cent). Individual home-work/study trips also showed a marked increase in the NPC area (+31 per cent, principally by rail); trips exclusively for business purposes increased by only 10 per cent in the same area.

4. PERCENTAGE OF MOBILE HOUSEHOLDS
REMAINED CONSTANT

Although the percentage of mobile households[2] remained constant overall, at 33 per cent for the corridor and 22.5 per cent for the IDF/NPC leg, in the NPC area the number of mobile households using rail increased slightly (+1.5 points).

The increase in traffic originating in the NPC area can therefore be attributed to a significant increase in train travel by mobile households in that area (Table 2).

Table 2. **Average number of trips (by area of residence on the leg)**

	Per household		Per mobile household	
	1992-93	1993-94	1992-93	1993-94
CORRIDOR				
Total	**4.2**	**4.4**	**12.8**	**13.2**
IDF residents	2.8	2.8	10.3	10
NPC residents	8.5	9.3	16.9	18.4
IDF/NPC LEG				
Total	**2.6**	**2.7**	**11.7**	**12.3**
IDF residents	1.8	1.8	10.7	10.9
NPC residents	5.2	5.6	13.1	14.1
Rail (IDF residents)	0.5	0.5		
Road (IDF residents)	1.3	1.3		
Rail (NPC residents)	2	2.8		
Road (NPC residents)	3.1	3.9		

5. DISPARITIES IN MOBILITY TRENDS BETWEEN USERS OF
DIFFERENT MODES ON THE LEG

It was among rail users that changes in mobility patterns were the most marked. The percentage of executives and professionals -- the vast majority of train passengers -- increased year on year (42 per cent to 47 per cent in the IDF area, 24 per cent to 32 per cent in the NPC area). The percentage of passengers in the 35 to 45 age group decreased.

Among road users, the only significant development was an increase in the percentage of users in the 15-24 age group, particularly among residents of the NPC area.

Lastly, it was among two-person groups that there was the highest take-up of the train service.

The percentage of air-only users in the IDF area increased at the expense of competing modes. For households in the NPC area, the decline in road-only users was offset by the increase in rail-only users (Table 3).

Table 3. **Trends in modal split in the corridor**

	IDF residents		**NPC residents**	
	1992-93	1993-94	1992-93	1993-94
Single mode				
Air only	9.5	12.0	0.0	0.0
Rail only	17.0	16.0	10.5	13.5
Road only	47.5	47.0	67.0	65.0
Two modes				
Air + Rail	3.0	3.0	0.0	0.0
Air + Road	6.0	6.0	0.0	0.0
Rail + Road	14.0	12.0	22.0	21.0
Three modes	3.0	4.0	0.5	0.5

Weighted base:
IDF: 2 030 households (1992-93)/1 225 households (1993-94).
NPC: 2 080 households (1992-93)/1 230 households (1993-94).

5.1. Panel methodology

5.1.1. Preliminary stages in panel selection

The statistical unit used was the household. Panel selection was based on three reference surveys (see study outline):

- a main reference survey (by telephone);
- a final telephone survey;
- additional field surveys at boarding points (stations, airports).

5.1.2. *The main reference survey served as the basis for recruiting the panel (of 10 000 households)*

Its objectives were to:

- provide an overall reference framework for household mobility, which would be representative in terms of volume and the structure of the long-distance travel marked on the Northern-Europe high-speed line, by trip destination area and by population category (panel make-up, administration and control was based on this survey);
- produce a segmentation that would explain mobility (ensuring that variables remained fairly stable) and serve to maintain the representativeness of the panel sample over time;
- establish a pool of potential panellists.

5.1.3. *Final survey (filter survey -- 600 telephone interviews)*

The filter survey was used to select mobile households specifically in the IDF area of the corridor with a view to increasing their percentage on the panel.

5.1.4. *Boarding point surveys*

These were carried out in order to:

- identify highly mobile households which used public transport modes (uncommon among the general public) to ensure that they would be represented on the panel;
- assess the percentage of non-residents among passengers using the corridor.

5.1.5. *The panel*

The reference population was households living in the IDF and NPC areas whose head of household was under 75 years of age. The survey measured trip generation by residents of both these areas in France and only in those areas.

The panel observation period was split into annual waves, the first of which covered the period October 1992 to September 1993.

The objective was to conduct analyses on the largest consistent sample possible, essential for identifying changes in mobility behaviour. With this end in view, it was important to retain as many of the panellists recruited at the beginning of the observation period as possible so that behavioural changes could be more accurately observed.

The optimum stratification methods used meant that the reference survey was not sufficient to supply all the mobile people needed for the panel. The final telephone survey and the boarding point surveys were used to recruit additional mobile panellists.

The size of the panel and its sources of recruitment (i.e. the number of panellists recruited in the three separate surveys, by mobility strata) were based on:

- optimum sample distribution calculations: over-sized corridor-mobile strata, which made for greater precision for a given sample size;
- the findings of the reference survey in terms of corridor mobility and overall mobility.

Interview frequency and data collection methods: postal questionnaire sent out every three months (mobile households); telephone interviews every six months (non-mobile households).

NOTES

1. The findings reported are taken from preliminary reports on the findings produced by SOFRES, the French market research company responsible for panel management. This summary report deals with general mobility aspects through a cross-section snapshot approach: a further summary report will analyse mobility behaviour on the basis of an unchanged panel.

   This operation was conducted with the collaboration of the three modes concerned through the responsible Ministries [the Surface Transport Directorate (DTT), the Roads Directorate (DR), the General Directorate for Civil Aviation (DGAC)] and the operators (SNCF, USAP, AdP) as well as the SES, the Research and Scientific Affairs Directorate (DRAST), the National Institute for Transport Research and Safety (INRETS), the Paris Transport Union (STP), the Channel Tunnel Secretariat and the Commission of the European Communities.

2. See definitions at end of article.

Study outline

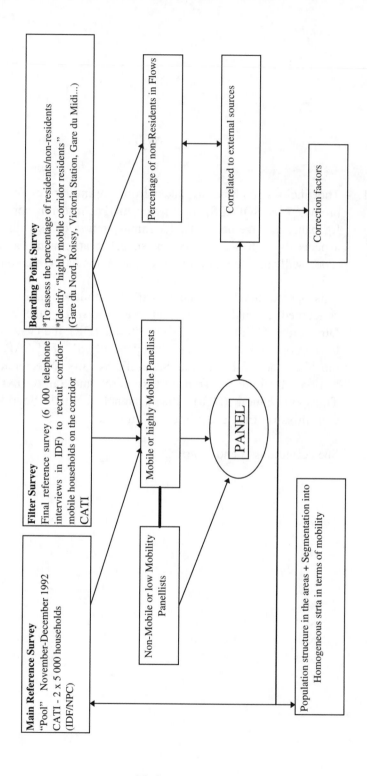

DEFINITIONS

- **Corridor.** All potential origins/destinations between two geographical areas considered as forming the North-Europe high-speed corridor, i.e. London and the London area, Belgium, the Netherlands, the Bonn, Cologne, Dusseldorf and Essen region in Germany, the Nord-Pas-de-Calais and the Ile-de-France areas.

- **Leg** : That part of the line between any two areas in the Northern-Europe high-speed corridor, e.g. Ile-de-France/Nord-Pas-de-Calais, often referred to as the IDF/NPC leg.

- **Individual trip.** Trip by one household member from an origin to a destination point for a specific purpose.

- **Household trip.** Travel by a group consisting of all or some members of the household from an origin to a destination point for a specific purpose (a household trip may therefore include one or more individual trips).

- **Mobile household.** A household on the corridor with at least one member who has travelled (in the corridor) in the past twelve months (or quarter, as the case may be) to another destination on the corridor, whatever the purpose of the trip.

- **Total corridor mobility.** The total corridor mobility of a household living in one of the areas of residence is equal to the number of household trips (or household journeys) made in the preceding 12 months (or three months) to other destinations in the corridor, whatever the trip purpose.

- **Corridor mobility (business/leisure only).** Corridor mobility for business trips (or journeys) or leisure trips only.

237

BIBLIOGRAPHY

M. Houée, P. Salini (1991), *"Suivi du TGV-Nord Européen, C'est parti!"*, *Notes de Synthèse de l'OEST*, No. 55, December.

J.F. Lefol, V. Salvy (SOFRES, France), M. Houée (METT, France) (1994), "Studying the impact of the North-European high-speed train on mobility behaviour: an original methodological approach", in: *PTRC Proceedings of Seminar A, Pan-European Transport Issues*, pp. 101-112, 12 -- 16/09.

SOFRES (1995), *"Évaluation de l'impact du TGV Nord-Européen, Comparaison avant-après mise en place du TGV Paris-Lille (Année 1-Année 2)"*, November.

FRANCE

Daniel Le Maire
Transportation Adviser
Eurotunnel

TRAFFIC INDUCED BY THE CHANNEL TUNNEL: INITIAL RESULTS

1. Introduction

The Eurostar passenger services and the Shuttle services for accompanied private cars have been in commercial operation since December 1994. The monitoring of operating results has shown the existence of induced traffic. This additional traffic, generated by the fixed link, had been estimated by means of forecasts compiled prior to the start of the services. This report summarises the initial operating results.

2. Induced traffic forecasts

The forecasts were compiled over the years in two stages. In the first stage, conventional economic models for forecasting diverted traffic flows were used to calculate price-induced traffic. Channel crossing price elasticities, estimated from surveys of stated preferences in the various market segments and the price elasticities given by price-time models fitted to time series, made it possible to calculate the volume of induced traffic for passenger services according to various scenarios for changes in cross-Channel prices. In the second stage, a separate estimate of induced traffic was compiled taking into account effects other than those of prices, such as:

* the characteristics of the Shuttle or Eurostar services;
* changes in land use on either side of the Channel;
* traffic generated by the Eurodisney complex;
* changes to the Tunnel's hinterland (Charles de Gaulle Airport);
* the company's marketing policy.

The resulting induced traffic is shown below (Table 1).

Table 1. **Eurotunnel -- Induced as % of total traffic**

Forecast of December 1995	1996	2003
Car passengers	11%	9%
Coach passengers	19%	13%
Eurostar passengers	18%	19%

The curiosity effect was excluded from the forecast. In addition, the induced traffic estimate did not allow for any redistribution effects, meaning changes in the structure of flows derived from the 1991 survey (now being updated with the 1996 O&D surveys), which was used to calibrate the models.

3.   Categories of induced passenger traffic

In the light of almost two years of Shuttle and Eurostar operation, the three categories of induced traffic taken into account in commercial strategy are as follows:

*   The increase in trip frequency among cross-Channel travellers, particularly among those using the Tunnel;
*   New crossings via the Tunnel replacing trips which formerly would have been made on the same side of the Channel;
*   Traffic actually created, meaning new trips generated by passengers who would not have travelled at all if the Shuttle and Eurostar had not been introduced.

This traffic is induced either by the Shuttle or the Eurostar services themselves, or by the activities made more accessible by these new services. By extension, an attempt can be made to explain the process by measuring the improved accessibility to existing and new activities. The following table summarises the relationship between accessibility and categories of induced traffic.

Table 2. Category of induced traffic and accessibility

Accessibility characteristics	Frequency increase	Redistribution effect	Traffic created
Time/price	X	X	X
Other (train frequency, comfort, etc.)	X	X	X
Attraction to existing activities	X	X	X
Attraction to new activities	--	X	X
Curiosity/novelty	X	X	--

It is particularly difficult to analyse the process, since the opening of services was accompanied by the following structural changes in cross-Channel demand (Table 3):

* The "artificial" growth of crossings whose purpose is the purchase of duty-free goods (day-trippers) rather than transport;
* Changes in the distribution of flows with a heavier concentration of traffic on the shortest route: Dover/Folkstone-Calais;
* The gradual market penetration of the Tunnel services, which makes it difficult to distinguish between induced traffic and traffic diverted from competitors.

Table 3. **Trend in cross-Channel traffic**

	Increase in traffic (% per year)		Concentration of traffic on DOCA* (%)		Share of Shuttle on DOCA* (%)	
	Cars	Coaches	Cars	Coaches	Cars	Coaches
1993/19 90	7.5	7.1	-	-	-	-
1994	6.9	7.3	57	76	-	-
1995**	16.0	10.3	61	79	28	13
1996***	9.9	10.7	67	83	42	30

*   DOCA = Dover/Folkestone-Calais route.
**   First full year of operation for car traffic.
*** From January to September 1996 -- first full year of operation for coach traffic.

The Shuttle and Eurostar services have also generated some traffic because of their novelty, reflecting the public's curiosity, the bandwagon effect and the fact that some non-European travellers had to use the services on their package trips in Europe. This novelty effect has been analysed in the case of the Shuttle and some information on the effect is available for the Eurostar.

4.   Follow-up surveys

Eurotunnel's follow-up surveys have been conducted among its car passengers.   Since the opening of the service, questionnaires have been distributed to travellers during their Shuttle trip and from whom a further selection is made for a specific telephone survey on diverted and induced traffic.

Three survey campaigns have been carried out:

(i)   August-September 1995: first period of summer services;
(ii) October 1995-March 1996:   off-season period but with rapidly expanding traffic;
(iii) June-September 1996: second summer season of full operation.

The telephone survey identified the new trips and distinguished between those prompted by the curiosity (novelty) factor and those linked with the other characteristics listed in Table 2. The analysis covered different segments of UK passengers and focused on French travellers after the first campaign covering all continental travellers.

According to the results in Table 4, the curiosity effect was very marked among UK travellers at the start of operation but decreased substantially for day and standard trips in the second summer of operation and disappeared altogether for short stays. In contrast, it seemed to become more pronounced among French passengers, who are less inclined to make day-return trips.

The proportions of induced traffic among French passengers, excluding the curiosity effect, were lower than for UK travellers. The special case of UK day-trippers should be pointed out, for they accounted for the highest proportion, rising from 30 to 40 per cent from the summer of 1995 to the summer of 1996.

This effect can be explained by two overlapping causes: promotional prices for the purchase of duty-free goods and lower fares due to a price war between the Shuttle and the ferries.

Using the latest survey, it can be estimated that induced traffic (excluding the curiosity effect) accounts for 18 per cent of UK Shuttle passengers and only 10 per cent of French passengers. The survey results therefore exceed the forecasts.

The same applies to Eurostar for which, in the summer of 1996, the proportion of induced traffic was about 18 per cent, to which should be added about 10 per cent of traffic that could be classified under the curiosity effect, mostly consisting of non-Europeans.

5. Conclusion

Although it is too early to draw definite conclusions from the modelling of traffic induced by the Shuttle and Eurostar services, it is possible to highlight the curiosity effect and to say, at the present stage of operation, that the volume of induced traffic matches the forecasts. The initial results recorded, however, seem to suggest that the volume is slightly higher for the Shuttle's car traffic.

Table 4. Passenger survey by telephone - Private car traffic induced by the Shuttle (as % of total traffic)

Category		Survey 1 August-September 1995				Survey 2 October 1995-March 1996				Survey 3 April-September 1996			
Passengers	(Induced as % of total traffic)	No. of surveys	Curiosity	Other	Total	No. of surveys	Curiosity	Other	Total	No. of surveys	Curiosity	Other	Total
UK	Day trips	106	21.7	30.2	51.9	51.9	5.0	30.0	35.0	73	8.2	39.9	48.1
UK	Short stays	94	13.8	12.8	26.6	100	4.6	21.1	25.7	25.7	0.0	13.6	13.6
UK	Standard trips	159	10.1	11.9	22.0	109	14.8	13.9	28.7	93	3.2	9.8	13.0
Continental		94	14.9	9.6	24.5	--	--	--	--	--	--	--	--
French		--	--	--	--	102	8.8	5.9	14.7	103	12.6	9.7	22.3

BIBLIOGRAPHY

Blanquier, A. (1994), Traffic and revenue forecasts for the Channel Tunnel project, Applied Econometrics Association -- Transport Econometrics Conference, 20-21 January, Calais.

Le Maire, D. (1992), Channel Tunnel traffic forecasts -- Institutional and methodological issues, Rail High Speed and Regional Development Seminar, Fondation de los Ferrocarriles Españoles, 2-3 December, Madrid.

Le Maire, D. (1994), *35 Années d'évaluation de projets de Tunnel sous la Manche*, Applied Econometrics Association, International Colloquium, 20-21 January, Calais.

FRANCE

Olivier MORELLET
INRETS
Arcueil

THE CONTRIBUTION OF IMPROVEMENTS IN TRANSPORT SUPPLY TO THE GROWTH OF LONG-DISTANCE PASSENGER TRAFFIC IN FRANCE

This purpose of this note is to describe briefly how INRETS estimated the contribution made by improvements in transport supply-- and especially in infrastructure -- to the growth of long-distance passenger traffic in France between 1980 and 1992.

SCOPE

Only journeys made by passengers between different regions were taken into consideration; metropolitan France (excluding Corsica) was divided into forty-two regions. Furthermore, of these journeys only those equal to or greater than 100 kms (including terminal journeys for those journeys for which the train or plane was the main means of transport) were taken into account. Lastly, coach journeys were excluded since there are very few scheduled long-distance domestic coach services in France.

Thus defined, this traffic constitutes "French long-distance passenger traffic".

METHOD

Estimate of traffic and average speed for 1992 with the socio-economic context and transport supply of the time

For each route the number of journeys made in 1992 were estimated for the various transport modes from the statistical data available.

Then, the average length of journey in kilometres (including terminal journeys for public transport) and the average total journey time per journey were estimated from the results obtained by applying INRETS' MATISSE model to the actual situation in 1992.

Estimate of traffic and average speed in 1992 assuming that one of the factors determining the trend of traffic was unchanged since 1980

The MATISSE model takes the following factors into account:

i) The socio-economic context, defined each year by the volume of final consumption of French households and their level of car ownership;

ii) The growth of air travel, due to the fact that passengers of the most recent generations travel more by air than older generations, all other things being equal;

iii) Changes in the user cost of the private car related to changes in fuel prices;

iv) The construction of new motorways, whether tolled or not;

v) The introduction of the TGV (Paris-Sud-Est and Paris-Atlantique for the period 1980-1992);

vi) Changes in rail fares: they rose for short journeys and fell for long journeys during the period 1980-1992;

vii) The increase in the frequency of services and possibility of fare reductions on air routes.

A variation in factor i) results in the model in a variation in the mobility of the various types of passengers on each route.

Also, a variation in one of the factors ii) to vii) results in a variation in a number of generalised costs which are representative of the way the various types of passengers perceive the level of service provided by the various means of transport on each route. A variation in generalised costs itself results in changes in the total number and modal split of journeys on each route, which take place gradually over a period of about five years. The change in the number of journeys for all means of transport combined corresponds to the "traffic induction" caused by the medium-term change in transport supply, *with unchanged location of population and economic activities.*

With the aid of the model, it was therefore possible to estimate what would have happened in 1992 if one of the factors i) to vii) had remained unchanged since 1980. The difference between the results obtained and the actual data for 1992 represents the contribution, plus or minus, of the factor in question to the growth of traffic and average speed over the period 1980-1992.

VALIDATION

The validity of the functional forms and numerical values of the parameters in MATISSE was verified by comparing the results of the model with empirical data available in a number of cases, the most relevant of which are the following:

i) effect of changes in the price of fuel on total long-distance traffic;
ii) effect of the construction of new motorways on total motorway traffic;
iii) effect of the introduction of the Paris-Sud-Est and Paris-Atlantique TGV on the routes in question;
iv) trend of traffic on domestic road, motorway, rail and air routes between 1980 and 1992;
v) changes in the number of journeys as a function of the distance between points of departure and arrival, for constant regional characteristics.

With the exception of the last one, these cases do not represent "with-without" situations but "before-after" situations. This is not a drawback, however, insofar as the model is able to dissociate the effects of changes in the socio-economic context from those in transport supply.

It should be noted that as yet the model does not take into account the effect of an improvement in transport supply on a given route on the number of journeys on other routes. As a result, the effect of improvements in transport supply on total long-distance traffic may be slightly overestimated.

FINDINGS

All told, the simultaneous changes in the factors i) to vii) listed above were accompanied from 1980 to 1992 by an increase of slightly more than 40 billion passenger-kms in French long-distance passenger traffic, all means of transport combined.

The attached figure shows the contribution of the various factors to this increase, in terms of the number of passenger-kms that were added or subtracted by the factor in question, by individual means of transport and for all means of transport combined:

i) The increase in households' final consumption, the continuing rise in the level of car ownership and the growth of air transport -- factors i) to ii) -- contributed just under 60 per cent to traffic growth;

ii) The fall in the user cost of the car and especially the price of fuel -- factor iii) -- accounted for just under 20 per cent of traffic growth;

iii) The remaining 25 per cent or so were accounted for by the development of motorways, the TGV and air services and, marginally, changes in rail and air fares -- factors iv) to vii).

In this connection, it may be noted that the simultaneous evolution of factors iv) to vii) over the period 1980-1992 was accompanied, all other things being equal, by an increase of 7.4 per cent in the average speed per passenger-km and of 7.6 per cent in the total number of passenger-kms for French long-distance passenger traffic.

In the example under consideration, therefore, the increase in speed took place with an almost constant total transport time (including terminal journeys for public transport).

This is an intriguing finding insofar as no assumption of this kind was made directly in the model. It is probably a coincidence since the same model gives a *slight increase* in total transport time if we consider the changes in factors over the period 1980-1988 and a *slight decrease* when the period 1980-1984 is considered.

REFERENCE

Morellet, O., P. Marchal (1995), *MATISSE, un modèle de trafic intégrant étroitement contexte socio-économique et offre de transport*, INRETS report No. 203, December.

Contribution of the various factors to the increase in the number of passenger-kms in 1992 in relation to 1980 for French long-distance traffic (millions)

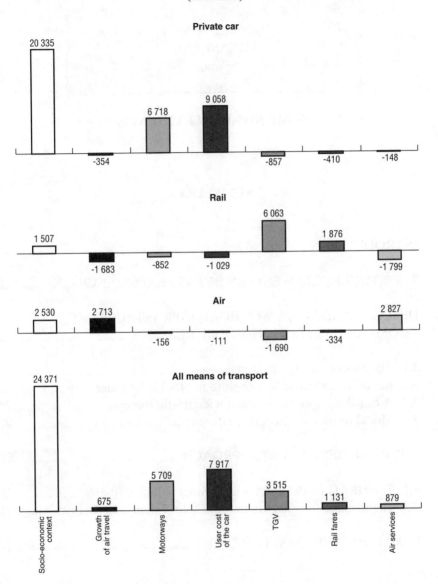

SWEDEN

Göran TEGNER
TRANSEK AB
Solna

SOME SWEDISH EVIDENCE

SUMMARY

1. INTRODUCTION

This paper deals with the relationship between road infrastructure and the possible impacts in terms of induced mobility within the urban scene. In Chapter 2, an *ex post* survey of the effects of opening a part of the first ring road in the Stockholm region is presented.

In Chapter 3 an *ex ante* analysis of the on-going Stockholm Traffic Agreement is penetrated with the time horizon 2005. Results from a travel demand model are presented, with focus on the probable changes in car traffic volumes caused by new road infrastructure.

In order to present an attempt to check such *ex ante* results, in Chapter 4 we present some results from a recent *ex post* study on the evolution of road traffic in Stockholm County during the last 25 years by means of a time-series model over vehicle-kilometres produced.

Our findings are summarised in Chapter 5, in which some conclusions are also drawn.

2. THE STOCKHOLM WESTERN BYPASS EXPERIENCE

The famous case of the M25 in London is often taken as evidence that there is no ideal way to enhance road capacity in large urban areas, as travel demand always exceeds capacity. Therefore, it is stated that a new road facility will only add to congestion and environmental damage.

However, it is often recognised that building bypasses around smaller and medium-sized cities helps to relieve the negative impact from motorised traffic on such city centres.

Figure 1. below shows that improved urban road capacity could divert car traffic from central road links to a new infrastructure such as a bypass without leading to an increase in traffic volumes on the older route alternatives.

Figure 1. **Traffic impact of a new bypass in Stockholm in 1966**

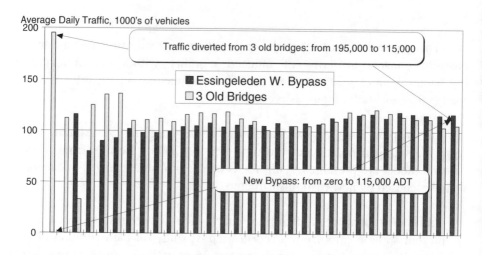

Before 1966, in central Stockholm, all major road traffic coming from the south-west and bound for the central business district -- like most of the traffic from southern Sweden, passing Stockholm and going to the north -- had to pass over three bridges, the Liljeholmsbron, Västerbron and St Eriksbron. In 1966, a new part of the Inner City Ring Road, the Western Bypass, called *Essingeleden* was opened for traffic.

The three old bridges carried around 60 000-65 000 daily vehicles a day each. Most of these flows were the same vehicles using all three bridges, going to the inner city and represented the daily flow pattern with origin in the south-western suburbs and with destination either in the inner city or the northern suburbs (and *vice versa*).

The new Western Bypass took over some 115 000 vehicles within one year after opening, which is near to maximal capacity for a 2x3 lane city motorway. With some yearly variation, the flow on Essingeleden has amounted to 115 000 daily vehicles on average.

The three old bridges which, before the opening of the new ring road, together carried 195 000 vehicles (65 000 ADT vehicles each), experienced a reduction in their load to, on average, 115 000 vehicles per day (38 000 ADT vehicles each). The reduction of traffic flows on the three old bridges was 40 per cent and this reduction has prevailed during the whole period from 1966 to 1996. In the meantime, the total volume of traffic passing the inner city cordon has increased by 11 per cent.

The total traffic volume due to the augmented capacity in the corridor (both the three old bridges and the new bypass) has increased by 18 per cent, from 195 000 to 230 000 vehicles per day (115 000 plus 115 000).

This empirical example shows that:

-- Augmented road capacity contributes to increased traffic volumes in the relevant corridor, in this case by 18 per cent;
-- A city bypass, constructed to divert traffic from central parts of an inner-city area, could relieve over-heavy loads on city roads and really **divert** them to the new bypass, more suited to carrying such loads;
-- An urban bypass -- at least in a medium-sized city like Stockholm -- could play its role as a bypass over a long period of time, even if road traffic as whole is steadily expanding;
-- The reduction of the former heavy traffic loads on the old route (40 per cent) has been **sustained** during a 30-year period, in spite of a substantial overall increase in car traffic volumes.

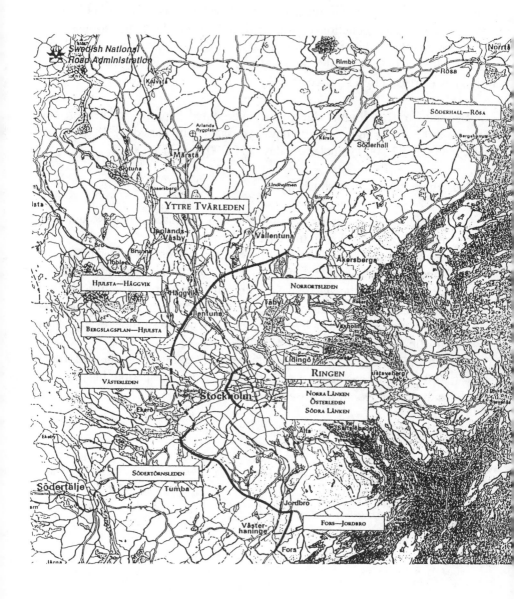

The Dennis Agreement
means that over SEK 40 billion is being invested in the traffic system in the Stockholm region, a little less than a half of which is in public transport. The intention is to improve the environment, increase accessibility and create sound potential for the continued development of the region. The Agreement is backed by the Liberal Party, the Moderate Party (Conservatives) and the Social Democrats in both the City and County of Stockholm.

Important milestones
The Agreement was signed on 29 September 1992 and covers the period 1992-2006. In April 1994, Parliament decided to provide government guarantees of SEK 11.5 billion for the road projects, the road toll system and information, park-and-ride facilities and measures in the inner city area for environmental improvements. The projects are to be financed by loans that are to be repaid by levying road tolls. In the political agreements, the starting point for the levying of road tolls has been tied to the completion of the first part of the Ring Road, *Norra Länken* (the Northern Link). A decision will be taken at a political checkpoint in 1996 on when work can start on the construction of Västerleden. At another checkpoint in 1998 (or later), Parliament or the Government will decide on the rate of construction and the possible increase in the government guarantees already awarded.

Public transport
Almost half the investments will be made in public transport, which means that tax revenues will be used in the normal way in the form of various allocations, including special funds for infrastructure and road funds transferred to public transport. Certain investments connected with roads are being financed by loans that are to be repaid by road tolls.

Road projects
These consist of a ring-road around Stockholm Inner City (the Stockholm Ring-Road), an orbital bypass (the Outer Bypass Route) and the facilities that are needed in order to be able to collect road tolls.

Swedish National Road Administration
The Swedish National Road Administration has, in its capacity as principal, been commissioned by the Government to finance and implement the road projects. Overall responsibility for this work rests with the Stockholm regional office of the Swedish National Road Administration.

Stockholmsleder AB
is part of the overall organisation for the implementation of the road investments. Since 15 December 1995, Stockholmsleder has been owned to 100% by AB Väginvest -- a wholly owned subsidiary of the Swedish National Road Administration. It is Stockholmsleder's task to raise loans and be responsible for the financial control of the project.

3. DEMAND AND SUPPLY OF ROAD INFRASTRUCTURE -- SOME CROSS-SECTION MODEL RESULTS

3.1. The Stockholm Traffic Agreement

The Stockholm Traffic Agreement (sometimes called the "Dennis Package" or "Dennis Agreement") contains the following three types of measures to solve the urban transportation planning problems in the Stockholm region:

-- A ring road system programme with one inner ring completed and one outer ring road system;
-- A substantial upgrading and extension as well as new environment-friendly public transport systems (commuter rail service and new track, metro extensions and a new tangential light rail line);
-- A system of vehicle tolls at the Inner Ring Road system and on the Outer Western Bypass to reduce car traffic and to finance the road programme.

The Agreement calls for the expenditure of SEK 36 billion on the traffic system over a 15-year period. Road building will be wholly financed by tolls on vehicular traffic. The public transportation will be financed jointly by the County and the State. The State will also provide an investment grant of SEK 3.8 billion for the enhancement of public transportation.

3.2. Reduced car traffic by one third in Stockholm Inner City

Compared to the existing transport system, the "Stockholm Traffic Agreement" leads to substantial changes in the trip flows in the region. Public transport usage increases and car usage decreases. Public transport ridership is estimated to increase by more than one-fifth in the entire region.

Reduced car traffic flows will be one of the major impacts of the Traffic Agreement. With the investments in ring-road bypasses, public transport improvements, road user charges and all other measures included in the Traffic Agreement, the Agreement is estimated to reduce car usage by 7 per cent in the entire Stockholm region compared to a do-nothing scenario. The major impact on road traffic will, however, be a substantial diversion of car trips from the most congested areas to the new ring-road bypasses. This is especially valid for the Stockholm Inner City.

The Traffic Agreement is estimated to reduce car traffic flows in the Inner City area by one-third. Half of this substantial reduction is due to the diversion to the new ring-road bypass around the city, and the other half is due to a shift in the mode choice from car to public transport trips.

3.3. A broad assessment -- systemwide traffic forecast and cost-benefit analysis

A broad assessment -- systemwide traffic forecast and cost-benefit analysis -- has been carried out. According to a 1990 Swedish parliamentary law, decisions on infrastructure investments in the field of transport should be based on social cost-benefit analyses (CBA). Such a CBA calculus should consider all costs and benefits to the society as a whole.

The basis for calculation of the benefits is defined in terms of willingness to pay, e.g. for shorter travel times, reduced number of accidents and reduced noise levels. The economic evaluation of the impacts is thus based on a judgement of the value of the resources in its best alternative usage. A consistent cost-benefit analysis of a transport package requires that all identified effects are quantified into monetary units. The impacts of such a traffic agreement as the "Dennis Package" in the Stockholm Metropolitan Area is to be evaluated against a do-nothing alternative, that is, the existing transport system. The year 2005 has been chosen as a relevant future time horizon.

The overall benefit/cost ratio is calculated so that the part of the total benefits that could be quantified and evaluated in monetary units will balance the total costs.

The overall assessment has been carried out by using a forecasting system called the FREDRIK/EMME/2 travel demand and supply model package, operated at 1 043 traffic zones for the entire County of Stockholm.

TRANSEK Consultants Company has developed the traffic planning system FREDRIK, which is a computer model system to handle travel demand in urban and regional areas in a user-friendly way. This planning tool consists of a system of nested logit models simulating travel behaviour in terms of

259

choices of the trip-makers. This comprises the number of trips generated, between which areas, by which mode of transport the trips are made and along which travel routes and transit lines the trips finally are decided to take place. This system is integrated with the EMME/2 transportation planning package.

Together, the two systems -- FREDRIK and EMME/2 -- form a complete transportation model system for integrated road and public transport planning for urban and regional applications.

3.4. Model results for Stockholm County

3.4.1. The generalised cost approach

The well-known **generalised-cost concept** is used both in the travel demand context and in the social benefit-cost context. This means that the following travel time and cost components form part of the perceived total efforts for a door-to-door trip between origin and destination:

-- Walk time (to a stop/station for public transport and to the parked car for car trips);
-- Waiting time (which is zero for car trips);
-- In-vehicle time;
-- Transfer and transfer time (for public transport);
-- Travel costs (in-vehicle costs and parking costs for car trips and fares for public transport).

These travel time components are weighted according to empirical research findings in the following way:

Table 1. **Official travel time values and relative weights for travel time components, for transit planning in Sweden, 1990 prices**

Travel time value (in 1990 prices) Relative weights		Bus trips 3.60 US $/hour	Rail trips 3.60 US $/hour
In-vehicle travel time weight		1.0	1.0
Walk time weight		2.0	2.0
Wait time weight	< 10 min	2.0	2.0
	10-30 min	1.0	1.0
	> 30 min	0.5	0.5
Transfer time weight	< 10 min	2.0	2.0
	> 10 min	3.0	3.0
Time spent staying weight	< 10 min	1.4	1.1
	> 10 min	1.6	1.3
Delay time weight		4.0	4.0
Addition for transfer		= 5 min in-vehicle time	= 5 min in-vehicle time

Source: Swedish National Road Administration: Impacts of Transit Investment, 1992 (in Swedish).

The travel time values that are implicit in the travel demand models and, at the same time, applied in the social benefits-costs analysis are the following:

Table 2. **Travel time values in urban transport, Sweden, 1-1-1997 price level**

Trip purpose	Travel time value in SEK/hour	Travel time value in ECU/hour
Work trips	35	4.10
Leisure trips	26	3.00
Commercial traffic	120	14.10
Heavy trucks	204	24.00

Sources: Swedish Institute for Transport and Communications Analysis, Report No. 1995:13.

3.4.2.   Travel demand in 2005 with new infrastructure and road tolls

The Stockholm Traffic Agreement consists of a complete Inner City Ring Road project (with the Northern, Southern and Eastern Links), while the Western Link is the *Essingeleden*, the Western Bypass built in 1966 and commented on in Chapter 2 above.

The Northern and Southern Link will be referred to below as "2 new road links". Together with the Eastern Link, we will refer to this complete Inner City Ring as "3 new road links". An outer orbital Western Bypass, e.g. a part of the second ring, forms the second large-scale road project in the Traffic Agreement. This is referred to as "4 new road links" below.

A wide range of travel demand-supply model studies have been carried out to analyse the impacts of the traffic package, which consists of:

-- ring roads;
-- public transport projects;
-- an inner city cordon toll system,

and which is briefly described in Section 3.1. above.

The travel demand-supply analysis is carried out for the following disaggregation of the transport market in Stockholm County:

-- 1 043 * 1 043 traffic zones;
-- 8 trip purposes;
-- 4 travel modes (walk, bike, car and public transport);
-- 3 time periods (morning and afternoon peak, and 9-15 hours).

Thus, the analysis is fairly well segmented on a geographical level and for various trip types, modes and time-of-day.

In Figure 3. below, the model estimated effects of various scenarios is presented as average daily traffic volumes (in terms of car vehicle-kilometres) on the road network in Stockholm County.

Figure 3. **Road traffic volumes in Stockholm County, various scenarios**

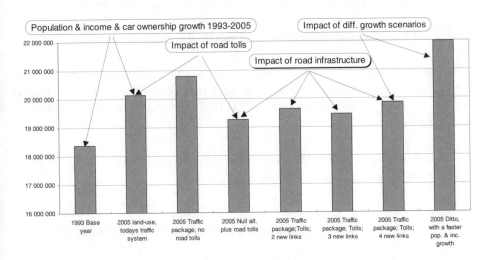

The first comparison is made between the 1993 base year scenario and the year 2005 scenario with only forecasted land-use effects (but with today's traffic network). The calculated increase in road traffic volume is almost a 10 per cent (9.6 per cent) growth from 18.37 million v-kms a day to 20.13 million v-kms in a twelve-year period.

The proposed road user toll system is calculated to have a substantial impact on the total demand for road vehicles, a reduction of 4 per cent (from 20.13 to 19.26 million v-kms per day) in the entire region and a 20 per cent reduction in the Inner City.

The last two bars in the figure illustrate the influence on total road traffic volumes in the Stockholm region of two different growth scenarios, one with a modest growth in population and income and the other with a more rapid growth rate on both population and income. The difference amounts to 11 per cent for the same year, 2005 (from 19.85 to 21.99 million v-kms), which is much more than the predicted effect of traffic growth in the coming twelve-year period and also greater than the road toll effect for the whole region.

Compared to these forecasted changes in the traffic levels, the corresponding changes due to various levels of the road infrastructure seem to be rather modest. The bars shown as "impact of road infrastructure" reveal a maximal difference of 3 per cent between the "2005 null alternative plus road tolls" and the alternative "2005 traffic package; tolls, 4 new road links". The impacts of the proposed new road infrastructure will be elaborated below.

3.4.3. The estimated impacts on road traffic demand

The morning car trip time is estimated to amount to 55.5 minutes as an average for the Stockholm region, with only part of the complete ring around the Inner City. Slightly less than 231 000 car trips are associated with this scenario.

A calculation of part of the road traffic demand curve with a varied number of new road links is presented in Figure 4. below:

Figure 4. Calculated trips and trip time for car traffic in 2005

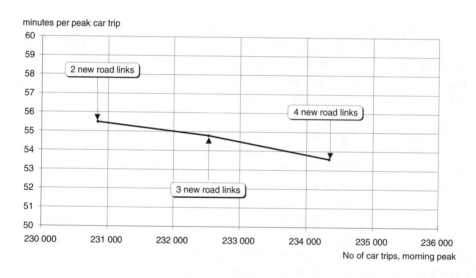

Adding another new road link project, i.e. the Eastern Ring, which completes the full first ring ("3 new road links") reduces the trip time by 0.7 minutes (corresponding to a -1.3 per cent decrease). The corresponding demand effect is calculated to be an increase in the number of car trips by 0.7 per cent and to a travel time elasticity of -0.58.

264

Adding then the Western Outer Bypass reduces car trip time even more, to 53.6 minutes or by almost 2 minutes (-3.4 per cent). Car trip demand expands by 3 500 trips in the morning peak period or by 1.5 per cent, according to the forecasts made. This corresponds to travel time elasticity of -0.44. As the demand model is non-linear[1], the elasticity is specific to this scenario and is, therefore, not constant.

As the demand model is elastic and contains both mode choice, destination choice and trip frequency choice effects, a change in the road infrastructure will affect, among other things, the modal split between car and public transport trips.

Figure 5. **Estimated mode choice effects of road infrastructure in 2005**

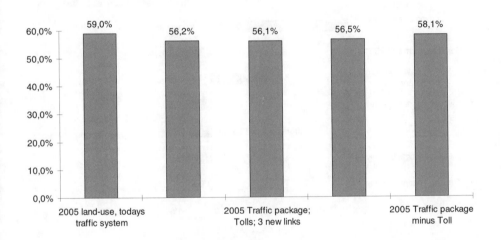

In the 2005 base scenario with only the future land-use effects, a 59 per cent car trip mode choice is calculated. Including public transport projects, "2 new road links" (the northern and southern link) as well as road user tolls, is altogether estimated to reduce the share of car trips to 56.2 per cent.

Adding another road link, the Eastern Bypass would not, in this specific case, influence the modal split more than marginally (and would indeed *reduce* car traffic).

Then adding the new Western Bypass (the Outer Ring Road) is estimated to increase the modal share for car trips from 56.2 to 56.5 per cent compared to the "2 new road links" alternative.

The modal effects are identified, but not very important in their magnitude.

The various types of estimated effects from the model forecasts are summarised in Figure 6. below:

Figure 6. **Estimated impacts of road infrastructure in Stockholm in 2005**

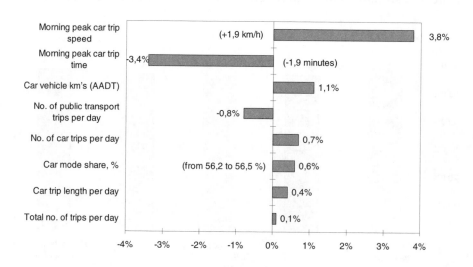

The demand model results indicate a minor influence (+0.1 per cent) on the number of total trips (car plus public transport) of the proposed new road links. Car trip length is estimated to increase slightly (by 0.4 per cent) in the comparison between 2 and 4 new road projects.

In the corresponding comparison, the mode choice effect is 0.6 per cent, as described above.

The number of car trips per day will expand by 0.7 per cent, and the number of public transport trips will decrease by 0.8 per cent due to the new facility. Total car traffic vehicle-kilometres (v-kms) is estimated to increase by 1.1 per cent, which is the product of more and slightly longer car trips.

However, these minor changes cause substantial improvements in car accessibility, as the morning car trip time would be reduced by 2 minutes or by 3.4 per cent, or -- seen as the car speed -- an increase of 3.8 per cent (almost 2 km/h). This is the consequence of a slight reduction in the level of congestion.

The impact of the road projects presented above could be compared to estimated impacts of the entire Traffic Agreement, containing ring road projects, public transport projects and a road toll system. The corresponding effects are illustrated in Figure 7. below.

Figure 7. **Estimated impacts of the Traffic Agreement in 2005 in Stockholm County**

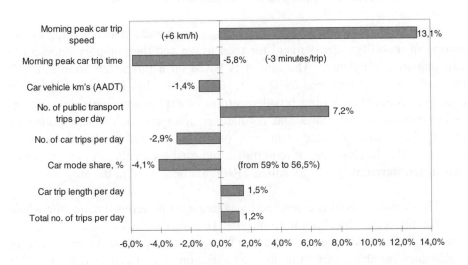

Compared to the road projects, the entire traffic package yields effects that are slightly more substantial. Total number of trips (car plus public transport) will increase by 1.2 per cent. The number of car trips will fall by almost 3 per cent, while public transport trips are calculated to expand by more than 7 per cent. This would, in turn, reduce the car modal split from 59 to 56.2 per cent, which is a 4 per cent drop in the mode share. The car traffic mileage will be reduced by 1.4 per cent in the entire region (while by 30 per cent in the inner city).

Car trip time at morning peak hours is estimated to drop by 3 minutes (or almost 6 per cent), with a corresponding speed increase of 6 km/h (or 3 per cent). The reduced level of congestion from the road tolls, as well as improved public transport, would bring substantial benefits in accessibility to the prevailing car users.

How reliable and realistic are these model exercises? In the next chapter, we will describe an *ex post* analysis of road traffic volumes in Stockholm during a 25-year period, to draw some conclusions on the role of infrastructure.

4. A TIME-SERIES *EX POST* APPROACH

4.1. The DRAG model approach for Stockholm, 1970-1995

The DRAG philosophy aims at creating an enhanced understanding of two aspects of mobility: the demand for road usage and the complex interactions affecting road accidents. The notion is based on a three-step approach, *risk exposure, accident rate and its severity*. A database has been created for the County of Stockholm with a broad spectrum of explanatory variables, such as socioeconomic factors, laws and regulations, road and public transport data, vehicle fleet data, climate data and other related information aiming at explaining the development of road traffic and road accidents *ex post*. A special statistical programme package, called TRIO[2] has been used in the analysis.

The demand model is estimated on aggregate time series data for the whole area (in this case, Stockholm County). The idea is to explain both traffic volumes (vehicle-kilometres) and road accidents by a wide spectrum of explanatory variables, exploiting the vast variation in the monthly data set. This technique is called DRAG (*Demand for Road use, Accidents and their Gravity*) and has been developed by Professor Marc Gaudry at the Transport Research Centre, University of Montreal, Canada.

In our application of the DRAG approach in the Stockholm region, the following time-series models have been carried out on a monthly basis for the period 1970-95:

-- An EXPOSURE model of total road mileage (vehicle-kilometres) for petrol passenger cars;

-- A FREQUENCY model of total number of road accidents with personal injuries and deaths;
-- A SEVERITY model of the:
  - number of light injuries per road accident;
  - number of severe injuries per road accident;
  - number of fatal deaths per road accident.

Analogous DRAG models have been carried out in Canada, Germany and are being developed in France and Norway[3.]

4.2. The demand for road use in Stockholm County, 1970-95

4.2.1. The model

In TRIO, a demand model function is specified as follows: :

$$\frac{y_t^{\lambda_y}-1}{\lambda_y}=\beta_0+\beta_k\sum(\frac{x_{kt}^{\lambda_k}-1}{\lambda_k})+u_t$$

where

y_t = the dependent variable for month t

β_0 = the constant term

β_k = the estimated regression coefficient

x_{kt} = the independent variable x_k:s value for month t

$\lambda_k resp \lambda_y$ = the so-called lambda-parameters for the independent variable x_k and for the dependent y-variable, i.e. a scale factor also estimated on the data set and which transforms the model or to a certain mathematical form. As a special case, when lambda is = 1, you get a linear model, and if lambda is = 0, you get a logarithmic model. This transformation is called "Box-Cox" transformation;

and

$$u_t = v_t f(Z_t)^{\frac{1}{2}},$$

$$v_t = \sum_{t=1}^{r} \rho_l v_{t-l} + \omega_t,$$

where

Z_t = a vector of heteroskedastic variables

u_t = the error term (the residual vector) depending on the heteroskedasticity

v_t = the error term (the residual vector) which is assumed to be dependent in the auto-correlation of the model

and finally

ρ_l = the so-called auto-regressive (time lag) parameters, which are also estimated and carry information about the time lag in the model

ω_t = the third stage vector of residuals.

4.2.2. Road traffic growth in Stockholm County 1970-1995

During the 25-year period 1970-1995, road traffic grew by 88 per cent in Stockholm County:

Figure 8. **Road traffic growth per month in Stockholm County, 1970-1995**

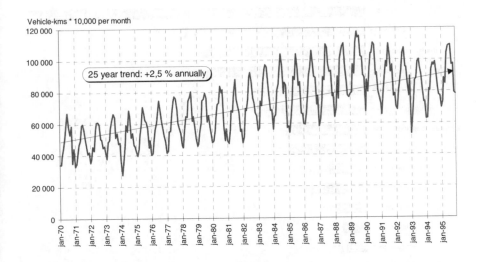

The seasonal variation is substantial -- some 50-60 per cent between peak and off-peak month (summer-winter). The average annual growth rate of the car traffic volume amounts to 2.5 per cent.

How much of this growth might be attributable to road infrastructure improvements and how much is a result of other factors? We will try to answer this question in Section 4.2.6 below.

4.2.3.   Overall transport trends in Stockholm County, 1970-1995

The rapid development of car traffic in Stockholm County during the last 35 years cannot be explained by any single factor. Rather, there is a wide range of factors which contribute to this augmentation. In Figure 9. below, some key factors of importance to car traffic growth are presented in per cent change between 1970 and 1995:

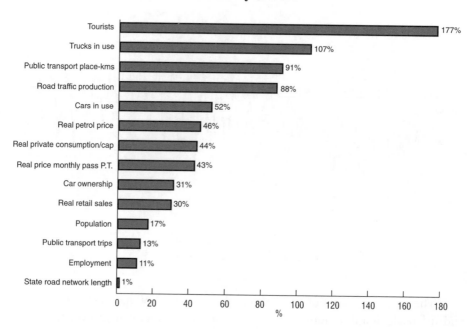

Figure 9. Overall transport trends in Stockholm County -- some key factors

Public transport supply has almost doubled and increased even more than road traffic vehicle-kilometres. But public transport demand has only increased by 13 per cent over the last 25 years. Real petrol prices have increased slightly more than public transport fares, 46 compared to 43 per cent. The car park, measured as cars in use, is in 1995 more than 50 per cent larger than in 1970.

The Stockholm County population has grown by 16 per cent in the last 25 years, i.e. some 250 000 more inhabitants; employment went up by 185 000 persons from 1970 to 1990, but declined by 115 000 persons between 1990 and 1994 due to the economic recession.

On the other hand, the length of the state road network has only expanded by 1 per cent, i.e. it is of almost the same length as in 1970. Most new road links have replaced older ones.

4.2.4. DRAG model results -- Estimated elasticities

Table 3. summarises the model results in terms of average elasticities. The "demand for road use" model for the period 1970-1995 for Stockholm County is presented in terms of average elasticities, with respect **to the number of vehicle-kilometres per month**, which is the dependent variable.

Table 3. **20 factors explain car traffic growth 1970-1995[4]**

No.	Dependent variable: Vehicle-kms per month Explanatory variables	Average elasticity 1970-1995	t-value
	Economic activities		
1	Employment (days)	+ 1.107	(4.72)
2	Retail sales per employed in constant prices	+ 0.267	(7.64)
3	Leisure activity (holidays per working day)	+ 0.211	(4.23)
4	Holiday *per se*	+ 0.554	(4.41)
5	Population per employed	-0.433	(2.09)
6	No. of tourists per vehicle-km	- 0.102	(3.98)
	The Car park		
7	No. of cars in use per employed	+ 0.536	(2.11)
8	No. of cars in use per employed (squared)	- 0.255	(-2.70)
	Prices & public transport		
9	Real petrol price	- 0.280	(-3.92)
10	Public transport improvements- dummy	(- 0.047)	(-0.72)
	Road network & restrictions		
11	New road links	+ 0.262	(3.78)
12	Parking restrictions in Inner City	(+ 0.046)	(0.80)
13	Temporary speed limits	(-0.022)	(-0.93)
14	Petrol rationing, Jan -74	- 0.098	(-2.98)
	Climate and calendar data		
15	Average temperature per month	+ 0.057	(5.27)
16	No. of snow days per month	- 0.029	(-3.39)
17	Share of day/night 06-24 with darkness	- 0.168	(-7.30)
18	No. of work-days per month	+ 0.632	(6.12)
19	No. of other days per month	(+0.0201)	(0.43)
	Special events		
20	The Kuwait war dummy	-0.051	(-1.04)
	Lambda 1-value for activity and price variables	*0.532*	(7.58)
	Lambda 2-value for variable no. 7	*1.507*	(0.43)
	Auto-regressive term: Rho: t-1	0.272	(+4.18)
	Auto-regressive term: Rho: t-2	-0.264	(-4.79)
	Auto-regressive term: Rho: t-12	0.129	(-1.80)
	Percentage explained by the model R^2	**96.5 %**	

Note! Elasticities within parentheses are not significant at the 90 % confidence level .

The vehicle-kms are calculated through petrol sales records per month, and adjusted for the fuel-efficiency of the car fleet, but also for the average monthly temperature. As the temperature falls below 8 centigrade (Celsius), fuel consumption increases per kilometre, and even more as the temperature falls beyond freezing point.

The 20 factors of the model explain 96.5 per cent of the total variation in traffic production (v-kms) during the last 25-year period.

Economic activities

The "locomotive" among the explanatory variables is the *employment variable*. A 10 per cent increase in the number of employed is estimated to enhance the number of vehicle-kms by 15 per cent. Increased employment produces higher personal income, which in turn leads to higher car ownership and this governs much of the activities in the urban area, such as private consumption and leisure activities. A one per cent population growth without any increase in employment, on the other hand, reduces car traffic by 0.4 per cent. To summarise, employed persons use the car, while others use public transport or the walk/bike mode.

The demand for transport is a derived demand. The demand for all those activities creates the demand for mobility, not income *per se*. That is why we have not inserted a household or personal income variable, but measured the demand via five activity variables.

As *real retail sales* increase by 10 per cent, road traffic increases by 2.7 per cent, according to the time-series model. This indicator measures the effect of shopping trips on total road traffic demand. The corresponding elasticity of 0.27 for Stockholm could be compared to a very similar result obtained in both Quebec (Canada) and in Germany. In Quebec, the corresponding elasticity has been calculated to 0.25 and in Germany to 0.24; thus, these findings are highly consistent with each other[5].

The car park

The car park in Stockholm County -- which has grown by 52 per cent from 385 000 cars in use in 1970 to 587 000 cars in use in 1995 -- has contributed to an increase in the road traffic volume. However, our analysis shows that the elasticity is 0.54. We have traced a non-linear impact: at extremely high loads on the road network, i.e. during the summer and holiday period, congestion itself seems to cause a *negative* effect by -0.25 on road traffic usage.

A similar low impact of the car park on road usage has also been revealed in a similar DRAG model for Germany, where petrol demand was estimated during a period between 1968 and 1983 (also on monthly data)[6]. The elasticity obtained was 0.11, which is even lower than our Stockholm result of 0.29 (on average). Given a certain activity level and other things being equal, the size of the car park does not have any decisive effect on car usage.

An increase in the *number of leisure days* by 10 per cent is estimated to increase road traffic by 7.6 per cent, according to the combined effect of leisure *per se* and of the number of holidays. If, on the other hand, a 1 per cent change in the number of work days is transferred to a 1 per cent increase in the number of holidays, the net effect will be a 3.5 per cent reduction in total car traffic volumes.

The road network

New road links might affect road traffic in several different ways. New urban land is "produced" or opened up, so to speak, by connecting new residential or commercial areas with a new road or street. In such a case, it would be natural to recognise an increase in road traffic, as the new road facility opens the new area for mobility.

Another case is recognised as a quality improvement, when a low quality road/street is replaced by a new, more comfortable road/street facility. It might be more straightforward: a wider road with more lanes allowing higher speeds. Car trip times would be reduced and, in this way, it is also natural to imagine the new road link might attract more road traffic.

However, in a third case, a new road facility might *reduce* total vehicle mileage in the entire urban area. This would be the case when a new road link replaces a former, cumbersome bottleneck. To avoid travel-time losses, car drivers used to reschedule their routes to another less direct route, simply to avoid excess congestion over the bottleneck. This would cause excessive vehicle-kilometres to be produced. But with the new road link, the bottleneck is gone, the road users can now take their shortest path not only in time but also in distance travelled and, as a consequence, the overall vehicle-kilometres might be reduced.

Using the time-series model presented above, we have traced both of these effects. On average, 10 per cent more new road links yields 2.6 per cent more road traffic kilometres.

One might argue that enhanced *parking restrictions* in the city centre ought to lead to a reduction in overall road traffic volumes. The reason should be that parking restrictions function like price rises. Our findings reveal, on the contrary, that car drivers, in order to avoid higher parking fees and penalties, probably drive more kilometres in total just to avoid being charged. After 25 years of a continuously sharpened parking policy in the city centre, road traffic has grown by 4.6 per cent in the whole area. However, this effect is not statistically significant; so the conclusion must be interpreted with caution.

Temporary speed limits on urban motorways (110 km/h reduced to 90 km/h during Summer 1979 and from Summer 1989 to Spring 1992) have contributed to a reduction in overall road traffic by 2 per cent. This effect is not significant; therefore, this effect should also be interpreted with caution.

Public transport

We have not been able to show any significant impact from the visible enlargement of the metro network in Stockholm (which took place in the 1970s and early 1980s) on road traffic volumes. This is not to say that there was no such influence; only that it has not been possible to reveal it through the time-series model used. Other public transport improvements (such as new bus networks and new bus terminals) seem to have a minor impact on car traffic - a road traffic kilometres elasticity of -0.05 is found. This means that such measures have contributed to reduce the car traffic volume by 5 per cent during the period 1970-95, although not significantly estimated.

Petrol price

The Petrol price affects the demand for road traffic (v-kms). As the petrol price is increased by 10 per cent in real terms, car traffic would be reduced by 2.8 per cent according to the estimated average price elasticity of -0.28 during the 25-year period. This direct petrol price elasticity seems to be of a reasonable magnitude. From other time-series models, e.g. the one by Marc Gaudry in Quebec, a gasoline price elasticity of -0.25 was estimated. The above-mentioned German study by Ulrich Blum reported a resulting gasoline price elasticity of -0.28, i.e. exactly the same size as our Stockholm results indicate.

Impact of new road links

We have tested a great number of traffic system variables that might have influenced the traffic growth rate in the Stockholm region during the last 25 years.

Traffic zoning might lead to an *increase* in the overall road traffic volumes, due to the fact that it forces the car users to divert from the shortest path and drive a longer route. A 9 per cent increase has been identified, although this variable is not significant. It should be interpreted with caution, and this phenomenon should be further investigated.

During the time period 1970-1995, some 35 different road projects have been identified. We have tested their impact on total road mileage using a two-way approach. In one approach, we have constructed a common "quasi-dummy variable", which takes a "one" if it is a real new road link, a "½" if it is only a ramp. Adding another link gives a "two" and so on. The variable "new link" and its time profile is shown below:

"Newlink" dummy-variable

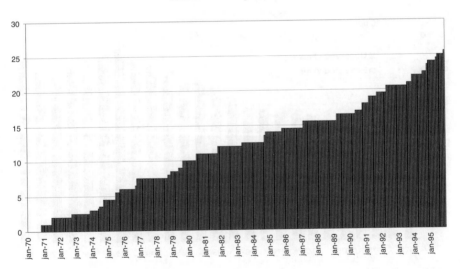

From the figure above, it could be seen that some ten new road projects were inaugurated in the 1970s. The next ten road projects were opened for traffic during a 12 to 13-year period; while some nine new road projects have been put in operation during the first half of the 1990s.

A 1 per cent increase in the number of new road links is estimated to cause a 0.26 per cent increase in the overall road traffic volume (v-kms).

Obviously, most new road projects might have a substantial *local* impact on traffic flows. Often, in the case of the new infrastructure facility being a bypass, it has contributed to a desired diversion of traffic flows away from central city streets. This means that disturbing motorised traffic would be rerouted to other more peripheral or orbital routes, which are less onerous for pedestrians and other sensitive categories of travellers.

4.2.5. *Comparison between model estimated and actual road traffic demand*

The performance of the vehicle-km model is shown below, where the observed and model-estimated traffic production (v-kms) are compared on a yearly basis:

Figure 10. Comparison between observed and estimated road vehicle kilometres in Stockholm County, 1971-1995

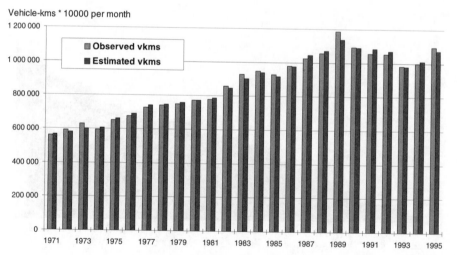

The overall correspondence between observed and estimated vehicle kilometres is quite good. For a single year, the deviations between model and reality vary between 0 and 3 per cent, with some very few exceptions:

--   In 1973, the model underestimates the observed road mileage by 6.5 per cent;

--   In 1989, the model underestimates the observed road mileage by 5.2 per cent.

In both cases, the time period could be characterised by an exceptional increase in road traffic over the past years.

4.2.6. The contribution of road infrastructure to road traffic growth

The single most dominant contributor to the road traffic expansion in Stockholm County during the last 25 years seems to be leisure and shopping activities, according to our model estimates. These activities explain one-third of the increase in the number of car-kilometres produced.

Figure 11. **Contribution to road traffic growth in Stockholm County 1970-1995, %**

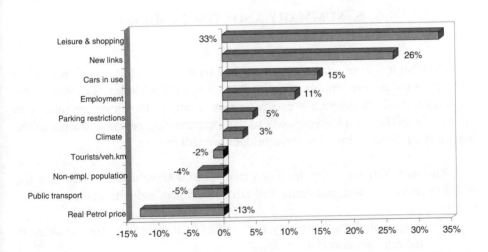

Rising employment adds an additional 11 per cent to the total. The 50 per cent increase in the car park (cars in use) contributes with a 15 per cent increase in the number of car-kilometres. Parking restrictions and the somewhat warmer climate together add to 8 per cent.

Factors which have contributed to a decline in road mileage are rising petrol prices, improved public transport services and a rising proportion of non-employed persons (during the last five years).

The road infrastructure factor, measured by the quasi-dummy variable "new road links", seems to have contributed to the total growth of car traffic by one fourth (+26 per cent). However, it is important to realise that this measure of the *ex post* impacts of road infrastructure is an indirect way of monitoring its impact. With this quasi-dummy variable we have tried to grasp the real travel time gains produced by the new road facility. As we do not have access to complete travel time matrices for each year of the entire time period, this has been a proxy method for such an ambitious approach.

5. SUMMARY AND CONCLUSIONS

In Chapter 2 of this paper, an empirical case study was presented illustrating the *ex post* impact of a city motorway in Stockholm. In 1966, a city motorway, the Essingeleden Western Bypass, a part of the first ring road, was opened for traffic. It added capacity to the three existing bridges, leading to the inner city of Stockholm. The three bridges are still in operation.

The new infrastructure facility carries 115 000 vehicles a day and the major impacts revealed, and conserved after 30 years of evidence, are:

-- Augmented road capacity contributes to increased traffic volumes in the relevant corridor;
-- A city bypass, constructed to divert traffic from central parts of an inner-city area, could relieve over-heavy loads on city roads and really **divert** them to the new bypass, more suited to carrying such heavy loads;
-- An urban bypass -- at least in a medium-sized city like Stockholm -- could play its role as a bypass over a long period of time, even if road traffic as a whole is steadily expanding.

In Chapter 3 of this paper, an *ex ante* study and forecasts of the ongoing Stockholm Traffic Agreement are presented, with the year 2005 as the time horizon. The method used for the traffic forecasts is a highly disaggregated full travel demand nested-logit model system, FREDRIK, with the EMME/2 system as the supply model of road and public transport network characteristics. The traffic package contains both new ring roads (the completion of the first ring and a second Western Bypass), enhanced public transport projects (e.g. radial rail upgrading and a new, tangential LRT line) and a road user toll system. The major findings from various studies of the impacts of new road infrastructure are:

-- Compared to variations in the assumptions of the possible growth rates in population, household/personal income and car ownership, the impact of a new road facility seems to be of limited scope;

-- The difference in total urban vehicle-kilometres produced between limited road building (2 new ring-road links) and the full road package (4 new ring-road links) is estimated to be 3 per cent. An explanation of this limited effect might be the fact that road user tolls reduce the overall demand for car traffic, something that has not been implemented in Sweden so far;

-- A wide range of changes in the road trip pattern is likely to occur, as new road space (comparison between 2 and 4 new road projects) relieves the present level of congestion. The major results from the model system are:

- The car trips will be marginally longer (0.4 per cent);
- The number of car trips will increase (0.7 per cent);
- The car mode share will increase marginally (from 56.2 to 56.5 per cent);
- The number of public transport trips will be slightly reduced (-0.8 per cent);
- The number of car-kilometres will expand (1.1 per cent);
- The peak trip time by car will be substantially reduced (-3.4 per cent);
- The peak car speed will be substantially increased (3.8 per cent).

All these figures are results of a wide range of assumptions and are predicted effects from the travel demand-supply model system. The future transport environment is, however, impossible to foresee. In real life, many other external factors will involve and influence the actual trip pattern and behaviour. How uncertain could these model results then be?

In the fourth chapter of this paper, an *ex post* approach has been adopted to estimate the role of the road infrastructure on car traffic levels in Stockholm County. This is achieved by using a time-series model based on petrol sales on a monthly basis during the last 25 years between 1970 and 1995.

Car traffic -- measured as the number of vehicle-kilometres produced -- has increased by 88 per cent, or by 2.5 per cent annually. The demand model contains some twenty explanatory factors, by which 96.5 per cent of the total variation in the v-km demand is explained. The most important findings from the time-series model, with respect to the role of road infrastructure, are:

-- New road links might increase road traffic, as the new road facility opens up new residential and commercial areas for mobility;
-- A new road facility might *reduce* total vehicle mileage in the entire urban area. This would be the case when a new road link replaces a former bottleneck. This relieves congestion and enables car drivers to take another, shorter path, with less vehicle-kilometres produced;
-- On average, the time-series model results indicate that all new road links established in the Stockholm region since 1970 have contributed to an increase by 26 per cent in overall car-kilometres.

To summarise, it seems clear that augmented supply creates its own demand, even for road space. The exact magnitude varies over time and in space according to the local circumstances, the overall socioeconomic climate and economic welfare.

It is still a challenge to assess both the *ex ante* and *ex post* impacts of new infrastructure and well worth devoting even more attention to theoretical and empirical research.

NOTES

1. Nested logit models.

2. TRIO is a statistical programme package for multiple regression model estimation of dependent variables of the types "level", "share" and "probability". TRIO has been developed by Prof. Marc Gaudry at the *Centre de Recherche sur les Transports* (CRT) at the University of Montreal, Canada.

3. *Source 1:* "Application of Econometric Model DRAG-2 to Road Travel Demand in Quebec", Proceedings of the Canadian Multidisciplinary Road Safety Conference VIII, June 14-16, 1993, Saskatoon, Saskatchewan. By M. Gaudry, CRT, University of Montreal, Quebec, F. Fournier and R. Simard, Société de l'assurance automobile du Quebec;
    Source 2: "Aggregate Time-Series Gasoline Demand Models: Review of the Literature and New Evidence for West Germany", by Ulrich C.H. Blum, Gertraud Foos and Marc Gaudry, *Transportation Research A.*, Vol. 22A, No. 2, pp. 75-88, 1988.

4. Model variant: acvehkmbc:64.

5. Source: "Application of Econometric Model DRAG-2 to Road Travel Demand in Quebec", M. Gaudry, F. Fournier and R. Simard, Proceedings of the Canadian Multidisciplinary Road Safety Conference, June 14-16, 1993, Saskatoon, Saskatchewan.

6. Source: "Aggregate Time-Series Gasoline Demand Models: Review of the Literature and New Evidence for West Germany", by Ulrich C.H. Blum, Gertraud Foos and Marc Gaudry, *Transportation Research A.*, Vol. 22A, No. 2, pp. 75-88, 1988.

BIBLIOGRAPHY

Göran Tegnér, Staffan Algers and Stein Hansen (1974), *"On the Evaluation of Comfort and Convenience -- A Choice Analytic Approach"*, Papers and Proceedings from Transport Research Forum 15th Annual Meeting, Vol. XV, No. 1, San Francisco, USA.

Göran Tegnér, Staffan Algers and Stein Hansen (1975), *"Role of Waiting Time, Comfort and Convenience in the Choice of Mode for the Journey to Work"*, Transportation Research Record No. 534, Washington DC.

Swedish Council for Building Research (1979), *"Sweden's state-of-the-art Report to the International Collaborative Study on Factors Affecting Public Transport Patronage"*, Document D7:1979, Stockholm, Sweden.

Göran Tegnér (1983), *"The Stockholm Experience -- Ten Years of Experience from Travel Demand Modelling -- and Ten Important Conclusions"*, paper presented at the World Conference on Transportation Research (WCTR) in Hamburg, 26-29 April.

(1984), *"Transportation Planning Problems, Travel Demand Modelling and Political Decision-Making -- the Stockholm Experience"*, paper presented to the Transport Research Conference, Zandvoort, Holland, September.

(1985), *"The Use of Service Standards in Urban Public Transport Planning"*, paper presented at the 46th International Congress of the International Union of Public Transport (UITP), in Brussels, Belgium, 19-24 May.

Göran Tegnér and Staffan Algers, TRANSEK AB, Solna, Sweden (1986), *"The Role of Quantitative Methods in Urban Transport Planning -- the Stockholm Experience"*, paper presented at the International Seminar on "The Management and Planning of Urban Transport Systems -- from Theory to Practice", University of Montreal, Canada, 25-29 August.

Göran Tegnér, Gunnar Lind, Esbjörn Lindqvist, TRANSEK AB, Solna, Sweden (1990), "*A Coherent Transport Strategy for a Better Environment in the Stockholm Metropolitan Region*", paper presented at the Council of Europe Standing Conference of Local and Regional Authorities of Europe, Improving Traffic and Quality of Life in Metropolitan Areas, Gothenburg, 12-14 June.

European Parliament Scientific and Technological Options Assessment (STOA), Directorate General for Research (1994), "*Improving Infrastructures and Traffic Management Systems in Northern European Cities: the Example of Stockholm Metropolitan Region*", in: "STOA Study on The Technological City - - ideas and experiments in urban organization of mobility, transport, production and services", Final Report, June.

G. Johansson-Sverder, P. Nylander and G. Tegnér, TRANSEK AB, "*Efficient Road Pricing -- an Assessment of Dynamic Road User Tolls in the Stockholm Region*", in: J.M. Baldasano Recio, L.J. Sucharov (eds.), Urban Transport and the Environment II, Computational Mechanics Publications.

SUMMARY OF DISCUSSIONS

SUMMARY

1. INTRODUCTION

Mobility cannot be treated as a conventional economic good, in that higher consumption does not automatically translate into a greater net benefit to the community. The reason for this is that private car usage generates negative externalities which have numerous and far-reaching implications. The existence of congestion demonstrates that infrastructure, rather than being a public good, should be viewed as a private good associated with externalities. The problem in the transport sector is that the cost of such externalities is not adequately covered by the price of transport. Since the restraint that would normally be exerted by appropriate pricing does not apply in this instance, it would be reasonable to assume that consumption of transport services is too high. Although it is true that the use of transport services can be justified in terms of other activities, the transport sector undoubtedly fails to make optimum use of scarce resources such as the environment. To complicate matters further, transport infrastructure is increasingly being tailored to a given mode or, in some cases, a given type of vehicle. By reducing journey times, such infrastructure enables users to make certain types of trip that had not been possible beforehand.

It would therefore be fair to ask whether the provision of better infrastructure, in terms of ease of use or faster journey times, generates greater mobility by encouraging individual users to avail themselves of the additional capacity available. If induced traffic is omitted from analyses, there is a danger that the failure to properly assess congestion or environmental nuisances will result in the anticipated benefits of a given project being overestimated. These were the areas on which discussions at the Round Table primarily focused. Participants reviewed these major issues and their implications in two stages. They first attempted to collate what was actually known about induced traffic (section 2 of this report, "The evidence for induced traffic") before proceeding with a more detailed analysis (section 3) of the methodological and policy implications of the evidence collected.

2. THE EVIDENCE FOR INDUCED TRAFFIC

The first step in attempting to gain an understanding of the nature of induced traffic is to clarify the theoretical concepts involved and, in particular, to define precisely what is meant by "induced traffic". In this respect, the Round Table decided to adopt the definition proposed in the report by Messrs. Cerwenka and Hauger, to the effect that new, induced traffic is the additional traffic which an enhanced transport supply (or the extension or upgrading of infrastructure) makes possible and which, as a result, is attributable to users who partly or fully realise this potential.

However, this definition does not cover all aspects of the process. The composition of induced traffic, for example, can vary within a given geographical area, over time, etc. Moreover, induced traffic has major implications for policy in that traffic is not simply a response to new infrastructure, but reflects a genuine need for mobility on the part of individual users. What matters most and can be measured through direct observation, is the volume of total traffic. It should be noted that induced traffic also has implications for the financing of infrastructure by the private sector, since the size of such traffic has a direct impact on the profitability of an investment. Determining the volume of induced traffic requires a comparison of two different types of parameter, one empirical (level of traffic if new infrastructure is built) and the other, theoretical (level of traffic without the new infrastructure). There can, therefore, be no certainty over the result; the best that can be achieved is an approximate estimate of induced traffic. Furthermore, the outcome will depend upon the time over which the phenomenon is studied, since induced traffic is a process and not a fixed constant.

Attempting to define induced traffic can be misleading. There is no reason to give priority to induced traffic over total traffic. The only traffic component which can be modelled is new traffic, since induced traffic cannot be measured directly. Again, it is only possible to measure total traffic. Defining induced traffic is not necessarily a useful exercise, therefore -- all that counts is the level of traffic before and after the provision of new infrastructure.

The provision of new road capacity does not, of itself, generate additional traffic, it simply accommodates it. Additional traffic is generated by economic and social activities. The volume and nature of such traffic will therefore be determined by a set of social activities. As a general rule, the provision of additional capacity brings about changes in travel patterns which may, as a result of the extra traffic generated, result in lower than expected increases in traffic speeds.

There is empirical, theoretical and historical evidence of the existence of traffic induced by new road capacity. However, this evidence does not offer a reliable means (i.e. *a priori* and *ex post facto* calculation) of determining the volume of induced traffic. There are, for example, many behavioural responses that can lead to additional traffic. The volume of such traffic varies substantially according to local circumstances and factors of a primarily macroeconomic nature. In the long term, induced traffic can be influenced by higher wages, the cost of using private cars and the price and attractiveness of other modes. At the local level, the volume of induced traffic will depend upon the size of the new investment in capacity (i.e. the higher speeds it allows), existing congestion, local geographical conditions (land use for different activities) and the existence and attractiveness of alternative roads. It should also be noted that the smaller the network, the greater the impact which new infrastructure will have.

In the case of new road infrastructure, as several independent forecasts show, mobility can be expected to increase on average by 10 per cent in the short term and by 20 per cent in the longer term, although the spread is extremely large in that induced traffic can vary, according to circumstances, from 0 to 40 per cent.

Many of the experts attending the Round Table commented that analyses of induced traffic are based on the assumption that conditions elsewhere remain unchanged, which does not make sense inasmuch as changes in the economic and social context (e.g. a factory closure) can also be responsible for induced traffic or variations in traffic volume and that traffic generation and changes in traffic volume are studied over the long term.

Induced traffic can only be observed within a clearly delineated spatial area, for which there are sufficient data available over a long period of time and in which there has been a significant improvement in the supply of infrastructure. This is rarely the case, however and undoubtedly explains the limitations of existing case studies. Furthermore, induced traffic does not correspond solely to the increase in traffic levels. There are significant non-linear effects characterised by simultaneous increases and decreases in different types of traffic.

What needs to be determined from the few complete examples available is the type of mobility involved. This can be ascertained from data surveys, even though there is no general rule which can subsequently be modelled. It may prove in the long term, for example, that households and firms relocate, thus influencing the volume of traffic. In view of this, analysing trends over a period of twelve months is not sufficient, several years of data are needed as input, since the novelty effect during the first year may generate a sharp increase in traffic which may not recur in subsequent years.

Individual users may be attracted by the novelty of new infrastructure, resulting in a surge in induced traffic followed by a gradual decrease over time. Indeed, there are several stages which can be distinguished in the generation of induced traffic. The first stage is one of equilibrium in the short term, followed by a second stage, in the longer term, in which other factors such as relocation come into play as users take full advantage of the opportunities afforded by the new infrastructure. It is not only households which move to new locations, firms too can relocate to take advantage of new transport capacity. It is therefore important to look at all aspects of the phenomenon of induced traffic.

Possible changes in user behaviour include changes in the time at which journeys are made, in routes and even in mode of transport, as well as relocation, as mentioned above, to take advantage of the opportunities offered by the new infrastructure. In considering the reasons for which a change may be made, it is clear that a change of route or in the time at which a given journey is made may be decided on a day-to-day basis. A change of mode, on the other hand, involves a change in routine, which users may be encouraged to make in response to the provision of new and attractive transport infrastructure. Habits may also change as a result of a move to a new job but, on average, people change jobs only every four or five years and move house, on average, every seven years (UK statistics).

These observations show that travel patterns need to be placed in a wider socio-economic context. Another example worth mentioning is the French high-speed train, the TGV, which has been shown to generate more frequent but shorter trips. Indeed, this type of pattern can also be seen in Europe in other areas of activity such as recreational trips. An enhanced transport supply can be seen as the product of a society which creates a transport supply in order to meet needs arising from social change (in this case, the time savings which allow users to travel more frequently). Mobility thus changes and will increase in response to societal change, even though it remains constrained by prices and time.

With regard to journey times, the Round Table touched upon the subject of constant travel-time "budgets" and noted that analyses and surveys appeared to indicate the existence of such a phenomenon. However, this view was contested by some of the participants at the Round Table who felt that there was no hard evidence of such practices. Nevertheless, in terms of mobility, it does seem as though users take advantage of infrastructural improvements to travel further in the same period of time by moving their homes, for example, to the outer areas of cities. This is a perfect illustration of the principle that the provision of new infrastructure generates traffic which will make full use of the new facilities.

The example was cited in the course of the Round Table of cities (reference was made above all to Munich) which had increased the supply of public transport but which, in doing so, had encouraged users to move to outer areas of the city where they became dependent on the use of cars. It is therefore not only new roads which induce road traffic; and the impact, in this instance, is particularly long-lasting. The supply of public transport can also induce user demand for new road infrastructure. This shows how hard it is to predict the consequences of providing new infrastructure of any kind, in this case because it was not possible to foresee the level of car ownership of households or the fact that households would use the car for tasks such as shopping.

It is clear from the analysis of different types of induced traffic that situations vary widely, thus reflecting the complexity of the real world. Large-scale infrastructure networks generate additional traffic but at the same time concentrate this mobility within a small number of heavily-travelled corridors, thus precipitating spatial reorganisation. Here again, understanding the subsequent changes in behaviour -- as reflected in altered patterns of mobility -- calls for another type of analysis, that of social change. What individual users are striving to achieve through their responses or changes in behaviour is a better quality of life, which proves that their reactions are based on social considerations. Every actor who makes a trip has a reason for doing so; induced traffic therefore corresponds to derived demand.

The final equilibrium attributable to induced traffic cannot be easily determined, given that rates of adjustment will vary according to local circumstances. There is no general rule that can be applied to all types of new infrastructure regardless of location. Changes in the use of land for residential or other purposes take place over a period of several years. During this time, the impact of factors which influence mobility, such as the cost of car use, road and railway developments, changes in rail fares (and air fares, too, as the case may be), as well as the quality of supply of these modes of transport, will remain unabated. Consequently, as observed earlier in this report, it is hard to determine the precise contribution of individual factors.

3. METHODOLOGICAL AND POLICY IMPLICATIONS OF INDUCED TRAFFIC

While it is a fact that induced traffic benefits from new road capacity, which is therefore a gross benefit to the community, it also contributes to increased congestion and damage to the environment, which therefore reduces -- sometimes substantially -- this gross benefit. The net balance will, in fact, depend upon the degree of existing congestion, with the result that in highly congested areas the net benefit will be reduced, or even negative, if the new investment adds too much traffic to an area that is already congested, with all the concomitant adverse environmental impacts. While the fact that there is induced traffic means that there are users benefiting from new infrastructure, the additional congestion resulting from such traffic places a greater burden on other users. In order to determine the full impact of induced traffic, account must also be taken of the externalities which need to be integrated into cost-benefit analyses.

In some cases, induced traffic can make all the difference in the decision as to whether or not to build the infrastructure, particularly if the latter is to be financed by the private sector, since the volume of induced traffic might be enough to make the investment profitable. However, it needs to be said that the equations are not that straightforward in that the rail sector, too, can generate road traffic. Much depends on local circumstances. It is therefore impossible to design a standard model. The instruments used must not be too sensitive to particular sets of circumstances.

To return to the issue of the assessment of induced mobility (i.e. the volume of induced traffic), it is clearly essential to have hard data available. Ideally, this should take the form of studies "with" and "without" a given infrastructure, but analysts must make do with studies of traffic "before" and "after" construction of the infrastructure. Moreover, it is not enough to have single sets of data before and after construction, several sets of observations are needed from the time the infrastructure is completed. Similarly, it is not enough to study simply a given section of infrastructure, the entire network needs to be studied in order to identify trends, particularly in view of the growing complexity of networks. Studies need to be designed to meet the precise objective pursued and not simply derived from other studies.

Furthermore, there is no single valid methodology for observing and gaining an insight into these phenomena. The best approach would probably be to combine complementary methods, ranging from surveys in the field to theoretical models that assume linkages between certain variables. Models can reveal straightforward causal links but cannot shed any light on the more complex interrelated causal links. It needs to be borne in mind that individual decisions may stem from other decisions. For example, the decision by a firm to relocate can result in the subsequent relocation of some of its employees. Thus, in addition to statistical and model-based approaches, there is a need for more qualitative observation procedures in the case of phenomena that are not induced by causal links. Models make it possible to interpret the data collected from surveys and to eliminate certain effects, such as increases in fuel prices. The ideal solution in some cases would be to have access to firms' statistics, but these are usually confidential.

Since what is important is not only the total volume of induced traffic but also the breakdown of such traffic in terms of trip purpose, the statistical analyses must be extremely detailed in order to shed light on phenomena which remain poorly understood. This argues in favour of collecting full sets of statistics both before and after the construction of new infrastructure in order to gain a better understanding of underlying trends. These trends can also be analysed by models, which should be seen as a complement to a purely statistically-based approach. There is no single approach better suited than another to the observation and interpretation of the phenomenon of induced traffic; instead, the best insight is likely to be obtained through a series of simultaneous analyses. Moreover, surveys alone do not provide sufficient information, but need to be complemented by models in order to interpret the results of surveys, given the lack of instruments for measuring individual behaviour.

Surveys must meet certain fundamental requirements: panels must be stable and users must be representative but not too mobile (therefore no relocation). This shows to what extent reliable statistics are essential, which is one of the conclusions reached by the Round Table. However, the need for high-quality statistics must be balanced against the fact that attempting to obtain highly detailed measurements of induced mobility, simply in numerical terms, would probably be a mistake. Induced mobility is a phenomenon which can only be approached in a highly approximate manner.

The need for reliable statistics can be readily understood if consideration is given to the extent to which basic statistics are crucially important parameters for understanding phenomena and deciding upon the requisite action. It is first necessary to measure a phenomenon before comparing the results of different analyses. Since the collection of statistical data is a necessary step in gaining insight into a given phenomenon, the Round Table suggested that a portion (a very small one in this case) of the money spent on building infrastructure be used to carry out socio-economic surveys of the impacts of the infrastructure in question. In time, this would constitute a valuable source of information which in most cases is simply not available at present. Issues relating to new traffic could thus be integrated into analyses and separated from any ideology. By performing such analyses at regular intervals (every five years, for example), it would thus be possible to incorporate issues which only become apparent in the long term, such as changes in spatial organisation.

With regard to the more policy-related implications of induced traffic, it is clear that although, as noted in the first part of this summary, major systems like high-speed rail generate additional mobility, at the same time they slow the pace of relocation and concentrate travel movements within a limited number of major corridors. As a result, they initiate spatial reorganisation. But is it in the best interests of the community for travel movements to be concentrated within major corridors? While the consideration given to the need for speed reflects the value which society places on speed and time saved, rising levels of inactivity (unemployment) may lead to the emergence of contrasting perceptions of time among the members of that society. While some members of society will continue to place a high value on time savings, other will see matters differently and conflicts may arise between those in favour of new infrastructure and those opposed to it. These conflicts will be centred on the way in which social space, and thus time, are represented and appropriated.

Major infrastructure projects encourage growth in urban areas because of the range of choice they offer to individual users. However, by promoting spatial polarisation around a limited number of major centres, infrastructure increases the density of these centres and thus fuels growth in transport.

It is clear that one of the messages to emerge from the Round Table is that mobility can be shaped by infrastructure policy. However, an understanding of the reasons for changes in behaviour clearly shows, as this summary has already emphasized, that the underlying causes are rooted in social practices. In order to predict changes in mobility, it would therefore be advisable for planners to analyse social trends, such as trends in property purchases.

In this respect, the Round Table again emphasized the important role that models based on sets of given assumptions could play in the identification of potential trends. Some models are of such complexity, however, that policymakers remain deeply sceptical of their ability to predict future trends. Nonetheless, policymakers must not dismiss the input which science can provide in the form of analyses that remain pertinent regardless of the complexity of the technical instrument used, particularly in view of the fact that the results of a given case of induced traffic cannot be transposed to another location. The aim must be to establish the basic reasons for behavioural changes and to do so may require the use of models.

Induced traffic poses the fundamental question as to whether or not mobility is desirable. While greater accessibility is desirable, however, the same is not necessarily true of mobility. It all comes down to the basic question of how to cover the cost of mobility. The cost of mobility in terms of the impact on the environment should be paid for by the user of infrastructure.

This is one of the more direct implications of induced traffic with regard to transport policy, in that the costs of mobility are not covered by those who use the various modes of transport. Either the infrastructural costs are not covered (public transport), or the externalities are not paid for in full (road transport). If the objective is to restrict induced traffic, then transport needs to be appropriately priced, i.e. prices must be sufficiently high to cover the economic, social and environmental costs incurred by traffic. This may consist in greater differentiation of taxes.

Once appropriate road pricing has been introduced at a level which will reduce traffic volume, the portion of the road infrastructure thus made available could be assigned to public transport or environmentally-friendly modes of transport. Indeed, every schoolchild should be taught the importance of taking such environmentally-friendly modes of transport into account whenever their use is feasible.

4. CONCLUSIONS

The economic crisis may challenge society's pursuit of goals such as speed by querying the economic efficiency of speed and the time savings it affords. In fact, situations and individual responses vary substantially, reflecting the complexity of the real world. However, there can be no doubt that the phenomenon of induced mobility is likely to remain with us in the future. It is unfortunate that the statistical data currently available from existing case studies are not sufficient to allow us to determine all the potential implications of induced traffic. Once again, it would be helpful if every major infrastructural project were to be monitored with regard to its socioeconomic implications. Such monitoring would require the collection of data over time, i.e. at different periods both before and after construction of the infrastructure. Various methods could then be used to determine the volume of induced traffic; indeed, these methods should preferably be used in conjunction, given that no single method is better than another for the measurement of induced traffic.

In more practical terms, survey techniques and models need to be improved, even if this should prove costly. The instruments used for evaluation also need to be perfected if decisionmaking processes are to be improved.

At a more basic level, the problem of induced traffic raises the issue, as noted earlier in this report, of how mobility should be priced. Mobility must be priced high enough to cover the cost of the numerous externalities in the transport sector. This is the only way in which to ensure that induced traffic does not continue to grow in an anarchical fashion, but in accordance with an economic rationale.

Lastly, consideration must be given to the links between infrastructure policy and other policy. Infrastructural measures are only valid if they are part of an overall policy approach which avoids the compartmentalisation of policy measures. There should be no surprise at the phenomenon of induced traffic, given that housing policy has encouraged people to move out of inner city areas into residential areas on the outskirts of cities. As a result of this trend, demand for infrastructure in the outer areas of cities has grown and traffic levels on such infrastructure have risen. There is therefore a need to ensure the overall coherence of policy measures. It might thus be advisable to avoid giving responsibility for land-use planning and transport policy to different Ministries.

LIST OF PARTICIPANTS

Dr. Derek WOOD, Q.C.
Principal
St. Hugh's College
GB-OXFORD OX2 6LE

Chairman

Prof. Dr. Peter CERWENKA
Institut für Verkehrssystemplanung
Technische Universität Wien
Gusshausstrasse 30/269
A-1040 VIENNA

Co-rapporteur

Dr. Georg HAUGER
Institut für Verkehrssystemplanung
Technische Universität Wien
Gusshausstrasse 30/269
A-1040 VIENNA

Co-rapporteur

Prof. P.B. GOODWIN
Centre for Transport Studies
University College London
Gower Street
GB-LONDON WC1E 6BT

Rapporteur

Prof. J.M. MENENDEZ   **Rapporteur**
ETSI de Caminos, Canales y Puertos
Dpto. Ingenieria Civil. Transportes
Planta 5ª
Ciudad Universitaria s/n
E-28040 MADRID

Dr. François PLASSARD   **Rapporteur**
Directeur de Recherche CNRS
Laboratoire RIVES (UMR CNRS 5600)
École National des Travaux Publics de l'État
F-69518 VAULX EN VELIN

Monsieur Jean-Pierre ARDUIN
Service des Nouvelles Infrastructures et de la Grande Vitesse
SNCF
10 place de Budapest
F-75009 PARIS

Monsieur le Professeur Dr. G.J. BLAUWENS
Universiteit Antwerpen (UFSIA)
Prinsstraat 13
B-2000 ANTWERPEN

Professor Ulrich BLUM
Technische Universität Dresden
Fakultät Wirtschaftswissenschaften
Lehrstuhl für Volkswirtschaftslehre,
insbes. Wirtschaftspolitik und Wirtschaftsforschung
Schumannbau C264
Münchner Platz
D-01062 DRESDEN

Monsieur Yves DELACRETAZ
Collaborateur scientifique
École Polytechnique Fédérale de Lausanne
EPFL DGC-TEA
CH-1015 LAUSANNE

Mr. Faustino GOMES
TIS - Transportes, Inovaçâo e Sistemas, A.C.E.
R. Vichena Barbosa 11
P-1000 LISBOA

Mrs. Kathrin GRÜTZMANN
Steinbeis-Transferzentrum
Angewandte Systemanalyse - Stuttgart
Schönbergstrasse 15
D-70599 STUTTGART

Prof.Dr. Rer.Nat. Günter HAAG
Head
Steinbeis-Transferzentrum
Angewandte Systemanalyse - Stuttgart
Schönbergstrasse 15
D-70599 STUTTGART

Dr. Christian Overgaard HANSEN
Tetraplan
Badstuestraede 8, 3
DK-1209 COPENHAGEN K

Monsieur Michel HOUEE
Chargé de mission
SFS/DAEI
Ministère de l'Équipement, du Logement,
des Transports et du Tourisme
Tour Pascal B
F-92055 PARIS LA DEFENSE CEDEX 04

Monsieur Olivier KLEIN
Laboratoire d'Économie des Transports (LET)
ENTPE
rue Maurice-Audin
F-69518 VAULX-EN-VELIN CEDEX

Mr. Werner KOVACIC
Bundesministerium für Öffentliche Wirtschaft
und Verkehr
Radetzkystrasse 2
A-1030 WIEN

Mr. Odd I. LARSEN
Chief Research Officer
TØI - Institute of Transport Economics
P.O. Box 6110 ETTERSTAD
N-0602 OSLO

Monsieur Daniel LE MAIRE
Transportation Adviser
Eurotunnel
B.P. 69
F-62231 COQUELLES

Prof. Peter J. MACKIE
Deputy Director
Institute for Transport Studies
University of Leeds
GB-LEEDS LS2 9JT

Prof.Dr. Rico MAGGI
Socioeconomic Institute
Universität Zürich
Haldenbachstrasse 44
CH-8006 ZURICH

Mr. Jan MARTINSEN
Head of Division
Norwegian Public Roads Administration
Directorate of Public Roads
Box 8142 Dep.
N-0033 OSLO

Mr. Olaf MEYER RÜHLE
Principal Consultant
PROGNOS AG
Missionsstrasse 62
CH-4012 BASEL

Prof. Rainer MEYFAHRT
Kasseler Verkehrsgesellschaft (KVG)
Königstor 3-13
D-34117 KASSEL

Monsieur Olivier MORELLET
Chef de la Division
Transports Interrégionaux de Personnes
INRETS
2 avenue du Général Malleret-Joinville
F-94114 ARCUEIL CEDEX

Prof. Antonio MUSSO
Dipartimento di Ingegneria Civile
Università di Salerno
15 via Domenico Cirillo
I-00197 ROME

Professor Marco PONTI
President
TRT Trasporti e Territorio SRL
Piazza Arcole 4
I-20143 MILAN

Mr. Jesus RUBIO
Jefe del Area de Planeamiento
Ministerio de Fomento, Direçción General de Carreteras
P^a de la Castellana, 67-8ª Planta
Despacho C-828
E-28071 MADRID

Ass.Prof.Dr. Josef M. SCHOPF
Institut für Verkehrsplanung und Verkehrstechnik
Technische Universität Wien
Gusshausstrasse 30/231
A-1040 WIEN

Prof. Folke SNICKARS
Department of Infrastructure and Planning
Royal Institute of Technology (KTH)
Valhallawägen 79
S-100 44 STOCKHOLM 70

Mr. Göran TEGNÉR
Business Manager International
Transek AB
Solna Torg 3
S-17145 SOLNA

Professor A. VAN DER HOORN   **Observer**
Transport Research Centre AVV
Ministry of Transport, Public Works
and Water Management
P.O. Box 1031
NL-30012BA ROTTERDAM

Prof. Dr. Manfred WERMUTH
Technische Universität Braunschweig
Institut für Verkehr und Stadtbauwesen
Pockelsstrasse 3
D-38106 BRAUNSCHWEIG

Professor Dr. W. WINKELMANS
Head of the Department of Transport Economy
Rijksuniversitair Centrum Antwerpen
Universiteit Antwerpen
Middelheimlaan 1
B-2020 ANTWERPEN

ECMT SECRETARIAT

Mr. Gerhard AURBACH - Secretary-General

Mr. Jack SHORT - Deputy Secretary-General

ECONOMIC RESEARCH, STATISTICS AND DOCUMENTATION DIVISION

Mr. Alain RATHERY - Head of Division

Mr. Michel VIOLLAND - Administrator

Mrs. Julie PAILLIEZ - Assistant

Mrs. Jane MINOUX - Assistant

Ms Françoise ROULLET - Assistant

ALSO AVAILABLE

Why Do We Need Railways? ECMT International Seminar (1995)
(75 95 10 1) ISBN 92-821-1207-1   France FF230   Other Countries FF300   US$62   DM86

13th International Symposium on Theory and Practice in Transport Economics. "Transport: New Problems, New Solutions" ECMT (1996)
(75 96 03 1) ISBN 92-821-1212-8   France FF450   Other Countries FF565   US$112 DM164

Express Delivery Services. Series ECMT - Round Table 101 (1996)
(75 96 04 1) ISBN 92-821-1214-4   France FF110   Other Countries FF 145   US$28   DM42

Changing Daily Urban Mobility: Less or Differently?. Series ECMT - Round Table 102 (1996)
(75 96 06 1) ISBN 92-821-1216-0   France FF260   £34   US$50   DM76

The Separation of Operations from Infrastructure in the Provision of Railway Services. Series ECMT - Round Table 103 (1997)
(75 97 02 1P) ISBN 92-821-1221-7   France FF295   £38   US$58   DM86

New Trends in Logistics in Europe - Round Table 104 (1997)
(75 97 05 1 P) ISBN 92-821-1224-1   France FF215   £28 $US42   DM63

Prices charged at the OECD Bookshop.

The OECD CATALOGUE OF PUBLICATIONS and supplements will be sent free of charge on request addressed either to OECD Publications Service, or to the OECD Distributor in your country.

OECD PUBLICATIONS, 2, rue André-Pascal, 75775 PARIS CEDEX 16
PRINTED IN FRANCE
(75 98 07 1 P) ISBN 92-821-1232-2 – No. 50149 1998